Human Dependence on Nature

Humanity is dependent on Nature to survive, yet our society largely acts as if this is not the case. The energy that powers our very cells, the nutrients that make up our bodies, the ecosystem services that clean our water and air; these are all provided by the Nature from which we have evolved and of which we are a part. This book examines why we deny or ignore this dependence and what we can do differently to help solve the environmental crisis.

Written in an accessible and engaging style, Washington provides an excellent overview of humanity's relationship with Nature. The book looks at energy flow, nutrient cycling, ecosystem services, ecosystem collapse as well as exploring our psychological and spiritual dependency on nature. It also examines anthropocentrism and denial as causes of our unwillingness to respect our inherent dependence on the natural environment. The book concludes by bringing these issues together and providing a framework for solutions to the environmental crisis.

Haydn Washington is an environmental scientist and writer with 35 years' experience. He has worked as a plant ecologist, a CSIRO scientist, an environmental consultant, and is currently a Visiting Fellow at the Institute of Environmental Studies at the University of New South Wales, Australia. This is his fifth book on environmental issues and he is also the lead author of *Climate Change Denial: Heads in the Sand* (Earthscan from Routledge 2011).

Figure 0.1 River Oak (*Casuarina cunninghamiana*) in the Murruin wilderness, Blue Mountains, NSW, Australia (photo courtesy Ian Brown)

Human Dependence on Nature

How to help solve the environmental crisis

Haydn Washington

With a foreword by
Professor Paul R. Ehrlich

Routledge
Taylor & Francis Group
LONDON AND NEW YORK

from Routledge

First published 2013
by Routledge
2 Park Square, Milton Park, Abingdon, Oxon, OX14 4RN

Simultaneously published in the USA and Canada
by Routledge
711 Third Avenue, New York, NY 10017

Routledge is an imprint of the Taylor & Francis Group, an informa business

British Library Cataloguing in Publication Data
A catalogue record for this book is available from the British Library

Library of Congress Cataloging-in-Publication Data
Human dependence on nature: how to help solve the environmental
crisis/Haydn Washington.
    p. cm.
"Simultaneously published in the USA and Canada" – T.p. verso.
Includes bibliographical references and index.
1. Nature – Effect of human beings on. 2. Human ecology.
3. Dependency (Psychology) – Social aspects. 4. Environmental
degradation. 5. Environmental protection. 6. Environmental
responsibility. 7. Climatic changes – Environmental aspects.
8. Climatic changes – Social aspects. I. Title.
GF75.W37 2013
304.2 – dc23
2012015737

ISBN: 978-0-415-63257-7 (hbk)
ISBN: 978-0-415-63258-4 (pbk)
ISBN: 978-0-203-09556-0 (ebk)

Typeset in Sabon
by Florence Production Ltd, Stoodleigh, Devon

Dedication

For Henry David Thoreau and Thomas Berry, two champions of Nature who lived centuries apart, yet so elegantly put into words *why* our roots lie in the Earth.

'Our characteristics trace back to the forces that created the earliest simple organisms, and the physical features of our planet and other life forms have shaped the processes and traits that eventually produced modern human beings. But we biologists tend to be even more impressed by our utter dependence on the world that gave us evolutionary birth – on Nature, which nurtures us and to which we are tightly bound. When you've finished *Human Dependence on Nature* you'll be impressed too – and want to give a copy to everyone you know.'

Professor **Paul R. Ehrlich**, President of the Center for Conservation Biology, Department of Biology, Stanford University, California

'Endowed with unprecedented numbers, technological prowess, consumptive demand and a globalized economy, human beings are now undermining the very life support systems of Earth. The environmental movement has successfully raised concerns over issues like pesticides, acid rain, ozone depletion, toxic pollution, clear-cut logging and global warming, but has fundamentally failed in indicating that these problems are driven by deep underlying beliefs and values that shape the way we behave. A paradigm shift happens when we move from the centre of everything to being a creature embedded in and utterly dependent on Nature for our well being and survival. Haydn Washington's book provides the unassailable evidence that we are in an eco-crisis of our own making, making a strong case for an urgent need to change direction and seek ways to live in balance with the factors that sustain us in the biosphere.'

Professor **David Suzuki**, University of Columbia, author of *The Sacred Balance*, USA

'We are all indebted to Haydn Washington for helping us to understand in more detail the complexity of our dependence on nature.'

Lester R. Brown, President of Earth Policy Institute, author of *World on the Edge*

'This book's stern and detailed message about humanity's multifaceted involvement in Earth's biosphere is vital. Are you among the many who have been reluctant to recognize how today's industrialized human load profoundly damages Earth's ecological basis for our descendants' lives? Inability to face that reality has obstructed essential change. Were we to overcome habitual denial, we might commit to protecting rather than undermining the physical, chemical, and biological qualities of this planet essential for future human life. Read this book! Enable posterity to respect us, their ancestors, for our wisdom, instead of loathing us for our obstinate fantasies.'

Professor **William R. Catton, Jr.**, Washington State University, USA

'We are entering the Anthropocene Epoch – so we are told these days. Humans will increasingly manage the planet. Haydn Washington provides a daunting account of how humans still need a biosphere enveloping their technosphere, a life support system they increasingly place in jeopardy.

His respect for the biosphere is inclusive, necessary for our human prosperity on landscapes we love, and enlarging into respect for the intrinsic value in nature. Enter the Anthropocene if we must, but life remains basically natural, and we should enter carefully, full of cares for ourselves and our wonderland Earth. Washington is a thoughtful, spirited guide, persuasively blending science and conscience.'

Professor **Holmes Rolston (III)**,
Colorado State University, USA

'This is a brave book that shows that unless we stop acting "like gods" who assume that we constitute the whole purpose of creation and recover the humility to respect nature, we are doomed. It articulates the ultimate questions that confront us with courage and points to solutions.'

Dr **Paul Collins**, author of *Judgment Day*

'Humans not only depend on nature – we are nature. Haydn Washington documents why. Not only does he bestow us with explanations of the scientific underpinnings, but he also helps us spell out the implications. If high-schoolers could not graduate without having read this book, our chances of survival would be greatly enhanced.'

Dr **Mathis Wackernagel**, President,
Global Footprint Network

'An illuminating and necessary discussion of humanity's absolute dependence on nature and our reluctance to accept that reality.'

Professor **Donald Spady**, Adjunct Associate Professor of
Pediatrics and Public Health, Faculty of Medicine
and Dentistry, and the School of Public Health,
University of Alberta, Canada

'Nowadays the majority of people are city dwellers and most have no idea that we humans are totally dependent upon nature for our survival. Until now scientists have been remiss in explaining this to the public and even to university students. In this book Dr Haydn Washington explains clearly the physical, biological, ecological, psychological and spiritual ways we depend on Nature and critiques the attempts by some to deny it.'

Professor **Mark Diesendorf**, Deputy Director
of the Institute of Environmental Studies,
University of New South Wales,
Australia

'Haydn Washington is among those who appreciate that if present trends in human activity continue unabated the ecological collapse of society is inevitable. Climate change is at present the most critical issue; but this is just one symptom humankind's gross over-exploitation of the Earth's natural resources and general insensitivity to the needs of the processes of life that underpin our existence. This thoughtful and thought-provoking book is a unique contribution to the growing literature on the gross excesses of modern society and the urgent need for a transition to a society that is truly in tune with and respectful of Nature.'

Professor **Stephen Boyden**, Fenner School of
Environment and Society, ANU, author
of *The Biology of Civilisation*, Australia

Contents

Figures

Foreword by Professor Paul R. Ehrlich

Understanding our roots

About a year ago I was asked to address the board of a UN-connected agency in connection with the Millennium Alliance for Humanity and the Biosphere.[1] I started my talk with a simple statement: 'Humanity, both genetically and culturally, is a small-group animal.' It's clear from what we know about human evolution that for the vast majority of the existence of Homo sapiens on this planet, social groups ordinarily contained 50 to 150 individuals, all sharing similar genetic endowments and cultures. Traces of this are easily seen today in the structure of human groups, even in the length of Christmas card lists. [obscured] roversial, indeed obvious. But a woman or [obscured] nine who was sitting next to her: 'That's [obscured] er heard!' My colleague responded 'What [obscured] an beings are not animals!'. In 2010 she [obscured] f William Jennings Bryan, the bald bible[obscured] l in 1925 declared he wasn't a mammal [obscured] ammals if they wanted to, but he didn't. [obscured] llowed as how Bryan was probably right, ... [obscured] uckled his young! What better anecdotes could illustrate the theme of this great book, the lack of understanding of human roots in the natural world. But at least the story of 2010 had a good ending – my colleague asked the lady, 'Are you a plant?'

Those of us who have spent our lives studying the genetic and cultural evolutionary processes that produced human glories such as Charles Darwin and Martin Luther King, and monstrosities such as Adolph Hitler and Joseph Stalin, cannot help but be impressed by our Earthly roots. Our characteristics trace back to the forces that created the earliest simple organisms, and the physical features of our planet and other life forms have shaped the processes and traits that eventually produced modern human beings. But we biologists tend to be even more impressed by our utter dependence on the world that gave us evolutionary birth – on Nature, which nurtures us and to which we are tightly bound. When you've finished *Human*

[Handwritten note: — Scopes 1925 — tru; not mamal — lack of under of hum roots in the nat wor]

Dependence on Nature you'll be impressed too – and want to give a copy to everyone you know.

Paul R. Ehrlich
Bing Professor of Population Studies
President, Center for Conservation Biology Department of Biology,
Stanford University, California

Note

1 MAHB – http://mahb.stanford.edu/

Acknowledgements

I would like to thank Routledge (Earthscan) for its support of this book; especially Louisa Earls, Associate Editor, and Helena Hurd, Editorial Assistant (Environment and Sustainability). I would like to especially thank Professor Paul Ehrlich of Stanford University for writing the wonderful Foreword. His writings have been an inspiration to me for many decades. I would also like to thank Professor Mark Diesendorf of the University of New South Wales for his detailed and helpful comments, especially regarding renewable energy. I would like to thank the other Earthscan reviewers of the book, Professor Donald Spady at the University of Alberta, Canada, and Professor Laura Westra at the University of Windsor, Canada, who made very useful comments on the draft. I would like to thank Dr Kevin Trenberth of the US National Center for Atmospheric Research for use of the water cycle diagram in Figure 2.1, Mr Max Oulton of Waikato University, New Zealand for use of the nitrogen cycle in Figure 2.2, the Millennium Ecosystem Assessment for use of Figures 3.1, 3.2 and 3.3, and Lord Robert May for use of the past extinction events in Figure 8.1. I would like to thank the Estates of Michael Flanders & Donald Swann for permission to use part of the 'First & Second Law' song from 'At the Drop of Another Hat' by Flanders & Swann (1963) (Administrator Leon Berger: leonberger@donaldswann.co.uk). I would like to thank Mr Ian Brown for his wonderful photo of a River Oak (*Casuarina cunninghamiana*) in the Murruin wilderness, Blue Mountains, NSW.

Introduction

This book is about something obvious – but overlooked and ignored. Many of us sometimes experience a moment when the scales drop from our eyes and we experience an 'Aha!' moment. We then see something we should *always* have seen. My hope is that this may happen here. This book is about the fact that humans are ecologically, bio-physically, psychologically and spiritually *dependent on the Earth*. It is obvious to anyone who has studied ecology, or spent time close to the natural world – yet our society acts as if it is not so. Thereby hangs a tale. How are we dependent on Nature, and in what ways? What services do ecosystems provide to us? What happens when we go too far, when we push ecosystems *beyond* their limit? How can we assess the impact we have on the Earth's ecosystems? How can we learn to live sustainably *within* the biophysical limits that the Earth imposes? Other books have sought to address this in part, yet the message is either still unclear, or we are in denial about it. It may well be both, and we shall discuss this. This book seeks to show how humans are pushing the Earth's ecosystems beyond their safe limits. Yet human civilization is rooted in the natural world and is reliant upon it. A recent TV series claimed proudly that Earth was 'The Human Planet', yet this is just human *hubris*. Earth is not the human planet, it is the planet on which humans evolved. Humans do not run the life support systems of planet Earth, Nature does. We ignore this truth at our peril, but sadly also at the peril of many of the family of life we share this world with.

Humanity is now more separate and divorced from Nature than ever before. To many of us this is not readily understood. Our contact with the natural world may only be with an urban park or occasional trips to the seaside or national parks. Most of us still cherish that time being close to Nature, and some of us realize it is a healing experience for mind and body. Yet how many of us think we are 'special', that humans are 'in control' of the world, that we are different from other species, an exalted God-like being at the top of the pyramid of life? Too many, as we shall see.

I have spent much of my life as an environmental scientist and activist walking in wilderness and national parks. Some of this was on solo trips, engaging with the land, with what has been called the 'genius of place' (Rigby

2003). I also own land on the edge of the largest wilderness in NSW, where I built my own house from local materials. I can sit on a cliff and look out for 50 kilometres over mostly wild land. I wrote my book *A Sense of Wonder* (Washington 2002) mainly through engaging with that natural world as both a scientist and a poet. *If you listen to the land you will learn.* I certainly did, just as Thoreau (1854) did at Walden Pond. To truly listen to the land, or to study it as an ecologist, is a profoundly humbling experience. It is also one of sheer 'wonder' at the complexity and harmony of the natural world. It is an experience that builds insight into the workings within the web of life, into the interwoven system that maintains the world we take for granted. It is a thing of sheer beauty. Such study of the natural world (unless one is immersed in anthropocentrism) gives one a sense of *perspective* as to the human place in the world. Humans are indeed a special species, with an intelligence and adaptability that have allowed our numbers to grow hugely. Yet we are still only *one species* among many, a species that relies on the world around us to survive. We seem to have forgotten this (or to deny it). Many traditional cultures developed lore or 'law' to ensure their living with the land was sustainable, truly *ecologically* sustainable in the long term. Modern industrial civilization has ignored these truths. We seem to be drunk with our own power. Yet the world and Nature's ecosystems have limits. We can transgress them, but not for long. This book reminds us of that dependency on the natural world. It reminds us that if we do transgress the limits for too long, then things fall apart and ecosystems collapse, and that rebounds on humanity. Indeed this is happening *now* (MEA 2005).

The majority of the human population lives in cities (UN 2007). With the advent of the computer age, many of us now spend less time in natural systems and don't grow up experiencing Nature or gain a feel for the land and how ecosystems work. It is said that children form their bond with the natural world by the time they are 12–15. If they have not spent time being *part of Nature* as children, then they may not relate to it as much as past generations did (to their great enrichment culturally and spiritually). This is a real problem, indeed it is one of the greatest problems we face, for we have forgotten the wisdom learned by earlier societies (Knudtson and Suzuki 1992). It may also seem strange, but schools by and large do not teach about how the world *really* works. Food does not come from supermarkets but from ecosystems. Timber does not come from timber yards but from ecosystems. Apart from synthetics, clothing does not come from stores but from ecosystems. Even our synthetic clothes are made from the residue of past ecosystems that formed into oil. Our energy is overwhelmingly provided by coal, which is the fossil relict of past swamp ecosystems. We now burn this and thus throw the CO_2 balance in the atmosphere out of whack, thereby causing rapid climate change. Yet modern society by and large *operates as if these things were not true*, and children still grow up being ignorant of them. Why don't we teach our children about human ecological dependency on Nature? After all, native peoples have been doing this since humans first evolved. We shall examine why this is, and how our modern view of the 'economy' plays a role in this. Just as society denies the reality of human-caused climate change (Washington and Cook 2011), it similarly ignores the *absolute and eternal truth* that humanity depends on Nature to survive. Always has, always will. Push the limits too far and things break down, as they are now doing.

What on Earth is going on? It is easy for ecologists and environmentalists to point out that society is blind, that what we are doing is 'crazy', unsustainable, and will lead to disaster. Indeed, many books state this. As an environmental scientist myself I would have to agree. But is it *useful* to make such statements? Of themselves their truth is not self-evident to many. Rather, the most interesting question is why (for much of society) these truths are *not* self-evident? The next question to ask is 'what can we do about it?'. We need to show to people why and how humans are dependent on Nature, why we have to live within the Earth's limits. We have to show how energy flows through ecosystems, and how nutrients are recycled in complex and intricate nutrient cycles. We need to explain about food webs. We have to explain about keystone species, about the fact that ecosystems can collapse or flip into a state quite different from that they started at, states we don't like. We also need to explain with humility that we are still ignorant of many things, that we don't understand everything, and that we probably never will and should not expect to (given the complexity of the natural world).

When we have gone through the ecological science however, we will also need to realize that 'facts' sometimes don't change people's views. Humanity is very good at *deluding* itself and believing what it wants to believe. It is called 'denial'. I have previously co-authored a book about climate change denial (Washington and Cook 2011). We shall similarly encounter denial operating in regard to the human ecological dependency on Nature. We shall even see that 'Nature' is itself denied by some. However, denial can be overcome and people *can* accept reality and solve problems, so I conclude the book with solutions.

It is the ecological reality of our situation I shall first discuss. This will be through chapters on energy flow, nutrient cycles, ecosystem services and ecological collapse. Then I shall look at our psychological and spiritual dependency on Nature. The key problem of anthropocentrism, of being focused almost exclusively *on ourselves* will then be examined. The role that denial plays in society's 'blindness' will be discussed, as well as the role of our modernist and postmodernist worldviews, and our addiction to growth economics. I will then bring this all together and ask 'Do we have a problem?'. Finally, I will look at solutions, at how we can acknowledge our ecological dependency and keep our roots in the Earth.

In this book I shall refer to 'Nature' with a capital 'N'. It is worth explaining here that this is not because I 'deify' Nature, make a fetish of it, or believe in any human/Nature 'dualism'. It is simply a mark of respect for the 'more-than-human world' (Abram 1996) that has nurtured humanity physically and spiritually since we evolved. Given the generosity and beauty that Nature has manifested to humanity, it is a respect I believe is well deserved. Our roots are in the Earth, always have been and always will be. And that is something wonderful we need to remember, to acknowledge and to cherish into the future.

1 Energy is life

The gathered power
Of a yellow star,
Slowly garnered
By the growing green . . .
Fire-friend,
We see within you
The endless years
Of our long journey.
Living starlight
You, the man-maker,
Will we pass the test,
Our time of growing?
Or will we fail the flame,
Your trust in man?

('Fire', Washington 2010)

Energy is life, or at least the prerequisite for life. We depend on Nature for the energy that powers the crops in our fields, the animals on our farms and the pets in our homes. We depend on it even for the energy that powers our own bodies. All the fossil fuels that power our civilization are carbon compounds trapped by photosynthesis in past ecosystems and preserved (fossilized) as fossil fuels millions of years ago. The petrol and diesel that power our cars and the coal that is burnt to make electricity makes use of an energy preserved from hundreds of millions of years ago, where the energy-rich long chain organic compounds created by photosynthesis survive in a condensed and fossilized form today as oil and coal. Our planet is bathed in a life-giving stream of energy flowing from the Sun. Through the wonder of photosynthesis, plants trap 1–2 per cent of the sunlight that falls on them (Hall and Rao 1999). This powers almost all of the Earth's ecosystems, the only exceptions being bacteria known as *chemo-autotrophs* that derive their energy from converting energy-rich chemicals in rocks (such as sulphur). So the ancient Egyptians had it right – the Sun is the font of life. Its light drives almost all the living world.

The second law of thermodynamics tells us that in Nature, energy goes from a useable form to an unusable form as 'entropy' (disorder) increases. Energy passes from a high energy state to a low energy state. It goes in one direction. As comic songwriters Flanders and Swann (1963) quipped, 'Heat won't pass from a cooler to a hotter ...You can try it if you like but you far better notter'. So unlike nutrients, you cannot 'recycle' energy, it moves in one direction, from the high-energy sunlight to low-energy heat. The direction can be reversed by human actions, but this takes energy to do this. Thus, ultimately, the amount of life the Earth can support is determined by the fixed amount of sunlight falling on the Earth, an amount that varies only slightly with solar cycles. Unlike our society's energy consumption, solar energy is not increasing exponentially. There is a fixed amount of life-giving energy that falls upon the Earth.

Productivity and food webs

We need to discuss a few ecological terms to get a grasp on energy flow in ecosystems. The first of these is Gross Primary Productivity (GPP), which is the total amount of carbon fixed by plants ('autotrophs' or 'producers') through photosynthesis. Incoming solar energy is trapped in sugars, which can then be used to make other compounds. However, plants use some of the energy fixed as sugars to run their own cells, and this is called 'respiration' (in this case it does not mean breathing). Respiration uses roughly half of the energy fixed in sugars by photosynthesis (Cain *et al.* 2008). The balance of the fixed carbon, once we subtract respiration, is called Net Primary Productivity (NPP). NPP represents the energy (fixed and stored as sugars) left over for plant growth and for consumption by herbivores (and 'detritivores' that break down plant matter in the soil). It is NPP then that is the basis of all the food chains and food webs that make up the Earth's web of life. More NPP means more opportunities for life, less NPP means fewer opportunities. NPP (the Sun's energy trapped as organic matter) is thus the fundamental foundation on which the rest of the living world is built. It is, however, a foundation of fixed size. We can degrade ecosystems (e.g. by land-clearing) so that we have less of this foundation, but we cannot build *more* of this foundation than the sunlight will allow.

The sugars produced in photosynthesis can be converted into starch for storage (for times of need), or can be converted to cellulose to build cell walls. They can be converted to 'lignin' also, the cement that makes cell walls rigid and 'woody'. They can have nitrogen added to make amino acids that link to form proteins. In forest ecosystems, over time the NPP tends to decrease as the forest matures, because leaf area and photosynthesis rates are lower. However, this should not be construed as a 'bad' thing (as some loggers tend to claim) where the forest is 'over-mature' or senescent. The decline in NPP over time in a forest is a natural function of ecological succession, and the older or 'climax' forest is better at nutrient recycling, water management and other ecosystem services (MEA 2005).

NPP is constrained by both physical and biological environmental factors. Sunlight is one. Climate is also clearly a key controller of NPP, especially rainfall. NPP increases with rainfall up to a figure of 2,400 mm a year (Cain *et al.* 2008), after which it decreases (owing to cloudy conditions, waterlogged soils, etc.). NPP also tends to increase with annual average temperature (provided there is enough water). Nutrient availability and the plant species present will also affect NPP, and in aquatic ecosystems, nutrient availability (e.g. phosphorus) controls NPP.

Energy is continually being added to ecosystems from the Sun, being trapped by plants (producers) and these plants are eaten by herbivores (known as 'first order consumers') that may be eaten by carnivores ('second order consumers'). This flow of energy in an ecosystem is called a food or 'trophic' chain (trophic is Greek for 'feeding') and the flow of energy through different species along such chains is called a *food web*. At each step in the chain usable energy is lost. This has led to what has been called 'Lindeman's

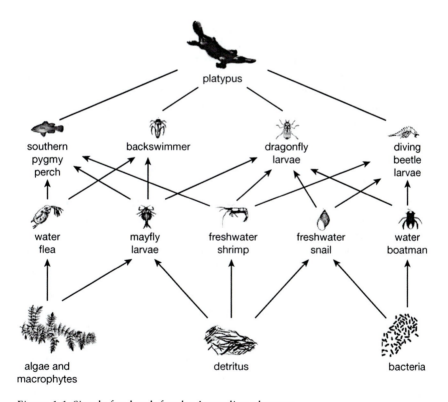

Figure 1.1 Simple food web for the Australian platypus.

Source: adapted from www.mghs.sa.edu.au/Internet/Faculties/Science/Year9/livingTogether.htm.

Law', where the next step in the food chain has only about 10 per cent of the biomass of the step before it. This is why most food (trophic) chains have only 4 or 5 steps, as the amount of energy remaining after this becomes too small to support a viable population of animals.

Figure 1.1 shows a simple food web for the Australian platypus. Of course, most food webs are much more complex and interwoven, and can be said to resemble a 'spaghetti diagram' (Cain *et al.* 2008). Carnivores can of course eat at several levels in the food web. For example, a predator may eat fruits or nuts, as well as the insects that eat these, and the animals that eat those insects. So food webs are *complex*.

Keystone species

There is another side to this complexity, as each species in a food web may not have equal importance or impact on other species. Not all members of the web affect each other evenly. Ecologists speak of 'interaction strength' as the measure of the effect of the population of one species on the size of another species population. Another way to look at it is that some species have more effect on how energy moves through a food web, and even on what species are present in an ecosystem. These are known as *keystone* species, and are important, little known, parts of ecosystems.

The classic example of a keystone species was identified in an experiment in the rocky intertidal zones in the Pacific Northwest of the US, where ecologist Robert Paine (1966) removed the sea star *Pisaster* to see what happened. Barnacles initially became more abundant, but were then crowded out by mussels and goose-neck barnacles. After two and a half years the number of species had dropped from 15 to 8, and even after the sea star was reintroduced, mussel dominance remained, as they had grown to sizes that prevented predation by the sea stars (Paine 1966). The sea star *Pisaster* was thus a keystone species that determined what the species mix ended up being in that ecosystem. It also actually maintained high species diversity in that ecosystem. Keystone species are found all around the world and include organisms from almost all ecosystem types.

There are three types of keystone species – 'predators', 'mutualists' and 'ecosystem engineers'. Keystone *predators* are often found at high levels in the food web, but are not necessarily the top predator. Some are in fact top predators, such as wolves and jaguars (Nowell and Jackson 1996) and dingos (Purcell 2010). However, the sea otter is one keystone species not found at the top of the food chain, for it is preyed on by killer whales (Orcas). Similarly, the sea star *Pisaster* is also preyed on by several other predators. Keystone *mutualists* are organisms that participate in mutually beneficial interactions with other organisms, and the loss of keystone mutualists would have a profound impact upon the ecosystem as a whole. For example, in the Avon wheat belt region of Western Australia, there is a period of each year when *Banksia prionotes* (Acorn Banksia) is the sole source of nectar for honeyeaters, which play an important role in pollination of numerous plant species. Therefore the loss of this one species of tree would probably cause the honeyeater population to collapse, with profound implications for the entire ecosystem. Other examples of mutualist keystone species are fruit eaters (frugivores) such as the cassowary, which spreads the seeds of many different trees around the rainforest. Some trees will not grow unless they have been through the digestive tract of the cassowary (Walker 1995).

In North America, the grizzly bear is a keystone species, not as a predator but as an ecosystem engineer. They transfer nutrients from the oceanic ecosystem to the forest ecosystem. The first stage of the transfer is performed by salmon (rich in inorganic nutrients) that swim up rivers, sometimes for hundreds of miles. The bears then capture the salmon and carry them onto dry land, dispersing partially eaten carcasses and nutrient-rich faeces. Bears leave up to half of the salmon they harvest on the forest floor (Reimchen 2001). The prairie dog is also an ecosystem engineer. Its burrows provide the nesting areas for mountain plovers and burrowing owls (NGP 2011). Prairie dog tunnel systems also help channel rainwater into the water table to prevent runoff and erosion (Outwater 1996; Miller *et al.* 2000). Another ecosystem engineer is the beaver, which transforms its territory from a stream to a pond or swamp (Wright *et al.* 2002). In the African savannah, the larger herbivores, especially the elephants, are ecosystem engineers that strongly influence their environment. The elephants destroy trees, making room for the grass species. Without these animals, much of the savannah would turn into woodland (Leakey and Lewin 1999). The caiman is an ecosystem engineer, and its removal from areas in the Amazon has led to a decline in fish populations (and hence fish catch), because of reduced nutrient cycling in the food chain which the Caiman made possible (Williams and Dodd 1980). The alligator is similarly a keystone species in the Everglades (Amsel 2007). The impacts of herbivores on savannah are altered in major ways by Tsetse flies, as only certain herbivores survive. The Tsetse fly may be small, but is also a keystone species (Elmqvist *et al.* 2010).

Overall then, keystone species are of great importance to keeping ecosystems healthy. Sadly, we don't know all the keystone species present on Earth, and we may in fact never know them all. We often only learn what species are keystone once they are lost or in major decline. We often fail to learn of the benefits provided by a species until it is gone. The Passenger Pigeon used to darken the skies with its huge flocks, and was deemed *inexhaustible*. However, it was sent extinct at the start of the twentieth century as a consequence of over-hunting. It was later realized that the pigeon had been eating huge amounts of acorns, and after its disappearance these were then eaten by deer and mice. This led to a boom in these mammals and thus in the ticks that lived on them, and in the spirochaete bacteria that lived in those ticks. This boom in spirochaetes caused an unexpected epidemic of Lyme's disease in humans several decades after the loss of the pigeons themselves (Pascual *et al.* 2010). We thus do not often know which species is a keystone species until long *after* we have sent them extinct. It is clear that many top carnivores are keystone species. The removal of the wolf from areas has led to an explosion in herbivores that overgrazed ecosystems (causing erosion and nutrient loss). The removal of the dingo, the top land predator in Australia, is implicated in the extinction of native animal species as a result of increased cat and fox predation (which the dingo had been controlling) (Purcell 2010).

One other term we should discuss is the 'trophic cascade'. This is about *indirect* effects within food webs. For example, when a carnivore eats a herbivore there is often a direct positive effect on the plant (primary producer). One key example is the sea otter eating the sea urchins that eat the kelp on the west coast of America. The sea otter was discovered to be a keystone species, but only when it was hunted for its fur almost to extinction. The sea urchin populations exploded and the kelp forest went into decline. So it is often through 'trophic cascades' that keystone species affect ecosystems. Trophic cascades are thus a series of changes in energy and species composition in an ecosystem. They are best known from aquatic systems, often through unintended releases of non-native (feral) species. The introduction of brown trout into New Zealand led to the decline of native fish, with some local extinctions. This happened through a trophic cascade where the trout reduced invertebrate (water creepy-crawlies) density and increased algae growth (Cain *et al.* 2008).

Diversity, stability, resilience and ecosystem services

Biologists speak of 'biodiversity', which is another name for plants and animals and the ecosystems they form. Biodiversity is made of three parts: the genetic diversity within a species, the species themselves, and the ecosystems that are made up of species (Cain *et al.* 2008). All three components are important. In regard to food webs and biodiversity, there has been much debate among ecologists on whether complex food webs (high biodiversity) are more *stable* than simpler food webs that are less diverse. 'Stability' is a term with many meanings, but is usually defined as the tendency of the community to remain the same in structure and function (Cain *et al.* 2008). The term is now avoided by some ecologists. For example, the UNEP project 'The Economics of Ecosystems and Biodiversity' or TEEB (Kumar 2010) talks about high biodiversity leading to 'less variability in functioning' rather than the term 'stability' as such. Stability is usually gauged by the size of the changes in organism populations over time. A less stable food web means greater potential for extinction. The question of greater diversity leading to stability has been hotly contested within ecology, with Odum (1953) and Elton (1958) believing this was the case, while May (1973) used food web models to suggest that food webs with high diversity are less stable.

However, rainforests and coral reefs do have high biodiversity and *do* indeed persist over time. The relationship of biodiversity and stability is still under research, but species diversity and species composition were important in determining the stability in a protozoan food web (Cain *et al.* 2008). Taken together, recent advances indicate that diversity can be expected, on average, to give rise to ecosystem stability. The evidence also indicates that diversity is not the driver of this relationship; rather, ecosystem stability depends on the ability for communities to contain species, or functional groups, which are capable of differential response (McCann 2000). Hooper *et al.* (2005) concluded that increased biodiversity leads to an increase in 'response diversity' (range of traits of species in the same functional groups in response to environment drivers or stresses) resulting in less variability in function over time. Also, more biodiverse ecosystems have greater productivity, greater drought tolerance, better water management, better nutrient cycling (such as more efficient use of nitrogen), greater community respiration, greater biotic resistance (to pests) and greater resilience (Elmqvist *et al.* 2010; Cain *et al.* 2008). More diverse ecosystems can absorb up to 30 per cent more CO_2 than monocultures (Daily 1997). More diverse ecosystems thus produce greater ecosystem services (see Chapter 3).

Keeping biodiversity is thus important to retaining the ecosystem services we rely on. There is thus a practical and selfish reason why we should keep biodiversity, as well as a strong ethical reason for keeping the wondrous web of life from which we evolved. Once 'stability' was much discussed in ecology, now the focus has shifted to *resilience*. Ecological resilience is the capacity of an ecosystem to withstand perturbations without losing any of its functional properties. The most common definition is that it represents the capacity of a system to cope with disturbances without shifting into a qualitatively different state. A resilient system has the capacity to withstand shocks and surprises, and if damaged to rebuild itself (Elmqvist *et al.* 2010). Hence resilience is the capacity of a system to both deal with change and continue to develop.

Thus we all run on sunshine, via plants and animals. We rely on the productivity of ecosystems, which is limited by sunlight, water, nutrients, species present and disease. One can artificially boost agro-ecosystems through nutrient addition in fertilizers, through irrigation, and through controlling pests and diseases. However, artificial fertilizers require energy to produce them (e.g. nitrogen is fixed from the atmosphere using energy from fossil fuels) or mine them from rocks (e.g. phosphorus). Irrigation also consumes energy, as does the production of pesticides. Pushing up the productivity of an ecosystem on a finite Earth from an ecological viewpoint is thus a *temporary* project that requires significant energy input. It also tends to put stresses on other parts of the system. Addition of artificial nitrogen fertilizers decreases the organic matter in the soil (Sullivan 1999), and at least half of the added nitrogen escapes to streams or groundwater, contaminating these (MEA 2005). Synthetic pesticides are themselves often a problem and often kill the predators of the actual pests (Daily 1997) and thus lock the farmer into an endless spiral of increasing pesticide use to control that pest.

How much is humanity's fair share?

The energy limits of the Earth's ecosystems thus cannot be ignored. On a finite Earth we just cannot keep increasing the amount of food, fibre and wood we produce. Energy is life, but the amount coming to Earth is *fixed*. The human species is now using about 12,000 times as much energy per day as was the case when farming first started; 90 per cent of this is a result of industrialization, 10 per cent to our huge growth in numbers (Boyden 2004). We can steal fossil energy from the past by using coal and oil, but only for a while. We could try and use radioactive minerals to produce energy, and in so doing create another whole set of ecological problems for the future (e.g. waste disposal, nuclear weapon proliferation). Or we could accept we have to live *within* the Earth's limited energy budget, an energy budget that maintains the whole web of life, not just humans. So how much energy is humanity's due? How much of the Earth's productivity should be controlled by just one species – ourselves? The NPP of the land amounted to about 132 billion tonnes dry weight of organic matter in 1986 (Vitousek *et al.* 1986). Of this the then human population of 5.7 billion humans consumed directly just over 1 billion tonnes as food. In addition humans co-opted 43 billion tonnes (32 per cent) of total NPP in the form of wasted food, forest products, crop and forestry residues, pastures and so on. Vitousek *et al.* (1986) concluded:

> We estimate that organic material equivalent to about 40% of the present net primary production in terrestrial ecosystems is being co-opted by human beings each year. People use this material directly or indirectly, it flows to different consumers and decomposers than it otherwise would, or it is lost because of human-caused changes in land use. People and the associated organisms use this organic material largely, but not entirely, at human direction, and the vast majority of other species must subsist on the remainder. An equivalent concentration of resources into one species and its satellites has probably not occurred since land plants first diversified.

They also note that 'humans also affect much of the other 60% of terrestrial NPP, often heavily', thus our impact is not just limited to the 40 per cent of NPP we co-opt directly. The estimates in this classic 1986 study are conservative, and we are now 25 years further down the path of expanding population and impacts. However, other scholars use different methodologies and come up with somewhat different figures. Rojstaczer *et al.* (2001) argued human use of NPP could be as high as 55 per cent, while Haberl *et al.* (2007) came up with a figure of 24–29 per cent of human appropriation of NPP. Whichever figure one uses, this remains a huge percentage of the net primary productivity of the planet that humans are appropriating. Of course, this appropriation is also still increasing as population, and possibly more importantly per capita *consumption*, continues to increase. The high and increasing appropriation of NPP by humanity is clearly a fundamental stress on ecosystem health. NPP is the foundation of all ecosystems, so if we pull out too many blocks from the foundation to put on the 'human' pile, then eventually other structures (natural ecosystems) *collapse*. And indeed they are, as Chapter 4 shows.

So how much is enough? How much is too much? Is 100 per cent of NPP our due, should we have it all? Those who believe Nature is just for human use might think so. Of course, if we actually tried for 100 per cent of NPP, then natural ecosystems would collapse everywhere, and civilization would also collapse. Something similar happened at Easter Island and at other past civilizations that pushed ecosystems too far (Diamond 2005). The fact that 60 per cent of ecosystem services are now being degraded or used unsustainably (MEA 2005) indicates that almost certainly the current level of NPP that humans appropriate is too high. We are using *far more* than our due. In fact, humanity's consumption of biomass is almost 100 times higher than the highest level of biomass appropriation by 96 other mammals (Fowler and Hobbs 2003). Clearly we are way *beyond* what could be considered 'equitable' in terms of our fair share of NPP. The energy stored by plants from sunlight cannot end up being *just for us*. Yet to date humanity has gorged itself to bursting point as a NPP glutton, perhaps without fully knowing the consequences.

Yet now we *do* know the consequences of gorging on the Earth's NPP, or at least ecologists do, and they have reported on this through reports such as the Millennium Ecosystem Assessment (MEA 2005). Clearly, civilization does ultimately need to live within the ecological energy budget of our planet. I am speaking here of the energy stored in NPP, not suggesting that we shouldn't make use of solar energy, which Chapter 9 shows is one of the key solutions needed. All the NPP cannot be 'just for us'; Nature needs it to provide the ecosystem services on which our society depends to survive (see Chapter 3). Apart from that, Nature has an ethical right to most of the NPP, an intrinsic right to survive and continue to evolve. That means ideas such as 'ever-moreism' (Boyden 2004), a belief in endless growth in population and consumption *just won't work*. Earth's energy budget won't allow it. Energy is life, but its amount is finite, and we have to live sustainably within that budget, within those limits. Yet most decision-makers are still looking for *more*, more of NPP energy as part of the mantra of endless growth. And there is the rub. Use too much, take too much energy for ourselves, and we impoverish the Earth. That impoverishment is a major ethical tragedy, where we close off the evolutionary options for much of the life on Earth. It is a betrayal of the future of those humans who come after us, to which we would pass on an impoverished world. It is also a major practical problem for those of us alive right *now*, dependent right now on the natural world we are starving of energy. This is the same world on which we rely for the ecosystem services that sustain us and keep the

Earth habitable. So energy is life, but humanity has become an energy vampire on the Earth's ecosystems, on life itself. Knowing this now, will we still seek to hoard it all – or will we *share*?

2 The great cycles

Heaven is my father
And earth is my mother,
And even such a small creature as I
Finds an intimate place in its midst.
That which extends throughout the universe,
I regard as my body
And that which directs the universe
I regard as my nature.
All people are my brothers and sisters
And all things are my companions.
                    (Chang Tsai, eleventh century AD)

Energy may flow through to us from the Sun, but the Earth is finite and has material limits. All life on Earth requires water and mineral elements to survive. For example: the water that makes up 70 per cent of our bodies; the phosphorus that is incorporated in our bones and in the molecule adenosine tri-phosphate (ATP) that powers our cells; the nitrogen that is combined in the amino acids that makes up the proteins in our muscles; the potassium that we need for cellular reactions and osmotic control; the sulphur that makes up some of the amino acids in our proteins. Even the very carbon we eat in our food and breathe out as carbon dioxide. If we only used these *once* then they would have run out long ago, and life would have faded away. Instead, they are part of the *great cycles*, where each is taken up and used by plants and animals (including humans) and then returned once again to the Earth. Both the hydrologic and sedimentary cycles are intertwined with the distribution of six important elements: hydrogen, carbon, oxygen, nitrogen, phosphorus and sulphur. These make up 95 per cent of living things (Daily 1997).

The water cycle

The easiest cycle to understand is perhaps the water cycle (see Figure 2.1). Water is evaporated from the sea (around 80 per cent of the water vapour produced comes from the oceans), but also from the land via the transpiration from the leaves of trees and evaporation directly from soil. This water vapour condenses and falls as 'precipitation' (a term for rain or snow). This precipitation on land either runs off, or if it is snow, some or all melts during summer to feed rivers. The rivers flow to the sea, and the cycle continues. In reality, the cycle is somewhat more complex, as some rainfall enters groundwater, some water vapour is added by volcanoes, and some water is taken into the crust through geological tectonic processes. However, overall we live with this great circle of water cycling, without which life could not function on Earth.

Humanity is *altering* the water cycle. We clear rainforest and other forest and vegetation and thus change the amount of transpiration from vegetation to the atmosphere. This may be of greatest impact regionally in terms of the clearing of the Amazon rainforest, where this slows the 'Amazon Water Pump'. This process moves water vapour into the atmosphere from tree transpiration and thus creates more local rainfall (Elmqvist *et al.* 2010). We also drain and clear wetlands and thus alter the water regime in those areas, and the capacity to regulate peak rainfall events and release water

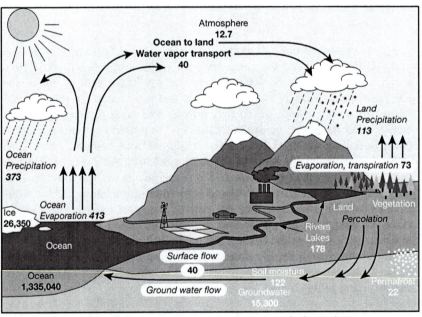

Units: *Thousand cubic km* for storage, and *thousand cubic km/yr* for exchanges

Figure 2.1 The water cycle.

Source: Trenberth *et al.* (2007), see: http://journals.ametsoc.org/doi/full/10.1175/JHM600.1.

steadily over time (Daily 1997). We pump out groundwater and lower the groundwater table, thus decreasing the natural groundwater pressure (e.g. in natural 'mound springs' in Australia fed by the Great Artesian Basin). Most importantly however, we *warm the climate*, with a 0.8 degree Celsius warming already here, and more in the pipeline. Each one degree Celsius we warm the atmosphere increases its water-holding capacity by 7 per cent (Trenberth 2011). This means that rainfall events and storms, hurricanes and cyclones (and also winter blizzards) can be *more extreme* and dump a lot of rain or snow in a short period. However, a warmer climate also means that evaporation over land is greater, which causes more droughts and fires and leads to desertification. A warming climate can thus mean *both* more extreme rainfall (and snowfall) but also overall greater dryness and desertification (Pittock 2009).

However, as we shall see, our effect on the water cycle is dwarfed by our effect on the cycles of the elemental nutrients essential for life. Here we will consider the cycles for nitrogen, sulphur, phosphorus and carbon. There are other important nutrients (e.g. potassium) but we shall concentrate on these four. First is the nitrogen cycle.

The nitrogen cycle

Nitrogen forms the basis of the amino acids that form all proteins used by life. Figure 2.2 shows the nitrogen cycle. Nitrogen gas forms 79 per cent of the atmosphere, so it fills our lungs with every breath, yet it is not available to us or to plants in this form. Instead, it must be turned into nitrates that can be absorbed by plants. In the natural world, this can be by the action of lightning in the atmosphere, or by nitrogen-fixing bacteria. These bacteria can be free-living, but most are found in nodules on the roots of plants (especially in legumes). There are also *denitrifying* bacteria in soils that gain energy by turning the high-energy nitrates back into nitrogen gas. Animals take up nitrogen as amino acids in proteins by eating plants (or other animals), and animal waste is then decomposed back down to nitrates. There is thus a great cycle of nitrogen moving from the atmosphere to the land and rivers, into plants and then animals and then back to ecosystems, where it is returned to the atmosphere as nitrogen gas. Nitrogen is one of the key major nutrients that limit plant growth on Earth. Humans now want more for agriculture, and we now produce vast amounts of nitrogen fertilizers, mostly using the energy from natural gas. Fossil fuel energy thus provides the energy for what has been called 'ghost acreage' that allows more food to be produced, as long as you have the fossil energy to do it (Catton 1982).

This has *consequences*. In regard to the nitrogen cycle, even in 1997 Vitousek *et al.* (1997) concluded that human alterations have:

- approximately doubled the rate of nitrogen input into the terrestrial nitrogen cycle, and the rate is still increasing;

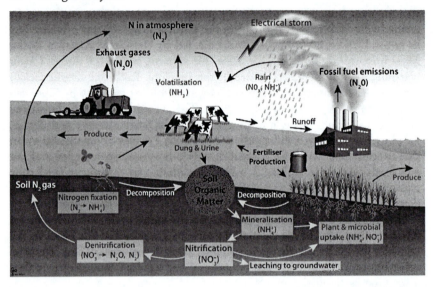

Figure 2.2 The global nitrogen cycle.

Source: The University of Waikato (Max Oulton), see: www.waikato.ac.nz/wfass/subjects/geography/people/max/ConceptDiagrams.shtml.

- increased concentrations of the potent greenhouse gas nitrous oxide (N_2O), and thus also the formation of photochemical smog;
- caused losses of soil nutrients, such as calcium and potassium, essential for long-term soil fertility;
- contributed substantially to the acidification of soils, streams and lakes;
- greatly increased the transfer of nitrogen through rivers to estuaries and coastal oceans;
- increased the quantity of organic carbon stored within terrestrial ecosystems;
- accelerated losses of biological diversity, especially of plants adapted to efficient use of nitrogen, and losses of the animals that depend on these;
- caused changes in the composition and functioning of estuarine and near-shore ecosystems, and contributed to long-term declines in coastal marine fisheries.

The disturbance of the nitrogen cycles through our addition of nitrogen fertilizers has thus been massive. This extra addition of nitrogen has led to more nitrous oxide (N_2O) being produced, a greenhouse gas 296 times more powerful per molecule than carbon dioxide. One unexpected effect has been the loss of soil nutrients such as calcium and potassium. When excess nitrate (a negatively charged chemical ion or 'anion') leaches from soils as a result of over-application, it draws out positively charged ions ('cations') such as calcium along with it. Excess nitrogen has also led to algae growth in aquatic ecosystems, and led to eutrophication and low oxygen levels that kill fish (MEA 2005). Excess nitrate also enters groundwater, where it represents a human and animal health problem for those that drink it. In groundwater, nitrogen forms nitrites that combine with haemoglobin in our blood, and this can cause asphyxiation. In babies it is known as 'blue baby syndrome'.

Over the past four decades, excessive nutrient loading has emerged as one of the most important direct drivers of ecosystem change. The total amount of 'reactive' or biologically available nitrogen created by humans increased ninefold between 1890 and 1990; 50 per cent of this applied nitrogen may be lost from fields into the natural environment (MEA 2005). The natural flux of nitrogen fixation is 100 million tonnes of nitrogen fixed by organisms naturally from atmosphere, and 10 million tonnes fixed by lightning. This gives a natural nitrogen flux of 110 million tonnes annually. Nitrate fertilizer production in 2008 was 131 million tonnes and the forecast for 2011 was 154 million tonnes, growing yearly by 1.4 per cent (FAO 2008); 30 million tonnes also comes from planted crop legumes and 25 million tonnes from fossil fuel combustion (Daily 1997). Therefore, humans are producing over 186 million tonnes of nitrogen, far larger than the natural flux (110 million tonnes). Nitrogen fertilizer has 90 per cent of its cost of production as energy use (from fossil fuels) to produce it, and is thus not sustainable in the long term (Elmqvist *et al.* 2010). Human activities have thus now more than *doubled* the rate of creation of reactive nitrogen on the land surface of Earth. The flux of reactive nitrogen to oceans increased by nearly 80 per cent from 1860 to 1990 (from 27 to 48 million tonnes) (MEA 2005). Massive use of nitrate fertilizers has meant it can now reasonably be called a major pollutant of the world's ecosystems.

The sulphur cycle

Sulphur is another essential element for life, present in two amino acids. Figure 2.3 shows the sulphur cycle. Like the nitrogen cycle, this has gaseous components as well as solid and dissolved forms. Within the terrestrial portion, the cycle begins with the weathering of rocks, releasing the stored sulphur. The sulphur then comes into contact with air, where it is converted into sulphate (SO_4). The sulphate is taken up by plants and microorganisms and is converted into organic sulphur compounds (e.g. the amino acids methionine and cysteine). Animals then consume these organic forms through the foods they eat, thereby moving the sulphur through the food chain. As organisms die and decompose, some of the sulphur is again released as sulphate, and some enters the tissues of microorganisms. There are also natural sources that emit sulphur directly into the atmosphere; for example, volcanoes emit hydrogen sulphide or 'rotten egg gas', and the breakdown of organic matter in swamps releases H_2S and SO_2. Sulphur dioxide and carbonyl sulphide are other gases in the cycle. Another gas shown under 'emission' from the ocean is dimethyl sulphide ($(CH_3)_2S$) which is released by plankton.

This then gets converted to sulphur dioxide in the atmosphere. In this way it returns quite large amounts of sulphur (35 million tonnes, NAU 2011) from the oceans to the atmosphere. Sulphur is also being removed from the biosphere by sedimentation, where it forms rocks that later get lifted. These and sulphur deposits in volcanoes then start to weather. The end result is another great cycle of element transport from rocks to atmosphere to life and so back through the cycle.

Humans have also altered the sulphur cycle. Emissions of sulphur to the atmosphere by humans are equal to or larger than those from natural processes (Daily 1997). Modification of the sulphur cycle has generated major problems such as acid rain and smog (Daily 1997). Sulphur is being added intentionally in fertilizers, but also unintentionally through the burning of sulphur-rich fossil fuels. It has been found that during volcanic eruptions, sulphate aerosols emitted to the stratosphere reflect sunlight and actually lower world temperatures for a couple of years. The Mt Pinatubo volcanic eruption in the Philippines is one example, where it lowered world temperatures by 0.5 degrees Celsius (Hansen *et al.* 2007).

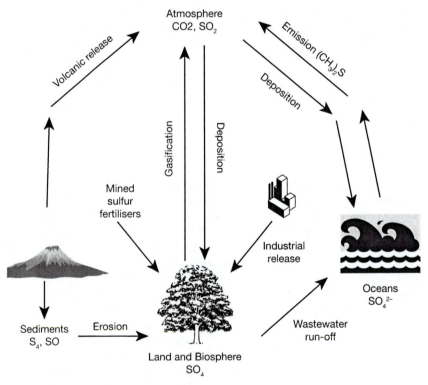

Figure 2.3 The sulphur cycle.

Source: adapted from Carnegie Mellon University, see: http://telstar.ote.cmu.edu/environ/m3/s4/cycleSulfur.shtml.

The action of volcanic sulphate aerosols has led to proposals for geo-engineering solutions to climate change. Geo-engineering means that rather than decreasing human emissions of greenhouse gases to actually *solve* the problem at the source, we instead pump large amounts of sulphur (as sulphate) into the stratosphere to shade the Earth. However, to compensate for a doubling of CO_2, the required continuous stratospheric sulphate loading would be 5.3 million tonnes (or teragrams) per year of sulphur (Crutzen 2006). World annual production according to the US Geological Survey is 68 million tonnes and world reserves are 5 billion tonnes (USGS 2011). In terms of resources, a sulphate injection strategy could thus be possible for some years. It has been estimated to cost around $125 billion a year, and would have to be done every one to two years, as the sulphur is naturally removed back into the lower atmosphere (Crutzen 2006). This removal to the lower atmosphere means the sulphur would come back to the Earth's ecosystems and cause significant acidification of rivers and lakes. Currently, substantial efforts (e.g. scrubbers on power stations) are taken to *stop* the sulphur we use from entering ecosystems, because of serious acid rain problems in the past (EPA 2011). Apart from the acidity question, this geo-engineering sulphur injection would turn our skies *white*, would not stop the acidification of the oceans resulting from increasing CO_2 (which threatens marine food chains), and may affect the Indian Monsoon, on which a large part of the world's population depends for food production (Pittock 2009).

The phosphorus cycle

The phosphorus cycle is another key nutrient cycle, for phosphorus is a major part of our bones (calcium phosphate) and forms a vital part of the molecule adenosine tri-phosphate (ATP) that produces energy in our cells. The phosphorus cycle is shown in Figure 2.4. Unlike the nitrogen and the sulphur cycles, this cycle has no atmospheric components (other than dust). Phosphate is present in rocks and weathers out, is taken up by plants (or flows to the sea) and then moves into animals and to decomposers and animal wastes, and then back to the ecosystem pool (or to the oceans). In the oceans it is incorporated into sediments, which can later be raised up to weather, and the cycle starts again.

Because phosphorus is one of the key limiting elements for plant (and animal) growth, humanity has altered the cycle by mining phosphate-rich rocks and guano (fossil faeces of sea birds) deposits. This has at least *doubled* the amount of phosphorus moving through ecosystems. Abelson (1999) notes:

> The current major use of phosphate is in fertilizers. Growing crops remove it and other nutrients from the soil . . . Most of the world's farms do not have or do not receive adequate amounts of phosphate. Feeding

the world's increasing population will accelerate the rate of depletion of phosphate reserves ... resources are limited, and phosphate is being dissipated. Future generations ultimately will face problems in obtaining enough to exist.

Use of phosphorus fertilizer and phosphorus accumulation in agricultural soils increased threefold between 1960 and 1990. The phosphorus flux to the oceans is triple that of background rates (MEA 2005). In 2008, 37 million tonnes of phosphate was mined, with a prediction that it would grow by 2 per cent a year, reaching 43 million tonnes by 2011 (FAO 2008). Most of the phosphorus used in agriculture in fact is not taken up by plants, but is lost and moves to waterways (either in solution or more commonly adsorbed on soil particles eroded from fields). The net loss of phosphorus from the world's cropland is estimated at about 10.5 million tonnes of phosphorus each year (Liu *et al.* 2008). Only 5–10 per cent of the added phosphorus to agro-ecosystems is recovered in crops, owing to the strong fixation of phosphorus on soils. In natural ecosystems, fungal mychorrhizae

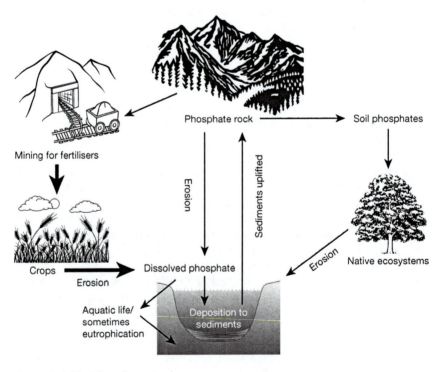

Figure 2.4 The phosphorus cycle.

Source: adapted from: http://andersonapes.pbworks.com/w/page/12868274/Pictures%20and %20Diagrams.

in the soil around plant roots are the main route of phosphorus transfer from soil to plant (Elmqvist *et al.* 2010). This means that farming that promotes mychorrhizae (such as organic farming or the use of biochar) makes better use of available phosphorus.

The huge addition of mined phosphorus puts a major strain on aquatic ecosystems, where phosphorus is the key limiting nutrient. This can cause massive algae growth and eutrophication, killing fish and sometimes flipping ecosystems into alternative, less diverse but stable states (that is they *collapse*). This is not only the case in freshwaters, as nutrient pollution has led Caribbean coral reefs (MEA 2005) to change to algae-dominated ecosystems with few fish (see Chapter 4). For years in Australia (with the most nutrient-poor soils in the world) we have splurged and applied large amounts of 'super' or super-phosphate fertilizer to force plant growth. At the same time, we are actively pumping out to sea the phosphorus-rich wastes that we call 'sewage'. In fact nothing could reflect the fact that our planning is not based on ecological reality than the way we treat our sewage. In ecological terms this is a key resource of nutrients, especially phosphorus, but also nitrogen, potassium and organic carbon; yet we pump it into rivers or the sea, where it causes major ecological problems. We thus impoverish *both* the land and the sea at the same time. Clearly, our planning has not been based on knowledge of the great nutrient cycles that power the world's ecosystems. However, we now *do* know this, yet we continue to do this, partly owing to the huge infrastructure costs needed to change our poorly designed sewerage systems, and partly because governments don't understand how crucial the resource is that is being lost.

Phosphorus is not a common element in the Earth's crust, and it is believed that we are close to reaching 'peak phosphorus'. That is, we are close to having found and mined around half of the known high phosphate rocks available on Earth. The expected global peak in phosphorus production is predicted to occur before 2035, after which demand will exceed supply (Cordell 2010), yet future access to phosphorus receives little or no international attention (Cordell *et al.* 2009).

The carbon cycle

There are many other nutrient cycles, indeed every nutrient needed by life has its own cycle, but the final cycle I shall consider here is the *carbon cycle*. The carbon cycle is one cycle of special importance to humanity. Carbon dioxide (CO_2) is an atmospheric trace gas that is fixed through photosynthesis (along with water) into sugars. Take for example the miracle of a 'tree', and if you don't take them for granted, they *are* in fact quite miraculous. It takes in CO_2 from the air through pores (stomates) in its leaves, and brings water from the soil, perhaps 100 metres upwards to its leaves. There, in the chloroplasts in the cells, chlorophyll uses sunlight's energy to combine CO_2 and water into high-energy sugars. These can then be turned into cellulose and lignin that make up the wood of the tree. The tree also uses some of these sugars as energy sources (through respiration), which breaks them down to CO_2 again, so at night the tree emits CO_2 (see Chapter 1). When the tree dies, it is decomposed by insects, fungi and bacteria. Some of its carbon will stay in the soil for a while as soil carbon. Much of the carbon, however, will be released as CO_2 back into the atmosphere. The tree has been through a great cycle, taking in CO_2, storing it while alive, and releasing it when dead. Carbon is also being added to and removed from the biosphere. Volcanoes release CO_2, and some CO_2 is also trapped in limestone and carbon-rich sediments, and then buried in ocean sediments. As a result of plate tectonics, some of this sedimentary carbon is taken into the mantle and melted into magma that then emerges again in volcanoes. Figure 2.5 shows a simplified diagram of the carbon cycle.

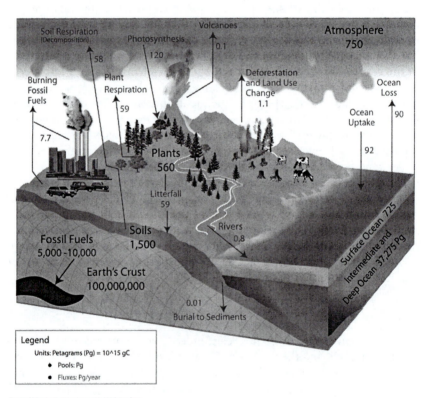

Copyright 2010 University of New Hampshire GLOBE Carbon Cycle
Data Sources: Adapted from Houghton, R.A. Balancing the Global Carbon Budget. Annu. Rev. Earth Planet. Sci. 007.35:313-347, updated emissions values are from the Global Carbon Project: Carbon Budget 2009.

Figure 2.5 The global carbon cycle.

Source: Globe Carbon Cycle Program (University of New Hampshire, funded by Inter-agency body involving NASA and US National Science Foundation. http://classic.globe.gov/fsl/html/templ.cgi?carboncycleDia&lang=en). Units are in Petagrams (10^{15} grams) = gigatonnes (Gt) = billions of tonnes of carbon. Note that 1 tonne of carbon = 3.67 tonnes CO_2.

There is a huge pool of carbon in the Earth's crust (100 million Gt), a large pool of carbon in the oceans (over 38 thousand Gt) and moderate pools in fossil fuels and soils (5,000–10,000 and 1,500 Gt respectively). The atmosphere and plants contain smaller reservoirs of carbon at 750 and 560 Gt respectively. Volcanoes emit only around 0.1 Gt, and 0.01 Gt is buried to sediments. It is important to understand that parts of the system can function as *both* sources and sinks of carbon. Plants fix 120 Gt of carbon and respire half (59 Gt) of that back to the atmosphere. Almost all the rest goes into litter and goes back to the atmosphere through decomposers and soil respiration. The oceans emit CO_2 as well as absorbing it, though they now absorb slightly more and have become a net carbon sink of 2 Gt a year.

So there is a natural balance in the carbon cycle, where carbon cycles again and again through ecosystems. That is why you probably contain some carbon atoms that were once part of Julius Caesar. That is why each of us certainly does contain carbon atoms that were once part of dinosaurs. The carbon cycle thus knits together the history of all life on Earth, and shows us the great continuity of the cycles operating within our world. They make us what we are. Of course, the carbon cycle can be thrown out of balance also, and humanity is doing just this. Emitting 8.8 Gt a year from fossil fuels and land use change may not sound like much, compared to the carbon pools shown in Figure 2.5, but it throws the cycle out of balance. The oceans mop up 2 Gt and vegetation mops up some also, but at least *half* the carbon humanity emits from fossil fuels stays in the atmosphere and warms this through being a greenhouse gas (Pittock 2009). Thus, by disturbing the carbon cycle, we force our climate to change, and to change faster than it has in a long time (Pittock 2009). In fact, disturbing the carbon cycle overall may just be the worst thing ecologically that humanity has done. It worsens many other environmental problems, and pushes the world that much closer to ecological catastrophe (Washington and Cook 2011). However, the reality is that ecological catastrophe is in train *already*. Climate change however *speeds up* that catastrophe.

So *in summary*, the great nutrient cycles, along with energy flow from the Sun, are the backbone of the ecosystem processes that run the world. It is no use having heaps of energy and no nutrients that are essential for life. It is similarly no use having oodles of nutrients but no energy flow to grow with. Life needs *both*. Yet humanity is altering both in increasingly major ways. Using nutrients efficiently in our farming is a good way of managing our agro-ecosystems and maintaining productivity. However, lack of any serious ecological grounding in our society has meant that we have fallen into false reasoning. We believe that if some nutrients (e.g. nitrogen or phosphorus) are good, then more is better! But *more* is not always better. Thus we artificially produce nitrate from the nitrogen in the air using fossil fuel energy, and we rapidly mine phosphorus-rich rocks. We pile these on our fields. And the difference in growth has been amazing. However, like many things in life, if something seems too good to be true, it probably is.

You can drive through the Australian countryside and pick the spots where farmers have put on super-phosphate recently, as the rich green of growing crops makes it obvious. What is *not* obvious is that a large amount of phosphorus is going into creeks and causing blue-green algae blooms and eutrophication in rivers and dams. Similarly, when we apply nitrogen and sulphur fertilizers, the acidification of ecosystems is not obvious. Also, because there have always been storms and hurricanes, the few per cent extra water vapour added to the atmosphere by climate change is not that obvious, even though extreme weather events are becoming more powerful and cost the insurance industry far more. The cost from extreme weather events went up fourfold in the last 10 years (Pittock 2009).

Looking at it from a geological perspective, the disturbance humanity makes to the great nutrient cycles may seem small, and sure to be corrected 'over time'. But that is *geological* time (millions of years) while humans are concerned primarily with the next 100 or 1,000 years at most. The environmental crisis is here now and will be played out over this century. The nutrient cycles are part of the backbone of the life processes that run our world. Disturbing them in major ways is thus a major contributor to the environmental crisis. Through writing this chapter, I have revisited the details of the nutrient cycles, and my overall feeling is *a sense of awe*. How wondrous are these interconnecting cycles that make it possible for life to continue to flourish on Earth?

When I consider that sulphur returns to the atmosphere from the oceans via the gas dimethyl sulphide, a gas produced by algae, it makes me 'wonder'. Not 'wonder if it's true', but wonder as in *marvel* at the evolved complexity in life that helps optimize these essential nutrient cycles. Another way to express this is that the function of these great nutrient cycles is simply beautiful and elegant. I suppose my overall feeling is one of being part of the Great Wheel of Life. My body probably contains atoms of *Tyrannosaurus Rex*, of the extinct giant Australian megafauna such as the Diprotodon, of the Dodo, and possibly of Alexander, Nefertiti and Caesar, Buddha, Christ and Mohammed, of Aristotle, Newton and Darwin. The great cycles thus link us all into a continuous tapestry of life. Accordingly, they deserve respect. We thus disturb the great cycles at our peril.

3 Ecosystem services – essential but overlooked

> Generations have trod, have trod, have trod;
> And all is seared with trade; bleared, smeared with toil;
> And wears man's smudge and shares man's smell:
> The soil is bare now, nor can foot feel, being shod.
> And for all this, nature is never spent;
> There lives the dearest freshness deep down things;
> And though the last lights off the black West went
> Oh, morning, at the brown brink eastward, springs—
> Because the Holy Ghost over the bent
> World broods with warm breast and with ah! bright wings.
> (From 'God's Grandeur', Gerard Manley Hopkins)

As the previous chapters have shown, it is clear that humanity does in fact *need* Nature. It is obvious but overlooked. It is thus a logical progression to say that Nature provides services (things we need) and benefits to humanity. The functioning of ecosystems in terms of delivering to humanity what are now called 'ecosystem services' was first described in a US report, 'Man's Impact on the Global Environment' (SCEP 1970), sponsored by the Massachusetts Institute of Technology in 1970 (Daily 1997). It listed nine environmental services that would decline if there was a decline in ecosystem function. These were pest control, pollination, fisheries, climate regulation, soil retention, flood control, soil formation, cycling of matter and the composition of the atmosphere. This was expanded by Holdren and Ehrlich (1974) to include soil fertility and the maintenance of the 'genetic library'. The services ecosystems provide were subsequently referred to as 'public services of the global ecosystem' (Ehrlich *et al.* 1977) and 'nature's services' (Westman 1977). Finally, they were termed *ecosystem services* by Ehrlich and Ehrlich (1981). 'Natural capital' was another idea coined by Vogt (1948) and further developed by Costanza and Daly (1992). This included non-renewable resources, renewable resources and ecosystem services to demonstrate the significance of ecosystems in providing the 'biophysical foundation' for the societal development of all human economies.

Daily (1997) states that ecosystem services are the 'conditions and processes through which natural ecosystems, and the species that make them up, sustain and fulfil human life'. They maintain biodiversity and the production of ecosystem goods such as seafood, forage, timber, biomass fuels, fibre, medicines and industrial products. Ecosystem services are the actual life-support functions such as cleansing, recycling and renewal, that also confer on humanity intangible, non-material, aesthetic, spiritual and cultural benefits. However, the term 'ecosystem services' has really come into vogue since the 2005 Millennium Ecosystem Assessment (MEA 2005), but what does it mean? It seeks to encapsulate the idea that Nature provides essential services to humanity that we depend on. Basically, 'ecosystem services' as a term highlights the theme of this book, that humanity is *dependent* on Nature. The MEA (2005) stated:

> Everyone in the world depends completely on Earth's ecosystems and the services they provide such as food, water, disease management, climate regulation, spiritual fulfilment and aesthetic enjoyment . . . the human species, while buffered against environment changes by culture and technology, is fundamentally dependent on the flow of ecosystem services.

Figure 3.1 shows how ecosystem services relate to human well-being (MEA 2005).

Ecosystem services are commonly defined today as the direct and indirect contributions of ecosystems to human well-being (De Groot *et al.* 2010). The MEA noted that few ecosystem services have been the focus of research, and thus the data are often inadequate for detailed global assessment of ecosystem services. The MEA was written by 1,360 experts from 95 countries. It split ecosystem services into four parts, being *provisioning services* (products obtained from ecosystems), *regulating services* (benefits obtained from regulation of ecosystem processes), *cultural services* (non-material benefits) and *supporting services* (those necessary for the production of all other ecosystem services).

Before we go on to discuss how these were broken down, we need to consider the big picture. Ecosystem services as defined above are *anthropocentric* in that they are all about the services (benefits) provided to humanity by Nature. Whether it be products, benefits from the regulation of ecosystem processes, non-material and cultural benefits or the supporting services that support the other three categories, these are about benefits to *us humans*. The definition of ecosystem services thus almost always focuses on ourselves, though in fact every species on Earth requires many of the ecosystem services listed below. The first two categories list ecosystem services as benefits from actual products derived from Nature (such as food, fibre, medicines and even water), and benefits from regulation of ecological processes (air quality, climate, erosion regulation). The third category is

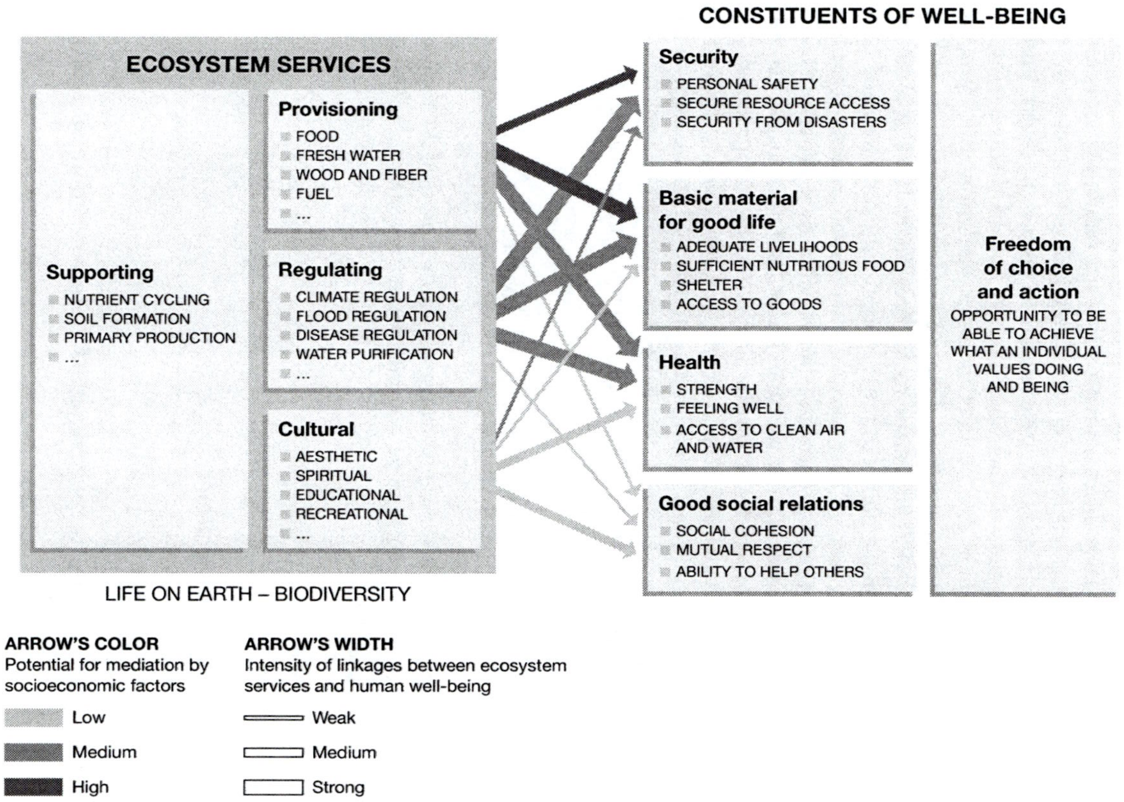

CONSTITUENTS OF WELL-BEING

Security
- PERSONAL SAFETY
- SECURE RESOURCE ACCESS
- SECURITY FROM DISASTERS

Basic material for good life
- ADEQUATE LIVELIHOODS
- SUFFICIENT NUTRITIOUS FOOD
- SHELTER
- ACCESS TO GOODS

Health
- STRENGTH
- FEELING WELL
- ACCESS TO CLEAN AIR AND WATER

Good social relations
- SOCIAL COHESION
- MUTUAL RESPECT
- ABILITY TO HELP OTHERS

Freedom of choice and action
OPPORTUNITY TO BE ABLE TO ACHIEVE WHAT AN INDIVIDUAL VALUES DOING AND BEING

ECOSYSTEM SERVICES

Provisioning
- FOOD
- FRESH WATER
- WOOD AND FIBER
- FUEL
- ...

Regulating
- CLIMATE REGULATION
- FLOOD REGULATION
- DISEASE REGULATION
- WATER PURIFICATION
- ...

Cultural
- AESTHETIC
- SPIRITUAL
- EDUCATIONAL
- RECREATIONAL
- ...

Supporting
- NUTRIENT CYCLING
- SOIL FORMATION
- PRIMARY PRODUCTION
- ...

LIFE ON EARTH – BIODIVERSITY

ARROW'S COLOR
Potential for mediation by socioeconomic factors
- Low
- Medium
- High

ARROW'S WIDTH
Intensity of linkages between ecosystem services and human well-being
- Weak
- Medium
- Strong

Figure 3.1 The relationships between ecosystem health and human well-being.
Source: MEA (2005).

actually an interesting ethical statement, in that it accepts that there are *non-material* benefits from Nature that are nonetheless important for humanity, such as spiritual values, inspiration, cultural diversity and 'sense of place'.

The final category of ecosystem services listed by the MEA is *supporting services*, and in a way this reflects the weakness of focusing on a 'benefits to humanity' approach. They differ from provisioning, regulatory and cultural services in that their impacts on people are often indirect (or occur over the long term). These are things that are essential to keep ecosystems running, and the first two chapters of this book discuss two of them: energy and nutrients. They don't fit in as a 'product' or just a regulation of the 'process', for they are *the processes themselves*. Thus we need photosynthesis and Net Primary Productivity (NPP) and nutrients for ecosystems to exist. Similarly, we need soil formation for plants to function optimally, and we need water to cycle through ecosystems. These are the fundamental processes that have to function to support ecosystems and the benefits they provide us. It is interesting to note, however, that we often know *least* about these essential supporting services, as we focus on the key products and processes that provide us obvious benefits. Sometimes we will then admit that there are 'non-material' benefits that Nature provides us, and that 'Man does not live by bread alone'. As the first two chapters have demonstrated, however, all too often we forget the essential importance of supporting services. They are fundamental, but so often overlooked.

Ecosystem services listed by Millennium Ecosystem Assessment

The MEA synthesis split these four categories into a total of 31 topics:
Provisioning Services are products obtained from ecosystems, including:

- food
- fibre
- fuel
- genetic resources
- biochemicals and medicines
- ornamental resources
- fresh water supply.

Regulating Services are benefits obtained from regulation of ecosystem processes including:

- air quality regulation
- climate regulation
- water regulation
- erosion regulation
- water purification and waste treatment

- disease regulation
- pest regulation
- pollination
- pollution and natural hazard regulation.

Cultural Services are non-material benefits through spiritual enrichment, cognitive development, reflection, recreation and aesthetic experience, including:

- cultural diversity
- spiritual and religious values
- knowledge systems
- education values
- inspiration
- aesthetic values
- social relations
- sense of place
- cultural heritage values
- recreation and tourism.

Supporting Services are those that are necessary for the *production of all other ecosystem services*. These include:

- soil formation
- photosynthesis
- primary production
- nutrient cycling
- water cycling.

Thus one can see 'genetic resources' as a product that Nature provides us. Food, fibre, fuel and medicines (and other biochemicals such as oils, gums, resins, etc.) are more obvious products that provide benefits to humanity. In terms of 'ornamental resources', animal and plant products, such as skins, shells and flowers, are used as ornaments, and plants are used for landscaping. Regulating services are pretty easy to understand. We need our air and water cleaned and maintained by ecosystems. However, it is not just a matter of water 'quality', it is also *quantity* over time. Forests and swamps absorb high rainfall and slowly release water to rivers over time. For example, the Mississippi forested wetlands used to store 60 days of river discharge, but through drainage and clearing only now store 12 days worth (MEA 2005). It is also clear that we need plants to bind soil and organic matter and microorganisms to stop it from eroding away when it rains. We need our wastes (such as sewage and agricultural wastes) to be broken down so they don't pollute, and so that their nutrients are recycled to ecosystems. We also need ecosystems to control expanding populations of pests such as insects. In a balanced ecosystem, most of the time predators control pest outbreaks. We may perhaps forget that ecosystems also regulate disease. Changes in ecosystems can directly change the abundance of human pathogens, such as cholera, and can alter the abundance of disease vectors, such as mosquitoes. We can also easily understand that ecosystems reduce pollution by filtering and absorbing it, breaking down dangerous chemicals, or burying them in sediments.

However, perhaps most of us don't recognize just how important *pollination* is. Evidence (admittedly incomplete) shows a global decline in the abundance of pollinators (Daily 1997). This has rarely led to a complete failure of crops, but has been shown to reduce crop yield (MEA 2005): 75 per cent of the world's crop plants (and many pharmaceutical plants) rely on pollination by animal vectors; 87 of 115 leading global crops (35 per cent of the food supply) have their productivity increased through animal pollination. The importance of wild pollinators for agricultural production is increasingly being recognized, and wild pollinators may also interact with managed bees to increase crop yields. A review of 23 studies found an exponential decay in pollinator visitation with distance to natural or semi-natural habitats (Elmqvist *et al.* 2010). Similarly, many of us may not know that many natural hazards are reduced by ecosystems. The presence of coastal ecosystems such as mangroves and coral reefs can reduce the damage caused by hurricanes or large waves. Forests and wetlands similarly moderate flood events after extreme rainfall.

The MEA (2005) showed true leadership by recognizing 'cultural ecosystem services' as a category, even though they are *non-material* and don't provide physical benefits. For example, the diversity of ecosystems is one factor that influences the diversity of cultures, an important but non-material influence. Many religions also attach spiritual and religious values to ecosystems and wild places, and also many 'non-religious' people feel spiritual value in Nature (Washington 2002). Ecosystems influence the 'types of knowledge' developed by different cultures. Ecosystems provide the basis for both formal and informal education in many societies. We cannot educate about Nature and its importance if we don't have natural ecosystems to take people to, so they can learn about them. Ecosystems also provide a rich source of inspiration for art, poetry, writing, folklore and architecture. Many people find beauty or aesthetic value in various aspects of ecosystems, as reflected in the support for national parks and wilderness. Ecosystems also influence the types of social relations that are established in particular cultures. Fishing societies, for example, differ in many respects in their social relations from nomadic herding or agricultural societies (MEA 2005). Many people value the 'sense of place' that is associated with recognized features of their environment, including aspects of the ecosystem (Cameron 2003). Many societies place high value on the maintenance of either historically important landscapes ('cultural landscapes') or culturally significant species. People often choose where to spend their leisure time based in part on the natural values of a place (MEA 2005).

The MEA has chosen to call this category 'cultural ecosystem values'; however, it could possibly better have been called 'non-material' values. Spiritual values, inspirational values and sense of place are not necessarily *always* dependent on culture, but rather reflect at the deepest level our personal 'witness' of the Earth and how we bond with life (see Chapter 5). So are these non-material ecosystem services discussed here in fact 'essential'? Most people would I think agree they are important 'benefits' that we humans derive from Nature. I would go further, however, and argue that they are indeed *essential*. Just as I would argue that the diversity of life is a 'plus' ethically, so too I believe cultural diversity is a plus (and endlessly fascinating). An early recommendation that the conservation of cultural diversity be included in the Principles of Ecologically Sustainable Development was made by Diesendorf (1997). The font of human creativity and art is tied up with inspiration, with the appreciation of beauty (described prosaically in the MEA as 'aesthetic values') and with a deep spiritual bonding to place, and a sense of wonder at life and the Universe (Berry 1988; Washington 2002). These are things that give us *meaning*, joy and happiness, that make us feel connected with life. At a fundamental level they thus deserve recognition as something not only necessary but *essential*. Their inclusion in the MEA I think shows an implicit (if unstated) understanding that the roots of the environmental crisis are tied up in our worldviews, ethics, philosophies and ideologies. We shall return to this aspect later.

Ecosystem Services and 'TEEB'

Six years after the MEA, 'The Economics of Ecosystems and Biodiversity' or TEEB (a project run by the UN Environment Programme) modified the list of ecosystem services down to 22 topics. The provisioning services in TEEB lump fibre and fuel into 'raw materials'. Regulating services lump pest and disease control under 'biological control' (with 'seed dispersal' added). Natural hazard regulation was replaced by 'moderation of extreme events'. Erosion regulation became 'erosion prevention'. A new category 'Maintenance of soil fertility and nutrient cycling' was added (Kumar 2010). However, in essence the provisioning and regulating services are much the same in TEEB as in the MEA. The major changes were in the next two categories. Cultural services became 'cultural and amenity services', while supporting services was axed and a new category 'habitat services' added. This 'habitat services' covered just 'migratory species' and 'maintenance of genetic diversity'. There is now no category that covers photosynthesis or NPP, though soil formation and nutrient cycling are covered under regulating services. TEEB states it omits supporting services (such as nutrient cycling and food chain dynamics), as it sees them as a 'subset of ecological processes' (Kumar 2010). This means, however, that the essential underlying importance of photosynthesis and NPP are now not recognized by TEEB as an ecosystem service.

The cultural services category has also been substantially reduced, through omitting many categories listed in the MEA. Those omitted include cultural diversity and heritage, 'sense of place' and 'knowledge systems'. Education values only get mentioned in terms of 'information for cognitive development'. Aesthetic *values* become just aesthetic 'information'. Similarly spiritual and religious values become just spiritual 'experience'. Thus overall, the idea of what is involved in cultural services is much reduced in TEEB. Indeed, the inclusion of 'amenity' in the new title 'cultural and amenity services' gives a view as to where it is coming from philosophically, as 'amenity' is about human use and comfort. As we shall see later, values in TEEB other than monetary receive only token status (less than one page on 'intrinsic value').

Although ecosystem services often increase in quality, quantity or resilience with increasing biodiversity, the measure of biodiversity that best predicts how to maintain resilience varies widely according to the ecosystem services being studied (Elmqvist *et al.* 2010). TEEB thus notes that it is not yet possible to account accurately for the role of biodiversity, nor the probable impact of its decline, on ecosystem services delivery in general. In other words, humans are reliant on ecosystem services, and these rely on biodiversity, but we are sending biodiversity extinct at a great rate. The trouble is we don't know (and may never know) *which* species are required for which ecosystem services.

So we can see that views change as to what ecosystem services *are* and what four categories they should be included in. As an environmental scientist I find the original MEA list of ecosystem services a more holistic, ethical and understandable breakdown of ecosystem services than that put forward by TEEB. I shall thus use the more holistic MEA description of ecosystem services. Having said that, in regard to provisioning and regulating services, there is good agreement between the two studies.

State of play of ecosystem services

So having waded through what ecosystem services 'are', what is happening to them? The MEA (2005) noted that human use of all ecosystem services is growing rapidly. Half of provisioning services such as food and water supply and 70 per cent of regulating and cultural services are *being degraded or used unsustainably*. Overall it concluded 60 per cent of ecosystem services are being degraded or used unsustainably. Many ecosystem services are being degraded primarily to increase food supply.

Take a moment to sit back and think about this. These are the categories of the essential products and processes that ecosystems provide humanity. However, half of the products ecosystems provide us and 70 per cent of the regulating services (and also cultural services) are in decline, being degraded or used unsustainably. The MEA came out in 2005, and this single statement should have rung (and continue to ring) alarm bells. However, recently at a talk I read out this statement and people expressed surprise. The message has not got through, or if it was heard it was not understood. The reason it was not understood may have been owing to jargon and poor communication, but mainly I suspect it was owing to society's on-going ecological ignorance, and our capacity to deny unpleasant realities (see Chapter 7).

The MEA concluded that degradation of ecosystem services could grow significantly during the first half of the century and stop achievement of the Millennium Development Goals. Any progress achieved in addressing these goals of poverty and hunger eradication, improved health and environmental sustainability is unlikely to be sustained if most of the ecosystem services on which humanity relies continue to be degraded (MEA 2005). The degradation of ecosystem services is harming many of the world's poorest people, and is sometimes the principal factor *causing* poverty (even if some poverty studies such as 'Rethinking Poverty' fail to mention this aspect, UN DESA 2009). The reliance of the rural poor on ecosystem services is rarely measured and often overlooked. As human well-being declines, the options available to people to enable them to regulate the use of natural resources (at sustainable levels) also declines. This increases the pressures on ecosystem services, and can create a downward spiral of increasing poverty and degradation of ecosystem services (MEA 2005). The MEA also noted that both economic growth and population growth lead to increased consumption of ecosystem services. Climate change and excessive nutrient loading were listed by the MEA as issues that will become more severe in the next 40 years.

The main problem, TEEB concludes, is that society does not think about or *value* ecosystem services. Although the delivery of ecosystem services often increases with increasing biodiversity, the way this happens varies widely according to the ecosystem service being studied. It is not yet possible to account accurately for the role of biodiversity, nor the probable impact of its decline, on ecosystem services delivery in general (Elmqvist *et al.* 2010). Ecosystem services are natural capital assets not included in our national accounts, and indicators such as GDP don't measure their degradation (MEA 2005). An important step towards the conservation and sustainable use of biodiversity and ecosystem services lies in accounting for the positive and negative 'externalities' associated with human activities. In economics, an 'externality' is a cost or benefit not transmitted through prices, and incurred by a party who did not agree to the action causing the cost or benefit. A benefit is called a positive externality, while a cost is called a negative externality. The impacts on the environment caused by humanity are thus overwhelmingly 'negative externalities'. Most resource management decisions are influenced by ecosystem services entering markets, and non-market benefits are often lost or degraded (MEA 2005). Many ecosystem services (such as purification of water, regulation of floods or provision of aesthetic benefits) don't pass through markets and are largely unrecorded.

For example, the water regulation benefits of wetlands don't appear under an ecosystem service category, but as higher profits for the water-providing sector. The non-market benefits of ecosystem services however are often high, and sometimes higher than the marketed benefits (MEA 2005), as Figure 3.2 shows.

The authors of TEEB argue that the lack of progress to protect ecosystem services after the release of the MEA stems not only from the failures of markets and systems of economic analysis and accounting (notably GDP) to capture values of ecosystem services, but also from our limited understanding of several points. These include how different services

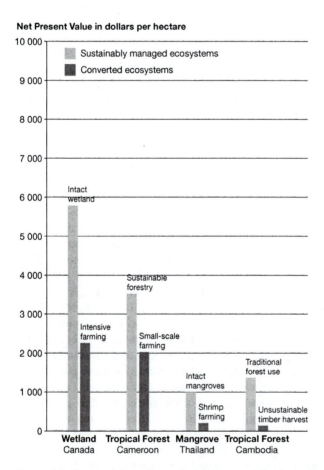

Figure 3.2 Economic benefits under alternate management practices. The net overall benefits from the more sustainably managed ecosystems are greater than those from the converted ecosystems, even though the *private* market benefits of the converted would be greater.

Source: MEA (2005, Figure 3.3).

are interlinked with each other, and the various components of ecosystem function and the role of biodiversity, and how different human actions change various ecosystem services (De Groot *et al.* 2010). Research on ecosystem services is now, however, finally increasing.

There are no markets for the largely public goods and services that flow from ecosystems and biodiversity, and so there are no established 'prices'. TEEB notes that this is in fact *market failure* (Sukhdev 2010). The reality is that markets exist only to trade *private* claims (Sukhdev 2010). Figure 3.2 (from the MEA) shows the economic benefits of managing four ecosystems under alternate management practices. The net overall benefits from the more sustainably managed ecosystems are greater than those from the converted ecosystems, even though the *private* market benefits of the converted would be greater.

The TEEB approach to deal with this is to reach a broader holistic economic approach that recognizes the benefits of natural capital. TEEB argues that economic valuation of Nature and public goods and services are both necessary *and* ethical and that 'shadow prices' can and should be calculated and presented (Sukhdev 2010). TEEB argues that so deep-seated is modern society's inherent *market-centric mindset*, that the mere device of demonstrating economic value for ecosystem services can become an important strategy for positive change (Sukhdev 2010). Thus at times it suffices just to recognize value (be it intrinsic, spiritual or social) to create a policy response favouring conservation or sustainable use. At other times it may be necessary to demonstrate the full economic value of an ecosystem service in order for policymakers to respond. The wetlands conserved near Kampala are an example of the latter, which had value as a result of their waste treatment function (Sukhdev 2010).

Valuing ecosystem services

So how do we *value* ecosystem services? Daily (1997) explains that ecosystem services are absolutely essential to civilization, but modern urban life obscures their existence. Once explained, the importance of ecosystem services is quickly appreciated by many people. However, the actual *assigning* of value to ecosystem services may arouse great suspicion, and for good reason, Daily concludes. This valuation involves resolving *fundamental philosophical issues*, such as the underlying basis for 'value'. This is a debate that has continued to the present day, and is arguably a key cause of the environmental crisis. The MEA (2005) touched on this issue, while TEEB (Kumar 2010) gave it more coverage. TEEB believes that abstaining from explicit valuation (on apparently valid scientific or ethical grounds) often amounts to no more than an acceptance of someone else's implicit valuation, which is then used to determine environmental trade-offs (Sukhdev 2010). It is not a risk-free exercise to demonstrate value by deriving and propagating 'shadow prices'. There is always the risk that misguided decision-makers or exploitative interest may want to 'use the prices for the wrong ends' (Sukhdev 2010). Indeed, having long experience of wilderness conservation (and doing my Ph.D. on wilderness) it is clear there will always be exploitation interests seeking to subvert any argument in the cause of making money from natural areas.

TEEB observes that the common metric in economics is *monetary valuation*, hence they use this. Some believe that the reliance on this has plagued many ecosystem services assessments, failing to show values that are critical to understanding the relation between society and Nature (De Groot *et al.* 2010). I share this concern. TEEB acknowledges that economic valuation functions as a system of 'cultural projection' that imposes a way of thinking and form of relationship with the environment, and 'reflects particular perceived realities, worldviews, mind sets and belief systems' (Brondizio *et al.* 2010). They note also that economic values are not objective 'facts', nor do they reflect universal truths. TEEB, however, argues that the right ethical choice is to compute these imperfect valuations for society to use. They believe valuations are a powerful feedback mechanism for a society that has distanced itself from the biosphere upon which its very health and survival depends. However, valuation can contribute to create a 'commodity fiction' or Western construct that Nature is pure materiality. The danger of this commodity fiction is that the commoditized environment becomes a contrived artefact of itself, as ecosystems and biodiversity can be owned and traded in the market system for money (Brondizio *et al.* 2010). However, TEEB concludes that mainstream economic beliefs of the values of ecosystems and biodiversity are *defined by people's willingness to pay for them*, and the existence or creation of markets. However, the neoclassical approach to valuation (people's willingness to pay) is based on the belief that there is no intrinsic value except as perceived by humans (Crabbe 2008). In short, while TEEB acknowledges the danger of monetary valuation, it thinks we have to value ecosystem services in monetary values to save them. This is a difficult ethical call, as we shall see.

So how to value ecosystem services meaningfully? As a 'value-articulating institution', environment valuation is not particularly inclusive of all environment values, given that values of some ecosystem services *cannot be monetarized* (Brondizio *et al.* 2010). TEEB points out that people may wish to participate in environment decision-making as 'citizens' instead of 'consumers'. Having warned of the problem of deriving value, TEEB says the extremes of how to value ecosystem services are 'people's willingness to pay' or 'allowing people to deliberate'. Brondizio *et al.* (2010) in TEEB argue there are three ways to articulate value:

1   **Contingent valuation method** – value is deemed to be pre-existing and needs to be 'discovered'. There is a separation between values and facts, and human and Nature. It works on the principle that you can substitute money for ecosystem goods and services.

2 **Deliberative or social process methods** – has a democratic stance, and value is 'constructed' in social processes, and unknown values evolve through deliberation.
3 **Multi-criteria methods** – involves complexity, value is understood in terms of ranked importance.

I can't help feeling the above does not provide much of a choice to derive the *value* of Nature. Clearly, none of the above gives Nature a voice. All of the above are anthropocentric, and none of them accepts that Nature has *intrinsic* value (see Chapter 6). The first believes that money can replace essential ecosystem services, which is clearly a delusion in terms of ecological reality. Leaving a pile of money to future generations will mean nothing if we have destroyed the life support systems (and half of the world's species) they will need to rely on. The second seems to think that value depends just on the group of people who 'construct' it. This may at first glance seem 'democratic' but is only a partial human democracy (of those involved in the evaluation) and again gives Nature no voice. The third basically seems to dodge the issue, and is made up of many small values, and weighting of values can be easily biased (Pascual *et al.* 2010). It still depends on the weighting one gives to each subset of values. I would thus argue that each of the above has problems and is unsatisfactory to value ecosystem services, both practically and ethically. We shall discuss intrinsic value further in Chapter 6, along with the dominance of anthropocentrism within academia and society.

From the above, TEEB states that the basic assumption is that society can assign values to ecosystem services and biodiversity, but only to the extent that these fulfil needs of *conferring satisfaction to humans*, either directly or indirectly (Pascual *et al.* 2010). The economic conception of value they admit is thus anthropocentric. Pascual *et al.* (2010) agree that this valuation approach should be used to complement *but not substitute* for other legitimate ethical or scientific reasoning (and arguments) relating to biodiversity conservation (Turner and Daily 2008). I would agree with the intent of this statement, but would argue that it is *naive* in terms of how the environment is degraded. Exploitation interests will seek to *only* use the monetary valuation, hence the concerns expressed by many. Of course, I can see the dilemma of the authors of TEEB, for what else can they *do* that has not been tried before? Intrinsic, non-material, scientific and spiritual values have been put forward time and again, and Western society has not listened, or listened and not acted.

TEEB states there are two paradigms for monetary valuation: *biophysical methods* and *preference-based methods*, the latter of which is more commonly used in economics (Pascual *et al.* 2010). Biophysical valuation uses a 'cost of production' perspective that derives values from measurements of the physical costs of producing a given ecosystem service. Thus it would consider the physical costs of maintaining a given ecological state.

Preference-based methods rely on models of human behaviour, and rest on the assumption that values arise from the *subjective preference of individuals*. This perspective assumes that ecosystem values are commensurate in monetary terms, and that monetary measures offer a way of establishing trade-offs in how ecosystems are used. Biophysical valuation makes more sense ecologically, as no substitution is possible between human-made and natural resources. However, perhaps not surprisingly, it is preference-based valuation that is mostly used, and it is this that TEEB used to derive its shadow prices (Pascual *et al.* 2010). Monetary valuation (by TEEB and others) is thus derived from people's willingness to pay for essential ecosystem services that they generally *don't understand*.

One other term is worth discussing in relation to valuing ecosystem services: 'discounting'. Proper *discounting* is central to valuing an entity such as an ecosystem service, where the vast majority of value lies *in the future*, and will always lie in the future. In other words, the value of an ecosystem service must consider its on-going value to future generations, which is unlikely to change (even for cultural services). Unlike many economic indicators, the value of ecosystem services cannot thus be discounted downwards over time.

So *in summary*, ecosystem services are the benefits ecosystems provide humanity and are essential for human well-being and survival. Yet 60 per cent of ecosystem services are being degraded or used unsustainably (MEA 2005). The main reason is society's ecological ignorance, and the fact that markets do not consider or value ecosystem services. TEEB (Kumar 2010) has sought to value ecosystem services and produce shadow prices. The way such prices are established, however, is anthropocentric and based on people's preference to pay. Nevertheless, TEEB does show that ecosystem services have major monetary value. Whether this will in fact be used by society and business to stop further degradation of ecosystem services remains to be seen.

So what is the dollar value of Nature? Costanza and Neil (1981) and Costanza and Hannon (1989) came up with a total monetary value of $34 trillion a year, being 2.4 times the world GNP at the time. Costanza *et al.* (1997) estimated the annual average global value of the world's ecosystems as being from $16 to 54 trillion, with an average of $33 trillion a year. This average was 1.8 times the world GNP at the time. Interestingly, the greatest single input was $17 trillion for nutrient cycling, followed by cultural ($3 trillion), and water treatment ($2.2 trillion). Only a modest $0.68 trillion was allocated to climate regulation (a figure bound to be given a larger estimate today). Alexander *et al.* (1998) developed estimates ranging from $3.4 to 17 trillion a year for ecosystem services. However, this only looked at impact on *marketed* value, and thus could not exceed the world GNP (then around 18 trillion US dollars). However, only a fraction of ecosystem services provide private goods traded in existing markets and that would be included in GNP (Costanza *et al.* 1997). Thus ecosystems *at the minimum* are providing monetary services greater than that from the world GNP, probably at least twofold greater.

TEEB (Kumar 2010) is the most recent approach to determining shadow prices ($/ha/yr) for ecosystem services in 11 biomes. It provides minimum and maximum values, though does not provide any average for the biome, nor does it provide the area of these biomes or a total figure for the Earth's ecosystems. Presumably this is deliberate, as TEEB believes one must consider each biome's value, not aggregate global value. This is complicated further by the huge range between minimum and maximum values found in TEEB. However, it is interesting to compare the figures of TEEB with those of Costanza *et al.* (1997). Costanza *et al.* list the value of coral reefs as $6,075/ha/yr, while TEEB lists them as $14 to $1,195,478/ha/yr. Similarly, Costanza *et al.* (1997) list the value for tropical forests as $2007/ha/yr while TEEB lists them as from $91 to $23,222/ha/yr. For the maximum value times the area of tropical forests (1.9 billion ha, Costanza *et al.* 1997) this comes to 44 trillion dollars just for tropical forests. Similarly, for coral reefs, the maximum value in TEEB times an area of 62 million ha (Costanza *et al.* 1997) is $74 trillion dollars a year. Clearly, the maximum monetary values in TEEB times the area of such biomes is many times *larger* than the current global GNP of $72 trillion a year. The minimum figures, however, would come out being lower than global GNP. To frame the above discussion in ecological reality, however, Daily (1997) points out that ecosystem services have *infinite use value*, because human life could not be sustained without them.

To conclude positively, ecosystem services have now been acknowledged as essential by UNEP and world governments, and attempts are being made to value them in monetary terms. Scientific research on ecosystem services is at last increasing (Kumar, 2010). There is also an increasing move by academics to apply *systems ecology*, which is a holistic approach based on the premise that an ecosystem is a complex system exhibiting emergent properties (where the sum is greater than the parts). A systems ecology approach helps to show that our current actions are unsustainable. So perhaps the tide has turned, and ignorance about (and denial of) ecosystem services may be on the decline. At last, ecosystem services may be coming into their own, and their essential importance may finally be being recognized.

4 Collapse

Things fall apart; the centre cannot hold;
Mere anarchy is loosed upon the world,
The blood-dimmed tide is loosed, and everywhere
The ceremony of innocence is drowned;
                    (From 'The Second Coming',
                         William Butler Yeats)

There are two collapses one can talk about. The first is the collapse of civilizations, often when they push the ecosystems they rely on into collapse. Many have written about the collapse of civilizations, summarized by Odum and Odum (2001) and Greer (2008). The most recent and authoritative work is Diamond's (2005) book *Collapse*. However, most people talk about collapse as if it will happen *all at once*, whereas Greer (2009) argues that in our civilization's case, it is likely to be a long descent. Here, however, I shall mainly talk about the collapse of *ecosystems*. We shall see, however, that the two collapses are related.

Ultimately, human existence depends on maintaining the web of life within which humans co-evolved with other species. The rapidity of current environment change is *unique in human history* (Gowdy *et al.* 2010). To those mesmerized by the myth of abundance and endlessly rising expectations of 'progress', the idea of nations or global society being on the verge of resource shortages, political chaos and even *collapse* may seem ludicrous (Rees 2008). However, Tainter (1995) has observed that 'what is perhaps most intriguing in the evolution of human societies is the regularity with which the pattern of increasing complexity is interrupted by collapse'. Diamond (2005) notes that many societies that collapsed did so at the height of their power, when the idea of collapse would have seemed ridiculous. However, today our populations are expanding, and the increases in energy use from fossil fuels, and our release of wastes, are weakening the very life-supporting functions on which we all depend for survival. Many entire ecosystems are degraded and verging on collapse. Past civilizations generally faced one environmental problem, while today we face many problems that reinforce each other (Brown 2011). Soskolne *et al.* (2008) ask how we can choose to 'sit idly by when all indications are that the path we are on is already leading to systems failure and collapse?'.

Returning to the collapse of ecosystems, I should make it clear that ecosystems are dynamic, that there is always change within ecosystems, and sometimes there can be natural events that lead to local ecosystem collapse. For example, cyclones and fires can change thousands of hectares of forest and change that ecosystem for decades. There are thus sometimes local 'pulses' in ecosystems that change over time (Gunderson and Holling 2002). Such recovery in ecosystems is part of the dynamism, where, owing to resilience, ecosystems bounce back from disturbance. However, the scale of ecosystem collapse discussed here is far *beyond* natural processes and beyond the resilience of natural systems to cope with. The structure of the world's ecosystem changed more rapidly in the second half of the twentieth century than at any time in recorded human history (MEA 2005).

It has been argued that there is a paradox involved regarding ecosystem collapse. If human exploitation leads to resource collapse, why haven't all ecosystems collapsed? The answer is partly the resilience of ecosystems, and partly that humans can learn and change their actions (Holling *et al.* 2002). Partly, also, it is that the statement sets up a 'straw person' to knock down. All human exploitation of ecosystems does not necessarily lead to resource collapse, as many indigenous cultures that used ecosystems sustainably have shown. It depends on the type and degree of exploitation we place on ecosystems. However, Nature's resilience is not 'magic', it just means that ecosystems have been able to absorb a great deal of damage. The environmental crisis, however, shows us that they cannot continue to do this forever, as discussed below. To understand what is going on means understanding that living systems do not proceed *evenly* in how they change in response to stress. Sometimes ecosystems *collapse*. Thus you can harvest a fishery for hundreds of years, steadily increasing the take of fish, and when you push the harvest just that one bit more, it is the proverbial 'straw that breaks the camel's back', and the fishery collapses. This happened with the Atlantic cod fishery off Newfoundland (see Figure 4.1), which collapsed in 1992 after hundreds of years of exploitation. The fishery has been closed for 13 years as of 2005, but there have been few signs of recovery (MEA 2005). 'Collapse' is a word that many don't like to use, as they think it is 'emotive'. Instead, the literature is full of terms such as 'irreversible non-linear changes' or 'regime shifts' or 'state changes'. Another way to describe collapse is 'sudden unexpected losses as ecosystems cross thresholds and degrade irreversibly' (MEA 2005).

However, we are all aware what happens to a house if you take out too many of its foundations, it *collapses*. The same thing can happen with ecosystems, and the term is in fact *entirely appropriate*, and this reality is not something we should hide under jargon. This situation of ecosystem degradation leading to collapse has been described as the 'rivet popper' analogy by the Ehrlichs (Ehrlich and Ehrlich 1981). If you keep taking out rivets from an aeroplane, at some point it will fall apart and crash. In terms of history, there are no recorded cases where 'sudden unexpected losses' in major ecosystems have been to the *benefit* of humanity. Where environment stresses are persistent or strong, ecosystems may pass a threshold and experience sudden and catastrophic structural change, a *regime shift* (Pascual *et al.* 2010). Such regime shifts can produce large unexpected changes in ecosystem services. Examples include state changes in lakes, degradation of rangelands, shifts in fish stocks, breakdown of coral reefs and extinctions as a consequence of persistent drought.

But is ecosystem collapse happening? Well, the Millennium Ecosystem Assessment (MEA 2005) identified that 60 per cent (15 of 24) of ecosystem services are being degraded or used unsustainably. The MEA also found that extinction rates were 1,000 times higher than those in the fossil record. Humanity's ecological footprint doubled in the last 40 years (Sukhdev 2010) and is now 1.5 Earths (GFN 2011). This is what it would take to *sustainably* provide for the demands we (collectively) are putting upon the Earth, our home. Of course we have only *one* Earth, which is why ecosystems are degrading and collapsing, and species are going extinct. We have *overshot* what the Earth can sustainably provide (Catton 1982). Between 1970 and 2007, the Living Planet Index fell by 28 per cent. This global trend suggests that we are degrading natural ecosystems at a rate unprecedented in human history (WWF 2010). According to the International Union for the Conservation of Nature (IUCN), a quarter of mammal species face extinction (Gilbert 2008). Conservative estimates indicate that 12 per cent of birds are threatened, as are over 30 per cent of amphibians and 5 per cent of reptiles. E. O. Wilson, the 'father' of biodiversity says that without action, by the end of the century, half the planet's species will be extinct (Wilson 2002).

Most of us tend to focus on what is happening on land, such as rainforest loss, but the state of the world's oceans is also alarming, where:

> Today the synergistic effects of human impacts are laying the groundwork for a comparatively great Anthropocene mass extinction in the oceans with unknown ecological and evolutionary consequences. Synergistic effects of habitat destruction, overfishing, introduced species, warming, acidification, toxins and mass runoff of nutrients are transforming once complex ecosystem like coral reefs into monotonous level bottoms, transforming clear and productive coastal seas into anoxic dead zones and transforming complex food webs topped by big animals into simplified microbially dominated ecosystems with boom and bust cycles of toxic dinoflagellates blooms, jellyfish and disease.
>
> (Jackson 2008)

Gretchen Daily (1997) notes that marine systems are interconnected, but not enough to ensure the regeneration of devastated areas. A 2011 report concluded there was a high risk of marine life extinction unprecedented in human history (IPSO 2011). Widespread fishery collapse has shown the oceans to be alarmingly responsive to the cumulative effects of human intervention. Fisheries have collapsed again and again. In fact, owing to overfishing, aquatic ecosystem collapse has been so severe that the biomass of fish in fisheries has been *reduced by 90 per cent* relative to levels prior to the onset of industrial fishing (MEA 2005). When told this, most people find this literally incredible, for they don't know. The media largely doesn't report this, nor does our education system get this across. Fisheries were taken for granted and pushed to the point of collapse, so now their total biomass is only a tenth of what they once had. We did this again and again to fisheries, and some still suggest we do it yet again.

In terms of the history of how humans have treated the natural world, we now enter (in the words of Winston Churchill) *a period of consequences* (Sukhdev 2010). Ecological scarcities, ecosystem degradation, biodiversity loss and climate change are affecting us severely around the world, causing water and food shortages, socio-political stress, and persistent poverty. The environmental crisis is increasing the level of ecological, social and economic risks that we and future generations will have to manage in our search for well-being for all (Sukhdev 2010).

The MEA (2005) discusses 'non-linear' changes, noting: 'Changes in ecosystems generally take place gradually but some are nonlinear where once a threshold is crossed the system changes to a very different state.' Non-linear change is not always experienced as dramatic ecosystem collapse such as that of the Atlantic cod fishery. Non-linear change also happens with human epidemics. If each infected person infects at least one other person, then an epidemic spreads. In this situation the non-linear change becomes an epidemic, what one could call a collapse in human health. Disease emergence was almost instantaneous in the outbreak of Severe Acute Respiratory Syndrome (SARS). Spanish flu killed 20–40 million in 1918 and today (owing to rapid transportation) it could now kill over 100 million people. Environmental stresses can assist such epidemics. For example, the warming of the African Great Lakes is a result of climate change, and may create conditions that increase the risk of cholera transmission (MEA 2005). When non-linear change in ecosystems occurs, it often leads to ecosystem collapse.

Examples of ecosystem collapse

Eutrophication. Eutrophication is the process by which a body of water acquires a high concentration of nutrients, especially phosphates and nitrates (owing to human disturbance of the nutrient cycles). These typically promote excessive growth of algae. As the algae die and decompose they deplete the water of available oxygen, causing the death of fish and other organisms. Once a nutrient threshold is reached, the aquatic ecosystem changes abruptly, with the appearance of large algal blooms and sometimes oxygen-depleted zones that kill animal life. In lakes, once an ecosystem is under stress from eutrophication, the loss of macrophytes (water plants) paves the way for continuous algal dominance. The loss of macrophytes removes a refuge used by zooplankton, which had previously been controlling algae. Loss of water plants increases mixing, re-suspension and turbidity, and decreases the uptake of nutrients, leaving phytoplankton to dominate the ecosystem. New 'buffering feedback' mechanisms reinforce the degraded ecosystem state (Elmqvist *et al.* 2010). In other words, this new impoverished ecosystem is *quite stable* and resilient. It resists being restored to the previous state, a state that humanity enjoyed, where we made use of the ecosystems services that the former ecosystem provided.

Fisheries collapse – as discussed earlier, the Atlantic cod fishery off Newfoundland collapsed in 1992 after hundreds of years of exploitation, and has not bounced back after more than 13 years closure. This is shown in Figure 4.1. The fact that total biomass of fisheries now is only 10 per

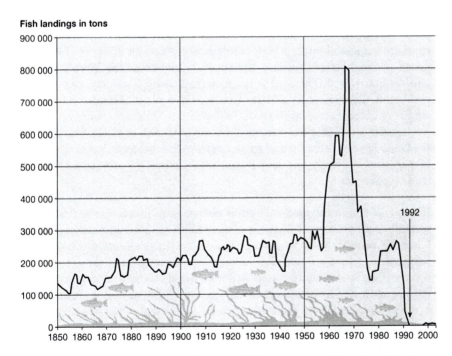

Figure 4.1 Collapse of Atlantic cod stocks off the east coast of Newfoundland in 1992.

Source: Millennium Ecosystem Assessment Synthesis, Figure 11, see: www.maweb.org/en/Synthesis.aspx.

cent of the biomass present before industrial-scale harvesting (MEA 2005) demonstrates the extent of fisheries collapse caused by recent massive overharvesting. Yet we are still often told today that 'there are plenty of fish out there, there is no need for regulation!'.

Species introduction. The introduction of the zebra mussel from Russia to the USA wiped out native clams, changed the energy flow and ecosystem functioning in aquatic ecosystems, and now costs the power industry over $100 million a year. The introduction of the comb jellyfish in the Black Sea caused the loss of 26 major fisheries, and is implicated in causing anoxic dead zones. The loss of sea otters from the Pacific coast of North America led to booming populations of sea urchins, which led to the complete loss of the diverse kelp forests (Cain *et al.* 2008). The introduction of the rabbit into Australia changed whole ecosystems, as did that of the fox and cat, which wiped out many native animals (Johnson 2007). The introduction of the cane toad into Australia caused massive deaths of native animals and continues to worsen as the toads invade new biodiverse areas (such as the Kimberleys, see www.canetoads.com.au/). The introduction of prickly pear (*Opuntia* spp.) into Australia resulted in the loss of hundreds of thousands of hectares of grazing land before biological control using the *Cactoblastis* moth was discovered (Cain *et al.* 2008). Invasive species can clearly lead to major regime change, where whole ecosystems can collapse. The introduced *Miconia calvescens* tree in Hawaii is known as the 'purple plague', and covers over 1,000 square kilometres, driving native species to local extinction (Pascual *et al.* 2010). The 'sensitive plant' *Mimosa pudica* is a similar problem in the swamps of the Northern Territory (Australia), while introduced *Melaleuca* from Australia is a similar threat in the Everglades in the USA. Species introduction to an environment where it has no predators or parasites is clearly one way to put major stress on ecosystems that can lead to collapse.

Change in dominant species in coral ecosystems. There has been a shift in several places from coral-dominated ecosystems to those dominated by algae. Nutrient run-off leads to eutrophication and algae dominance once the herbivorous fishes are removed through overfishing. Such change can take place within months, and results in a less productive and diverse ecosystem. Regime shift in Caribbean coral reefs in the 1980s started with increasing nutrient loading, along with intensive fishing that reduced the numbers of herbivorous fishes. The sea urchin *Diadema antillarum* became the key controller of algae (Pascual *et al.* 2010). When numbers of this species collapsed owing to a pathogen, the reefs shifted (apparently irreversibly) to a low diversity, algae-dominated system with few fish. This occurred over a period of two years, and the new regime is dominated by algae. It has lasted for more than 20 years in this apparently stable state.

Regional climate change. Climate change can trigger sudden changes in regions where ecosystems are already highly water-stressed. Regional climate change has occurred in the Sahel in North Africa, where the vegetation cover was controlled by rainfall. Land degradation has led to a reduction in water recycling and hence a reduction in rainfall over the last 30 years. In tropical regions, deforestation leads to decreased rainfall (MEA 2005). There seem to be two alternative 'steady states' (ecosystems in equilibrium) that can exist in tropical areas: rainforest or savannah. Which one dominates an area will change depending on the amount of clearing. The clearing of cloud forest (e.g. on the Andean slopes) results in a regime shift that may be *largely irreversible*. The cloud forest was established under a wetter rainfall regime thousands of years in the past. Water in this ecosystem now comes from condensation from clouds and mist. If the trees in the cloud forest ecosystem are cleared, then water input decreases markedly, and conditions are then too dry for the cloud forest to re-establish. Deforestation thus leads generally to decreased rainfall. The 'Amazon water pump' puts water vapour into the atmosphere from transpiration from the leaves, so removing trees decreases water vapour and hence rainfall. This forms a positive feedback that can lead to non-linear change in forest cover (or to put it more clearly, a rapid decline or collapse in the rainforest ecosystem) (MEA 2005).

Unsustainable bushmeat trade. Hunting of bush meat (i.e. wild animals) places pressure on many species in Africa and Asia (MEA 2005). Once the harvest exceeds sustainable levels, this puts these species at risk of extinction, while at the same time reducing local food supply. Once the populations of these animals crashes, the ecosystems they are part of may also then change markedly. Of course, hunting as a stress is not just limited to hunting for food. Animals are hunted for their skins, their novelty value to tourists, and for body parts that are used in traditional medicines (e.g. musk deer glands, tiger body parts, etc.).

Loss of keystone species. Keystone species are species that are located at the centre of a 'network of interdependencies' in an ecosystem. In other words, they are like the keystone in a stone arch, so if you remove it the arch comes crashing down. Similarly, if you remove a keystone species, the whole ecosystem changes or even collapses (see Chapter 1). Loss of keystone species has cascading effects on community diversity and ecosystem function (Elmqvist *et al.* 2010).

Threshold changes in ecosystems are not uncommon, but are infrequently encountered in the absence of stresses caused by people, and such stresses are on the increase (MEA 2005). Increased fish harvests raise the likelihood of fisheries collapse, higher rates of climate change boost the potential for species extinction, and increased nitrogen and phosphorus make eutrophication more likely. As human populations become more mobile and more trade occurs internationally, more and more species are being introduced into new habitats, where they can then become pests (as they are free of their natural controls such as predators and disease).

The MEA (2005) showed that there are sudden unexpected losses as ecosystems cross thresholds and degrade irreversibly, and that the increased likelihood of 'non-linear changes' stems from the *loss of biodiversity*, along with growing pressures from multiple direct 'drivers' of ecosystem change. Just as 'non-linear change' is used as a code for collapse, the term 'drivers of change' really means *stresses* on an ecosystem. Drivers of change means ecosystems are under stress, and this explanation is more easily understood by the community, and thus should be used. The MEA noted that most direct drivers of change are *constant or growing* in intensity in most ecosystems. In other words the stresses on ecosystems are increasing rapidly. The expansion of abrupt, unpredictable changes in ecosystems has harmful effects on an increasingly large number of people. The MEA states this is the key challenge today facing managers of ecosystem services.

Causes of ecosystem collapse

So what causes an ecosystem to collapse? An ecosystem may change gradually until a particular pressure on it reaches a threshold, at which point change occurs rapidly and the system shifts to a new state. There can be irreversible regime shifts, and it is impossible to know exactly *where* the dangerous thresholds lie (Elmqvist *et al.* 2010). Once an ecosystem has undergone a non-linear change (that is, 'collapsed'), recovery to the original state may take decades or centuries, and may sometimes be impossible. Although in many cases it may be possible to restore mildly degraded ecosystems, other ecosystems may be so altered that restoration is no longer possible. Given the current human impacts on the biosphere, it has been suggested that the notions of 'restoration and restorability' need to 'be expressed with many caveats' (Elmqvist *et al.* 2010). In other words, we would be fools to think we can restore *all* ecosystems that collapse. The MEA (2005) notes that lack of theories and models that anticipate thresholds means that once one passes the threshold there are 'fundamental system changes or even system collapse'. This is one point at which the MEA *does* actually use the term 'collapse'. Some of these non-linear changes can be very large and have substantial impacts on human well-being. The MEA notes that capabilities for predicting some non-linear changes are improving, but for most ecosystems (and most potential non-linear changes), *science cannot predict the thresholds where change will occur*. Thus we cannot say which particular ecosystems will collapse and at what level of stress, or when. Ecologist Paul Ehrlich (2011) has noted that ecosystems are 'complex adaptive systems', which under stress may collapse in ways we do not anticipate. Clearly the risk of collapse is very real, as history has shown us.

Impacts from human activities on ecosystems may be unpredictable and uncertain, producing 'major step changes, surprises and regime shifts' (Elmqvist *et al.* 2010). When faced with change through environment stress, ecosystems may pass a critical threshold, a point of no return, where the existing ecosystem structure collapses. As an ecosystem's resilience declines, the risk of collapse increases. Resilience may be eroded through human-induced environment change and loss of biodiversity. 'Tipping points' indicate a transition from one state to another. While science is increasingly able to predict some of these risks and non-linearities, predicting the thresholds at which these changes will occur generally is not possible. Users of particular 'indicators of stress' on ecosystems should not assume a linear relationship between biodiversity loss and its consequences. In other words, fishermen did not expect the Atlantic cod fishery to collapse when they pushed harvesting past what turned out to be the ecologically sustainable level. Today, we are in this situation with respect to many ecosystems, as many are close to a threshold. Stress them just that bit more and they will collapse.

Literature on ecological resilience offers growing evidence of 'regime shifts' when critical thresholds are reached, owing to discrete disturbances or cumulative thresholds (Pascual *et al.* 2010). The 'distance' to ecological threshold affects the economic value of ecosystem services. In other words, if an ecosystem is close to collapse, then clearly the economic values coming from ecosystem services are at major risk of being lost (perhaps for good). However, we have already discussed how it is basically impossible to know how close an ecosystem is to collapse. Traditional valuation methods for ecosystem services, when used in this situation of 'radical uncertainty' that we find ourselves in, are thus unreliable. It may be possible to develop 'early warning' indicators to anticipate the proximity to tipping points, but available scientific knowledge has not yet progressed far enough to anticipate shifts with precision (Pascual *et al.* 2010). Radical uncertainty thus poses a formidable risk to the meaningful economic valuation of ecosystem services. As resilience is reduced, then the probability of collapse or 'regime shifts' will rise. As ecosystems approach thresholds, what seem quite 'small' human impacts will lead to increasingly uncertain effects. It may not take much then to push ecosystems over the edge into collapse. The trouble is, we don't know where the tipping points are. Nature is the timekeeper – but we cannot see the clock (Brown 2011).

Does ecosystem collapse matter to us? Hopefully the other chapters in this book have shown that humans are dependent on Nature, so it *should* matter to us. There is a real (although unknown) possibility that net biodiversity loss will have catastrophic effects on human welfare (Gowdy *et al.* 2010). Certainly, we do know that humans are totally dependent on the ecosystem services that Nature provides. If enough ecosystems collapse then this will impact big time on human well-being, whether it is in regard to food, fibre, medicines or the other benefits that Nature provides for free to humanity.

Holding off collapse

Way back in 1972, the book *Limits to Growth* pointed out that our population growth and increasing consumption of resources would exceed planetary limits around the middle of the twenty-first century, most likely leading to societal collapse, though action could avert this (Meadows *et al.* 1972). This report was strongly criticized by those seeking to deny the environmental crisis. However, a 30-year review of the 'standard' model in the 'Limits to Growth' has shown that it has been remarkably accurate (Turner 2008). Accordingly, it has been argued that our choice is to act now to minimize the inevitable harms from the collapse of ecological systems or to 'wait for catastrophic environmental upheavals'. The longer we wait the more costly the consequences (Soskolne *et al.* 2008). Put in this light it would seem *obvious* that we must take action – so why don't we? Part of the problem is communication of the gravity and severity of the problem (which is why I wrote this book). The MEA (2005) states that one problem is: 'Limited capability of communicating to non-specialists the complexity associated with holistic models and scenarios involving ecosystem services, in particular in relation to the abundance of nonlinearities, feedbacks and time lags in most ecosystems.' This statement proves its own point through its jargon, which would be gibberish to much of the public. Scientific experts rarely know how to communicate clearly about the dangers of ecosystem collapse. This is especially so when they won't in fact use the term 'collapse', but instead use 'non-linear change' or 'regime shift'. So often to date, the warning has been put in words that the media ignores and most laypeople cannot understand. If you were to stop people in the street, how many would actually understand that the world's ecosystems are under stress to the point that they are collapsing? Perhaps a third is my guess. The rest don't get told the problem by the education system and the media, or don't understand the problem if it is raised. For some, if they do understand it, they may well *deny* it (see Chapter 7).

Biologist Jared Diamond (2005) notes that societies can in fact pull back from the abyss of societal collapse, and historically some have actually done so. However, Rees (2008) argues that today this would require a well-informed public, inspired leadership and the political will to take decisions *against the established order*. Scientific uncertainties about ecosystem processes clearly indicate a need for the precautionary principle in environment management. This is because of the potential for an unexpected irreversible collapse of the ecosystem services on which humanity relies. Some functions of natural ecosystems are not fully replaceable by *any* mitigation actions, an argument for caution in formulation of environment policy (Daily 1997). So we should take precautions in regard to the possibility of ecosystem collapse, given our dependence on these ecosystems. Weitzman (2009) uses the evidence for a small (but significant) possibility of a runaway greenhouse effect to argue for aggressive climate change mitigation policies. Weitzman's reasoning could also be applied to ecosystem services and the possibility of ecosystem collapse once a damage threshold is crossed. In terms of policy, the precautionary principle thus needs to be applied to ensure ecosystems don't collapse. However, some people in denial attack the precautionary principle on the basis that it 'abandons scientific rigour' (Plimer 2009). What the above discussion has highlighted in fact is that there *is* a large body of ecological evidence that indicates that the idea of the precautionary principle is both rigorous and urgently needed to stop ecosystem collapse.

Current efforts to adapt to climate change and other stresses will require a precautionary approach, and a much deeper understanding of ecosystem resilience. When there is uncertainty and ignorance about ecosystem functioning, or where there is a small possibility of disastrous damage (such as complete ecological collapse), current valuation techniques used to feed into cost benefit analyses are insufficient. A major challenge is how to design ecosystem management in ways that maintain resilience, and avoid crossing the tipping point into collapse (Elmqvist *et al.* 2010).

So how do we stave off collapse? The first point is to *accept we have a problem*, that ecosystems are collapsing and that more will collapse if we don't act to stop this. The second point is to respect Nature and accept its *intrinsic value*. If we respect Nature and its right to exist, we will take strong action to stop ecosystems collapsing as a result of the stresses our population and consumption cause. The third point is that while we always need more research, we *already know enough to act*. The bureaucratic stratagem of putting a problem on the back burner (by sending it off for 'more research') will only lead to more collapse and worse consequences for Nature and humanity. The fourth point is to get the message across that our society and economy *rely* on ecosystems to survive. Finally, we need the *political will* to drive action to stop ecosystems collapsing. That means we need grass-roots action to force politicians to do the right thing. Instead of mouthing platitudes about the 'national interest', we need politicians today to actually *think* about the interests of the land itself and its ecosystems that provide so much to us. That means living in an ecologically sustainable way, controlling population, controlling overconsumption (and greed) and solving climate change, and thus stopping ecosystems collapsing.

So collapse is not too extreme a word to use for what is happening to ecosystems around the world, yet so much of society seems unaware of this. Ecosystem collapse is happening and is accelerating. If it continues then it must lead to the collapse of the societies that depend on those ecosystems. Jared Diamond (1993) goes further and calls it a holocaust:

> An environmental holocaust is equally certain to prove disastrous, but it differs in that it's already underway. It started tens of thousands of years ago, is now causing more damage than ever before, is in fact accelerating, and will climax within about a century if unchecked.

He notes that our harnessing of the Earth's productivity, our extermination of species and our damage to the environment are accelerating at a rate that 'cannot be sustained for even another century'. Usable farmland, food stocks in the sea, other natural products, and environmental capacity to absorb wastes are decreasing. He concludes that as more people scramble for fewer resources 'something has to give way'. The first thing to give way is ecosystems that collapse – as they are. They are the canary in the coal mine warning us of grave danger. Diamond also reminds us of Dutch explorer and Professor, Arthur Wichmann who summarized the history of New Guinea exploration. His bitter last sentence was 'Nothing learned, and everything forgotten!'. Diamond (1993) notes that: 'Despite all our past self-destructive behaviour from which we could have learned, many people who should know better dispute the need for limiting our population and continue to assault our environment.'

Like Diamond, I too relate to this statement. Not much of what I write about here is 'new' as such, most of it has been said before, but society has *not listened*. We shall discuss why in Chapter 7. To sum up, most of humanity seems proud of our civilisation and its achievements. We are proud of the house we have built, without considering the cost involved in that building. However, speaking allegorically, while humanity may pride itself on the house it has built, we need to reflect that if the foundations collapse – then the house goes with it.

5 Psychological, cultural and spiritual dependence on Nature

Ah what beauty
So often hidden
Falling, feeling
Crowns the sky!
A lustrous band
Above circles
And the endless ancients
Flash in flame.
The pale glow
Of other galaxies,
And the white-blue fire
Of the hunter's star.
The painted cross
South sky ringing,
And white light trails
Of shooting stars . . .
Alone not ever,
Sweet song singing,
Alone no more,
The stars are watching.
    ('Stars', Washington
          2002)

Does humanity live by bread alone, or are we dependent on Nature in other ways? In particular, are there social, cultural, psychological and spiritual ways we *depend* on Nature? There are a whole range of non-material values we derive from Nature, and they can be categorized in different ways. Nature has social, cultural, educational and recreational values to humanity, so I will cover these first. However, Nature also has other key values that can be described as psychological or *spiritual*, and I will cover these next. I will then touch on the 'sense of wonder' we feel toward Nature, that encapsulates many of the above. I will also often refer to 'wilderness' or wild places as ways of discussing the non-material values that Nature provides us. This is not to say that Nature does not provide these in less wild places (for it does), merely that they are more obvious in wild places.

Social, educational, recreational and cultural values

A number of authors have written of the value of going to Nature to reflect on their society, and see it in a different *perspective*. Henry David Thoreau (1854) in part went to Walden Pond to do just this. There is also a stream of thought in the Bible (the 'Abraham' stream) that sees wilderness not as a wasteland, but a place where one went to ponder the ills of society (Oelschlaeger 1991). Wilderness provides society with numerous benefits and services, such as biological, physiological, personal, societal and educational, as well as research (Ewert and Shellman 2003). As well as seeing society in perspective, there is also the value of seeing *oneself in perspective* in wilderness. Wild Nature is also seen as a place of humility (Tempest Williams 1999). It is sometimes seen as an essential retreat from the pressures of modern life, a place to recharge one's batteries, an important sanctuary or refuge (Hendee *et al.* 1978).

The importance of solitude in wilderness is another value discussed by Thoreau (1854), and by others (Robertson *et al.* 1992). 'Freedom' is another important value of wilderness for retaining a free human spirit (Dasmann 1966; Stegner 1969; Nash 2001).

There are strong *educational values* to wild Nature also. It can be viewed as a 'living museum' that provides many opportunities to teach about biodiversity, geodiversity, ecology and other topics. There are relict or threatened species found in wild places, and in Australia the most famous of these is the Wollemi Pine discovered in 1994 (Woodford 2000). This has special relevance for me as I discovered the *second* site of this fascinating tree. While perhaps not as exciting as finding the 'first' site, it was nevertheless quite special.

Another significant category of values is what one might term 'recreational'. Wilderness has physical health benefits derived from bushwalking, climbing, canoeing, liloing, canyoning, skiing and so on (Duncan 1998). These are increasingly important as our lifestyle becomes more sedentary. There are also *cultural* or artistic values to wilderness, both visual (photography, painting), and literary, such as poetry and nature-writing (Prineas and Gold 1997; Tredinnick 2003). There is also the importance of *indirect enjoyment* of wilderness, such as enjoyment from looking out over wilderness from lookouts, from seeing films, wilderness photography, books and videos. Hence it is important to recognize that wild places are valued by people who rarely (or even never) go there, but who value it as they believe that wilderness has the right to *exist for itself*.

The Millennium Ecosystem Assessment (MEA 2005) acknowledged that one strand of ecosystem services was 'cultural services' that covered non-material benefits that ecosystems provide humanity. These included 'spiritual and religious values', 'education values', 'inspiration', 'aesthetic values', 'sense of place' and 'recreation and tourism' (see Chapter 3). The MEA was a true *leader* by including this category within ecosystem services.

In particular, the acknowledgment of spiritual, aesthetic and 'sense of place' values is significant. It acknowledges the reality that humanity evolved from the natural world, and that most of our history was lived intimately *within* Nature, to which we felt a deep connection.

Spiritual and psychological values

While I am an environmental scientist, I am also someone who has spent much of his life in wild places (especially the Wollemi wilderness), where I learned to 'listen'. *If you listen you will learn.* The word 'spiritual' puts some people off, so instead one can speak of the psychological and cultural benefits of Nature. I have had experiences there that led me to write the book *A Sense of Wonder* (Washington 2002). I am thus quite happy to recognize the *spiritual* dimension of Nature. However, modernism, the dominance of *markets* and the 'endless growth' myth have weakened this spiritual connection. Philosopher Thomas Berry (1988) noted:

> The difficulty presently is with the mechanistic fixations in the human psyche, in our emotions and sensitivities as well as in our minds. Our scientific inquiries into the natural world have produced a certain atrophy in our human responses. Even when we recognize our intimacy, our family relations with all the forms of existence about us, we cannot speak to those forms. We have forgotten the language needed for such communication. We find ourselves in an autistic situation. Emotionally, we cannot get out of our confinement, nor can we let the outer world flow into our own beings. We cannot hear the voices or speak in response.

Despite this Berry acknowledges that: 'We are constantly drawn toward a reverence for the mystery and the magic of the Earth and the larger Universe with a power that is leading us away from our anthropocentrism.'

When we speak of 'spiritual' values, I think we need to be careful not to get too bogged down in the meaning of 'spiritual'. What some people call 'spiritual values', others may simply call *psychological*. It is a sad reflection on our society that an issue can be dismissed as being merely 'spiritual', meaning that it is 'down at the bottom of the garden with the fairies'. Thomas Berry (1999) argues that the 'ever-renewing world' of Nature is both an abiding and sacred world and 'gives to human life a deep security'. It can give a sense of identity that leads 'to be integral with the Great Self of the universe' (Berry 1999). David Tacey (2000) describes spirituality as a 'desire for connectedness, which often expresses itself as an emotional relationship with an invisible sacred presence'. Tacey believes that the shrinking away from spirituality in our society has serious effects. He argues that our desire to change the world quickly 'runs out of steam' because it is not being replenished or directed by the spirit of the 'sacred' in the landscape. As many books have shown (this one included), the need to change the world is urgent, so our aversion to the concept of spirituality needs a real re-think. Tacey points out that the 'rational' mind assumes spirituality to be 'some kind of escapist madness or quaint delusion'. However, he responds by pointing out that there is nothing escapist about the 'desire to relate to the core of living creation'. Collins (2010) concludes that 'we can't save the natural world except by rediscovering the sacred in nature'. He goes on to note that if we destroy the natural world, our imaginations would shrivel up and we would lose the ability to perceive the deeper feelings that 'give meaning to our lives'.

The 'wilderness experience' has been a key theme in literature about wild Nature (Hendee *et al.* 1978). Robert Marshall (1930), the co-founder of the US Wilderness Society wrote: 'wilderness furnishes perhaps the best opportunity for . . . pure aesthetic rapture'. It has been said that 'we need the wilderness for our inner life, not simply for itself', and that without this we are 'shrivelled up in our souls' (Berry 2000). Berry goes on to say 'the loss of wilderness is a loss of dynamism and creativity' for humanity. Wild Nature has been seen as a source of inspiration and insight (Hendee *et al.* 1978), and inspiration was a cultural ecosystem service acknowledged by the MEA (2005). Wilderness has often been described as a 'cathedral' or temple, a place for reflection (DPWH 1991).

Another important spiritual value is *healing*. Wilderness 'may well have more psychological importance than hundreds of beds in a mental hospital' (Nash 1967). Wilderness can provide therapy, and even be of help to schizophrenics (Hendee *et al.* 1978). 'Wilderness practice' has been applied as a term for the process where wilderness heals people psychologically. Harper (1995) argues:

> People have always turned to wilderness to become whole again. We need only think of the many primary cultures that use intensified wilderness experience as a rite of passage to see these healing qualities at work. . . . we may find that wilderness holds the potential for transformative experiences that were perhaps never possible before.

Lopez has also stated that landscapes can 'give one hope' (in Tredinnick 2003). Others are bewildered that conservationists have made nothing of 'this evidence for the healing value of wilderness' (Roszak 2002). However, the healing power of the land has figured in nature-writing:

> When I got back home, I came up here . . . to connect with an order larger than myself, larger than the human. To become whole again. This country heals me. Land can do that. It is possible to participate bodily in landscape, even though it cares nothing for us in any sense we understand as human. We can be intimate with it. We can love it.
>
> (Tempest Williams 2003)

Lastly, wilderness is a place where it is easy to let down the barriers we create in society, where we can listen to the land, to *contemplate*. This ability has been called *dadirri* by Ungunmerr (1995), and 'witness' by Tredinnick (2003), and is highly valued by many other authors (Tempest Williams 2003). Of course, such a quality is not limited to wilderness areas, but is certainly an important part of the 'wilderness experience'.

The transformative power of wild Nature

Part of the deep psychological and spiritual importance of Nature is its ability to *transform* people. Such transformation can be life-changing and provide meaning to people. What earlier was called 'seeing yourself in perspective' can also be called 'self-realization' or *personal transformation*, where the wilderness experience can have a strong effect on how you see and understand yourself (Ewert and Shellman 2003). The fact that wild Nature can change people is testified to by the Nature poetry of many cultures (Washington 2002). This is not focused on 'wilderness' alone, but sometimes on less wild areas (such as the poetry of Wordsworth). Thoreau in the mid-nineteenth century was perhaps the first modern writer to explain the transformative powers of the wild. Some of his writing was done at Walden Pond, a wild area near Concord. In 'Sounds', Thoreau (1854) writes:

> I sat in my sunny doorway from sunrise till noon, rapt in a reverie amidst the pines and hickories and sumachs, in undisturbed solitude and stillness, while the birds sang around or flitted noiseless through the house . . . I grew in those seasons like corn in the night, and they were far better than any work of the hands would have been. They were not time subtracted from my life, but so much over and above my usual allowance . . . Instead of singing like the birds, I silently smiled at my good fortune.

In 'Solitude', Thoreau (1854) writes probably one of the most moving passages of what one might call a 'hierophany' or epiphany with Nature (Oelschlaeger 1991) or a 'transcendent moment' (Washington 2002). Thoreau writes:

> I was suddenly sensible of such sweet and beneficent society in Nature, in the very patterning of the drops, and in every sound and sight around my house, an infinite and unaccountable friendliness all at once like an atmosphere sustaining me. . . . Every little pine needle expanded and swelled with sympathy and something kindred to me, even in scenes which we are accustomed to call wild and dreary . . . that I thought no place could ever be strange to me again.

Similarly for John Muir, who started as a devout Christian, and over the years came effectively to espouse a 'wilderness theology – a profoundly insightful evolutionary pantheism' (Oelschlaeger 1991). In 1864, Muir was in a swamp near Lake Huron in Canada when he came across a cluster of rare white orchids (*Calypso borealis*), and wrote:

> I never before saw a plant so full of life; so perfectly spiritual. It seemed pure enough for the throne of its Creator. I felt as if I were in the presence of superior beings who loved me and beckoned me to come. I sat down beside them and wept for joy.
>
> (in Fox 1981)

Muir (1916) also wrote of intensely personal moments of transformation:

> To lovers of the wild, these mountains are not a hundred miles away. Their spiritual power and the goodness of the sky make them near, as a circle of friends . . . You cannot feel yourself out of doors; plain sky, and mountains ray beauty which you feel. You bathe in these spirit-beams, turning round and round, as if warming at a camp-fire. Presently you lose consciousness of your own separate existence: you blend with the landscape, and become part and parcel of nature.

Leopold (1949) in *Sand Country Almanac* speaks movingly of the land and argues for a 'land ethic' (see Chapter 6). Lopez (1988) writes of how the 'interior landscape' of a person is shaped by the exterior landscape:

> the shape and character of these relationships in a person's thinking, I believe, are deeply influenced by where on this earth one goes, what one touches, the patterns one observes in nature – the intricate history of one's life in the land . . . the shape of the individual is affected by land as it is by genes.

Lopez (1986) believes that: 'for some people, what they are is not finished at the skin, but continues with the reach of the senses out into the land'. Wilderness transformation is something that is by its nature *intensely personal*. Harper (1995) argues: 'wilderness is a way and a tradition in its own right. If we are willing to be still and open enough to listen, wilderness itself will teach us'. He also speaks of his own life after a breakup of a long-term relationship when walking to Big Sur (California):

> gradually I was overcome by the strangest sensation of webs of light extending out of me to every living thing and from them to me. I was sustained by all that surrounded me. The experience slowly dissipated as we climbed to the summit of the ridge, where I stood smiling, sweat in my eyes. And although I still had more grieving to do, the experience stands out as a clear turning point in my healing process, as well as in my life.

He goes on to write of the 'wisdom' in wilderness that teaches us and allows transformation from within:

> when we are truly willing to step into the looking glass of nature and contact wilderness, we uncover a wisdom much larger than our small everyday selves ... Wilderness is a leaderless teacher ... The only personal transformation that occurs arises from within ourselves.
>
> (Harper 1995)

Wilderness was transformative not only for himself, but also of many other people of all ages that he took there. Similarly, Thomashow (1996) carries out what he calls 'ecological identity' work with people, where they keep an ecological identity journal. He notes the importance of contemplation of the wild in carving out a personal vision:

> After 15 years of reading these journals, what I have found is that for many environmentalists, the direct experience of wild places has a transformational quality. Most of my students can distinguish an event, a time in their lives, or a critical series of incidents in which different strands of their lives seemed to converge, helping them carve a personal vision. Frequently, these events encompass the contemplation of the wild, or what they perceive as being 'immersed in nature'.

Berry (1999) notes:

> Without the soaring birds, the great forests, the sounds and coloration of the insects, the free-flowing streams, the flowering fields, the sight of clouds by day and the stars by night, we become impoverished in all that makes us human.

It has been observed that:

> humans need to see their lives in a larger context, as embedded in, surrounded by, evolved out of a sphere of natural creativity that is bigger than we are. Humans who cannot do this never know who they are and where they are; they live under some other and inadequate mythology.
>
> (Rolston 2001)

Esbjornson (1999) has a slightly different view on *cultural transformation* and wilderness:

> the repressed yearning for wildness that I believe resides in the hearts of most humans may ... enact the necessary comprehensive cultural transformation ... In wildness humans may recover their deepest humanity, and in wilderness the diversity of life may flourish.

Wild Nature is thus seen as a catalyst that might transform not just the person but the whole culture. Similarly, he argues that rather than being 'anti-human', wilderness is rather a place where we *recover our deepest humanity.*

A sense of wonder

Most of us (at least at times) feel a sense of wonder at the natural world. Many of us can remember this wonder from our childhood. Wilderness can be valued as a place that restores one's 'sense of wonder' in life (Washington 2002). This can also be called a re-enchantment of the land (Tacey 2000). Part of this sense of wonder is a feeling of being *one* with the land, of *belonging* (Thomashow 1996). This issue fascinated me so much I wrote the book *A Sense of Wonder* (Washington 2002). So, what is this sense of wonder at the natural world? Is it something innate that we are born with, or can anybody learn it? Is it something more common in different races, or merely different societies? Does the fact that only 10 or 20 per cent of people (in our society) get interested in environmental issues mean that only that percentage can *feel* the sense of wonder? Alternatively, does the growing interest in the environment in young people mean that the percentage of those who can feel a sense of wonder is growing? These are important questions.

It is common for environmentalists to list all sorts of 'scientific' arguments about *why* a natural area should be saved. It must be saved because it is a gene pool, a reservoir of biodiversity. It should be saved because there are 'x' rare or threatened species there. It should be saved because it has unique geodiversity. It should be saved because it provides clean air and clean water to humans who live nearby, and holds the soil that would otherwise wash away and choke our rivers. I know this list well, as I have run campaigns on these and similar arguments myself. These arguments are of course valid, and this book has listed similar reasons for valuing Nature. However, it seems that through our history of scientific analysis we have lost the ability to see Nature as an interlocking whole (Collins 2010). All too rarely do we say that an area of native bush should be saved because it is a place of 'wonder' that we love, or because it is a *sacred* place. To do so would be to have one's words dismissed as 'emotional' and to fail in one's task to protect a wonder-full area that we love. It is strange that we in our society have come to such a pass, if we cannot get emotional about the land we love – what *can* we get emotional about? Or is our passion dead?

The sense of wonder I am talking about here is very much a connection with the land. As such, the sense of wonder must be considered 'spiritual', even if one does not call it religious. A Christian, an Agnostic, a Buddhist, a Hindu, a Muslim . . . *all* can feel a sense of wonder, even if they call it by various names (Washington 2002). What I am talking about here is not something that should be trivialized and put on the shelf with the books on fairies, tarot and astrology. I am talking about the *fundamental* relationship of humanity with the land, land that has nurtured us for millions of years. I am talking about one of the deepest and most abiding loves of them all: the love of the land.

The sense of wonder is also about *empathy*. One must let down one's guard, open oneself up and let all one's senses absorb the beauty of the natural world. Aboriginal Elder Miriam-Rose Ungunmerr (see Tacey 2000) explains that there is a word in the Ngangikurungkurr language, *dadirri*, which is 'something like what you [white people] call "contemplation"'. Tacey (2000) states this is a spirituality of deep seeing and deep listening, a 'kind of spiritual spirituality'. This would seem to me to be part of the empathy that allows us to feel the sense of wonder. Miriam-Rose believes that the gift of *dadirri* is 'perhaps the greatest gift we can give to our fellow Australians' (Tacey 2000).

This sense of wonder is tied in with other terms, such as 'sense of place' (Cameron 2003), though it is not always a 'place' that is the focus of the wonder (for example, sometimes it is an animal or plant). There are also peaks in our sense of wonder, and I have called them 'transcendent moments' (Washington 2002) while others have called them a hierophany or epiphany (Oelschlaeger 1991). I have covered this here briefly, but I believe a sense of wonder is an important part of the human psyche. In fact, it is an ability that can play a key role in helping us solve the environmental crisis. The sense of wonder at Nature is thus not just 'a' value, but something of central importance, something that gives us *meaning*.

Anti-spirituality in Western culture

We should, however, ask ourselves if modern Western society actively *opposes* a deep spiritual connection to the land.

Tacey (2000) argues:

> The consumerist society reinforces our shrunken empty status. It is vitally important for capitalism that we continue to experience ourselves as empty and small, since this provides us with the desire to expand and grow, and this desire is what consumerism is based on. Consumerism assumes that we are empty but permanently unable to fulfil our spiritual urge to expand. It steps into the vacuum and offers its own version of expansion and belonging . . . If we stopped believing in the myth of our shrunken identity, the monster of consumerism would die, because it would no longer be nourished by our unrealized spiritual urges. Therefore true spirituality . . . is extremely subversive of the status quo. This is why consumer society is keen to debunk or ridicule true spirituality.

This is a deep insight, one very relevant to the discussion of consumerism later. We have talked about the sense of wonder and how it ties in with the love of the land. We have talked about how it is the birthright of us all. Then why do so few people today feel it? Why is it relegated to children, and only survives in a few adults (at least in Western society)? Where did we go so wrong that our society acts to *suppress* the sense of wonder at Nature, rather than celebrate and foster it? It is not like losing your handkerchief in the park, or misplacing your keys. It is the fundamental alienation of oneself from the natural world, so that the sense of wonder becomes one of the things we 'no longer have time for'. Clearly something is very wrong for us to have come to this state. Clearly *our whole worldview* must be at fault (Berry 1988). How could such a thing happen? How could we let it slip away?

In the modernist worldview we discuss in the next chapter (and even in many postmodernist ones) humans are seen as 'apart' from Nature, as superior beings who must conquer and subdue wild Nature. This has been called the humans/Nature dualism (Evernden 1992). Such an ideology is clearly deeply anti-spiritual. However, as we shall see in the next chapter, some responses to the human/Nature dualism have themselves been problematic and anthropocentric, involving *Nature scepticism* (Plumwood 2003) and the argument that Nature has become 'part of culture'. However, it is clear that Nature in Western society is no longer *sacred*, no longer the 'Earth Mother', but just a resource for human use. The underlying ideology of Western society is thus at great pains to suppress a sense of wonder and a spiritual connection with Nature. This is something that desperately *needs to change*.

Conclusion

There are clearly many non-material values that Nature provides humanity. Are they essential? Many would argue they are not, that they are peripheral add-ons or luxuries. Science by-and-large has ignored their value until recently. However, we have seen above how important these non-material values actually *are* to our physical, psychological and spiritual health. They give us *meaning*, and meaning is essential to a fulfilling life. Collins (2010) notes that we must undergo a 'deep spiritual change' to solve the environmental crisis. This will require that we make use of the psychological and spiritual values that Nature provides. For this reason, such values are indeed *essential*. In fact, I believe that it is through rejuvenating our sense of wonder at Nature that we can attain the deep ethical beliefs that will fuel the solutions to the environmental crisis. If we believe we are part of Nature, have a deep connection to it, feel a responsibility towards it, then we will act to protect it. We will then push our politicians to act to solve environmental problems. We are indeed truly psychologically and spiritually dependent on Nature.

How do we go about rejuvenating our sense of wonder at Nature? A few brief points are:

- Be there with Nature. Get out into the bush every now and again, into wild places so your spiritual batteries can be recharged. Tacey (2000) reports than many Australians feel in spiritual terms they are 'running on empty', and that one in five Australians suffer acute or chronic (often undiagnosed) depression. We are not alone in the world in feeling that way. By bonding with the land again we connect with a reality larger and other than ourselves. Quite simply, we *belong*.
- Take time to *ponder* at Nature, whether this is called meditation, empathy, prayer, contemplation or *dadirri*. Find a beautiful spot and let your defences down and empathize with the natural world. Meditate or just watch and witness. Perhaps you too will find, as Thoreau (1854) did, that 'Every little pine needle expanded and swelled with sympathy and something kindred to me'.
- Keep your *imagination*, creativity and artistic expression alive. These renew your sense of wonder (Washington 2002). Heidegger (1977) argued that by 'poetizing' we develop our imaginations and can thus perceive the divine.

The above is a good start, and surely is not so hard? The potential drawbacks of doing this are negligible. The potential gains are enormous: a world where we can live and let live, a world where we are in harmony with Nature, a world where we can solve the environmental crisis and live sustainably into the long term. It is a way forward to a world where (in terms of Nature) we are allies not enemies, equals not conquerors, relatives not despots. In this Western world of today, so many people feel isolated, lonely and unfulfilled. They know they have lost something, but are unsure what it is. The sense of wonder tells us something of great importance – if we only listen. Quite simply, we are Nature, Nature is us. *We are not alone. We never have been.*

6 The great divide – anthropocentrism vs ecocentrism

Sweet is the lore which Nature brings;
Our meddling intellect
Mis-shapes the beauteous forms of things:
We murder to dissect.
Enough of Science and of Art;
Close up those barren leaves;
Come forth, and bring with you a heart
That watches and receives.
(From 'The Tables Turned',
William Wordsworth)

If I was to run around shouting 'Me! Me! Me!', I am sure you would soon get sick of me. Yet that is what humanity has essentially been doing over our recent history. Humanity has become *self-obsessed*. We tend to focus on ourselves, or at least the majority of us in Western society do. We focus on our society, our economy, and only lastly on the Nature that supports us. Even Green political parties fall into this trap. Now people love to pigeon-hole other people and make camps of 'them' and 'us', and this has been called one of the great problems of human nature (Diamond 1993; Ehrlich and Ornstein 2010). However, I do not seek to pigeon-hole people when I make an essential recognition of a 'great divide' in terms of our worldview, ethics and values in how we think about Nature. I have come to understand over the years that there is a fundamental 'great divide' within humanity: whether one believes in the *intrinsic value* of Nature. Anthropocentrism (also called homocentrism) regards humanity as the central element in the Universe; *ecocentrism* is instead focused on a Nature-centred system of values.

I did my Ph.D. ('The Wilderness Knot', Washington 2006) on the con-fusion and tangled meanings around 'wilderness'. I will thus at times refer to wilderness here, as it illustrates perfectly the issue of intrinsic value, and the problems of anthropocentrism. Those of us who believe in intrinsic value will almost always be ecocentric and not anthropocentric; we will under-stand that humans are dependent on Nature. We will understand that humans should respect Nature, and feel a responsibility towards it to be a guardian and protect it. Those who don't believe in the intrinsic value of Nature may not be any of the above. They are most likely anthropocentric, they may take a 'Cornucopian' view that technology can solve *any* problem, they may believe that humanity not only should but 'must' dominate Nature. They probably don't respect Nature or feel any responsibility towards it. They probably fear it. The divide between these two groups has probably never been so great as it is today, for humanity is now more divorced from the natural world than ever before. More than half of us now live in cities (Starke and Mastny 2010), being isolated from wild Nature. But how did we get to this stage? Was humanity *always* like this, or is this self-obsession with ourselves something that has been fostered by modern culture? Is it a cultural maladaptation (Boyden 2004)?

Anthropocentrism

One of the main issues addressed by environmental ethics is the dilemma of anthropocentrism versus ecocentrism and of intrinsic value of Nature vs utilitarian (i.e. just for human use) or instrumental value (value as a means to acquiring something else) (Norton 1995; Zack 2002). The idea of anthropocentrism has dominated modern societies since at least the sixteenth century (Smith 1998). The relevance in discussing anthropocentrism here is whether our self-absorption affects how we can *understand* Nature (or our reliance upon it). The universality and insidious aspect of anthropocentrism in modern culture has been attested to by Naess (1973), Godfrey-Smith (1979) and Smith (1998). Anthropocentrism (as a value system) of course gets disseminated around the world by globalization. Globalization offers no template for either an economically viable or an eco-sustainable future, but serves only to disembed economic life further from agriculture and Nature than did early capitalism (Westra 2004). There has also been a clear tendency for philosophers to focus on the human mind. Descartes after all observed 'I think therefore I am', situating his ground of being within the mind, rather than seeing the self as being part of a larger natural world (Taylor 1986). It has been noted by Naess (1973) that some scholars argue that most forms of human knowledge are *inherently* anthropocentric, and that we are incapable of acknowledging ecosystem importance. It has been claimed that by being human 'we can only be anthropocentric: we seek our own good, not what we suppose is nature's' (Lowenthal 1964). However, this is actually a sterile ideological claim, not a fact. Taylor (1986) points out that humans *can* take an animal's standpoint 'without a trace of anthropocentrism', and make judgements of what is desirable from that standpoint.

A central assumption of Western moral thought is that value can be ascribed to the non-human world only in so far as it is good 'for the sake of humans' (Godfrey-Smith 1979). The Western attitude towards Nature thus has a decidedly anthropocentric bias. It is an unquestioned axiom of our present code of ethics that the class to which we have obligations is the *human* class. However, an important distinction in this debate has been called the 'anthropocentric fallacy'. This explains that just because humans can only *perceive* Nature by 'human' senses does not mean we cannot attribute intrinsic value to it (Fox 1990; Eckersley 1992). By way of comparison, men (even white men) are quite capable of cultivating a non-sexist or non-racist consciousness. They don't 'have' to be sexist or racist, and can clearly attribute value to women and dark-skinned people. Similarly, humans are quite capable of cultivating a non-anthropocentric consciousness (Fox 1990), and attributing intrinsic value to Nature. To understand the environment will always involve human imagination, but Smith (1998) asks does this mean that 'humans should always be the measure of all things?'. Just because we are human does not in fact mean we have to be egotists and focus on ourselves. As we shall see, humanity has not always been this way.

It has been noted that the very posing of a question 'what is the use of wilderness?' reflects an anthropocentric system of values (Godfrey-Smith 1979). From a genuinely ecocentric point of view, this question would be as absurd as the question 'what is the use of happiness?'. Western culture is now ingrained with a 'doctrine of inherent human superiority' over other species, and this has become 'an unfounded dogma of our culture' (Taylor 1986). Taylor argues for a 'biocentric outlook', but notes that this cannot be 'proven' as such, since worldviews are not deductive systems or theories. It is thus not so much a question of 'proof' as taking an ethical stance and worldview. If one takes a biocentric (or ecocentric) worldview, then it can readily be justified, but first one has to *take that view*. The worldview one takes determines one's core underlying values. It has been noted that if we conceive of Nature as a 'machine', then the human mind retains a God-like position *outside* of the world. If the worldview of 'Nature as a machine' rose to prominence in the seventeenth century (following the work of Descartes and Newton) owing to its compatibility with a divine creator: 'it remains in prominence today largely due to the deification of human powers that it promotes' (Abram 1992). Seeing Nature as a machine, something less than ourselves, thus allows us to pretend we are something *more*.

But to return to an earlier question, has humanity *always* been anthropocentric? Surviving art suggests that Palaeolithic humans viewed wild Nature as the 'Magna Mater' (Great Mother), of which they were a part (Oelschlaeger 1991). More recently, many native cultures have stated that they see themselves as part of Nature (Knudtson and Suzuki 1992). Being part of Nature often led to the establishment of lore (or in Australia 'law') about how to live sustainably within natural ecosystems. This has been called the 'Wisdom of the Elders' (Knudtson and Suzuki 1992). However, I am not suggesting that tribal peoples did not make mistakes and cause damage to ecosystems, especially when first arriving in new lands. There exists good evidence to believe that the arrival of native peoples in new lands did contribute to extinction of megafauna around the world (Diamond 1993). Some native cultures also collapsed because they misused the ecosystems upon which they relied (Diamond 2005). However, some native cultures *did* learn from their mistakes, and developed rules of living in an ecologically sustainable way. Western society has yet to show that it has done this and learnt from its mistakes, hence the environmental crisis continues. So, has humanity *always* been anthropocentric? Clearly the answer is 'no', as we have for most of our existence taken a more ecocentric view of the world. Many cultures had a deep spiritual connection with the land, and saw (and some still see) Nature as *sacred*, and this survives through their art and poetry (Abram 1996; Tacey 2000; Washington 2002). Our egotistical anthropocentrism is thus an invention of the last few centuries.

Ideologies – modernism

Chief among the things that have aided anthropocentrism are our ideologies, and chief among them is *modernism*. Modernism took a strong anthropocentric view of the world as being essentially a resource for human use. 'Modernism' is central to how humans treat wild Nature today, and as a historical movement began with the Renaissance. Modernism continued the humanization of wild Nature initiated by the early agriculturists, and operated through science, technology and liberal democracy. It consists of several processes that intertwine: the Renaissance, the Reformation, the Enlightenment and the democratic, industrial and scientific revolutions (Oelschlaeger 1991).

Modernism arguably underlies the emergence of a 'profound homocentrism' still dominant in the world, where Nature is conceived of as 'nothing more than matter-in-motion' (Oelschlaeger 1991). No aspects of modernism have had a greater effect on the idea of wild Nature than science and economics. Galileo's new science, Bacon's new logic, Descartes' mechanistic reductionism and Newton's physics are central. They represented a paradigm shift so radical 'that the very meaning of the word *nature* was changed' from an organism to a mechanistic paradigm (Oelschlaeger 1991). Descartes proposed that mind and matter are distinct, and that the natural world is a machine (Godfrey-Smith 1979; Abram 1992), while Newton provided an understanding of the natural world, where natural change was reduced to an illusory status, being rather the mechanical repetition of predictable phenomena. Nature in effect became an object of scientific study, and the idea of Nature as animate and living was replaced with the idea of a cold and lifeless mechanical Nature (Oelschlaeger 1991).

Intrinsic value and the revolt against modernism

Still, modernism and the dominance of a utilitarian view of Nature did not completely dominate Western culture. The idea that Nature has *intrinsic value*, a right to exist for itself, irrespective of its use to humanity, was resurrected by the writings of the Romantic poets such as Wordsworth, and later by the visionaries Thoreau and Muir (Oelschlaeger 1991). Now when discussing 'intrinsic value', one has to be careful as to what one means. The term carries a lot of philosophical baggage, and the debate to me resembles the religious debate about 'how many angels can fit on the head of a pin?'. It has been complicated by a past history of attack by pragmatism, debates about objectivism and subjectivism, and by claims equating it to hedonism (Monist 1992). Much of the discussion is about the term 'intrinsic' itself rather than whether Nature as such has intrinsic value. Philosopher G.E. Moore concluded that three things had intrinsic value: friendship, pleasure and beauty (then recanted later about beauty, Weston 1992). Several philosophers agonize about whether certain parts of Nature have *more* intrinsic value than others (Monist 1992). Taylor (1986) argues that intrinsic value is the wrong term, that we should use 'inherent worth'. However, to skirt this can of worms, I use *intrinsic value* here for the simple idea that the non-human world has value (worth) irrespective of whether it is of use to humanity.

Thoreau's (1854) 'Walden Pond' is a classic evocation of the intrinsic value of Nature where he writes of his essential identification as being one with Nature: 'The indescribable innocence and beneficence of Nature – of sun and wind and rain, of summer and winter, – such health, such cheer ... Shall I not have intelligence with the earth? Am I not partly leaves and vegetable mould myself?' John Muir (in Oelschlaeger 1991) also wrote eloquently about Nature:

> When I entered this sublime wilderness the day was nearly done, the trees with rosy, glowing countenances seemed to be hushed and thoughtful ... and one naturally walked softly and awe-stricken among them. I wandered on, meeting nobler trees where all are noble, subdued in the general calm, as if in some vast hall pervaded by the deepest sanctities and solemnities that sway human souls.

Aldo Leopold (1949) followed on from Thoreau and Muir in arguing for the wild, and spoke for the 'minority' of humans who find delight in Nature and believe in intrinsic value:

> There are some who can live without wild things, and some who cannot. These essays are the delights and dilemmas of one who cannot. Like winds and sunsets, wild things were taken for granted until progress began to do away with them. . . . For us of the minority, the opportunity to see geese is more important than television, and the chances to find a pasque-flower is a right as inalienable as free speech.

Leopold (1949) also developed what he called the 'land ethic', which:

> simply enlarges the boundaries of the community to include soils, waters, plants, and animals, or collectively: the land . . . A land ethic of course cannot prevent the alteration, management, and use of these 'resources', but it does affirm their right to continued existence, and, at least in spots, their continued existence in a natural state.

Deep ecologist Arne Naess (1984) argued: 'The well-being of non-human life on Earth has value in itself. This value is independent of any instrumental usefulness for limited human purposes.'

The intrinsic values and rights of Nature have been recognized in the World Conservation Strategy (IUCN 1980), which declares that because humans have become a major evolutionary force, they are morally obliged to act prudently in the interests of other species. The Millennium Ecosystem Assessment (MEA 2005) and the UNEP project 'The Economics of Ecosystems and Biodiversity' or TEEB (Kumar 2010) both acknowledge the intrinsic value of Nature, even if only in passing. Regarding intrinsic value, Rolston (1985) argues 'such values are difficult to bring into decisions; nevertheless, it does not follow that they ought to be ignored'. Taylor (1986) also distinguishes between 'respect' for Nature and 'love' of Nature, arguing we should respect Nature even if we don't 'love' unattractive parts of it. It has been argued that 'autopoetic entities' (those that self-renew) are deserving of moral consideration in their own right (Fox, 1990 in Eckersley 1992).

There does not appear to be a large literature on the intrinsic values of Nature. This can be easily explained by the dominance of anthropocentrism within Western culture and academia itself. Some people have argued that the intrinsic value of wilderness is obvious: 'the idea of wilderness needs no defence. It only needs more defenders' (Abbey 1977). Similarly, Wilson (1992) maintains that: 'wilderness has virtue unto itself and needs no extraneous justification', meaning that we should not have to *justify* an ethical stance of not humanizing 100 per cent of the Earth's surface. However, given the continuing loss of natural areas and ecosystem services around the world, clearly it *does* in fact need justification, if we are to solve the environmental crisis. Zimmerman (2001) discusses intrinsic value in an analytical philosophical approach, though almost nothing is said about the intrinsic value of Nature. The philosophical journal *The Monist* (1992) produced a special edition on the 'The Intrinsic Value of Nature' yet after this the literature on the intrinsic value of Nature has remained sparse.

If we have respect for Nature, we will approve the protection of natural areas as part of 'restitutive justice' (Taylor 1986), as a way of restoring the damage we have already done. Arguably it is in the recognition of intrinsic values that wilderness is unique among land uses (Robertson *et al.* 1992). Wilderness protection encapsulates a philosophy about what the *role of humanity* within the environment should be, and reflects a movement towards an 'ethic of responsibility' (Brown 1992). However, others have claimed that intrinsic values have been overlooked in the patriarchal conception of wilderness, and that: 'wilderness exists not for itself but for the . . . needs of humans' (Vance 1997). Intrinsic value has been 'assumed' (not proven) by environmentalists, argues Nelson (2003), who urges environmental philosophers to 'begin dealing with and answering questions about how we ground the claim that putative wilderness has intrinsic value'. In response, it has been argued that the compassionate ideology of 'humanitarianism' is part of the problem, as it denies Nature's intrinsic value (Soulé 2002). The need for 'holistic pluralism', being an ethical theory that asserts intrinsic value for all aspects of reality, is argued by Gorke (2003). Thus, the question of intrinsic value remains in play, even if the dominance of anthropocentrism within academia ensures it is something of a backwater. However, if we accept the intrinsic value of Nature, it makes it that much easier to change our worldview to one that respects Nature and allows us to live sustainably within it.

Ideologies – postmodernism

So under modernism, Nature had no value of its own, only value as something to be used by humanity. Nietzsche (1871) reacted against this modernist anthropocentrism, stating that man's procedure is 'to apply man as the measure of all things'. Postmodernism has been called a *geography of ideas* that developed in opposition to modernism. It is not readily defined, and in fact appears resistant to being defined (Butler 2002). Instead of espousing clarity, certitude, wholeness and continuity, postmodernism commits itself to ambiguity, relativity, fragmentation, particularity and discontinuity (Crotty 1998). Arguably, the postmodernist penchant to accept that everything is 'relative', and that we 'co-create reality' has meant that much of academia has defended the right of deniers to create their own distorted view of environmental science. It has increased scepticism about the existence of objective truth. Cohen (2001) notes that this 'epistemic relativism turns scientific facts into mere "social constructions"'.

Some themes within postmodernism that are relevant to this debate are:

1 'reason' as defined by Western society is itself suspect (Derrida 1966);
2 the denial of grand narratives (theories organizing overall meaning) (Lyotard 1992);
3 that it is impossible to prove the *real* from a 'simulacra' (Baudrillard 1983);
4 concern for the 'other' (Kristeva 1992).

One can legitimately ask whether many of the postmodernist streams of thought have been any less anthropocentric than modernism. Hence the need to discuss postmodernist views of Nature, especially given the dominance of postmodernism within academia. Some postmodernist attacks on wilderness appear to share an anthropocentric view, similar to that which a number of authors (Taylor 1986; Oelschlaeger 1991; Marshall 1996; Reason and Bradbury 2001; Abram 1996) ascribe to Descartes. For some postmodernists, wild Nature as an independent entity appears to be reduced to just a discourse operating within human minds (Baudrillard 1983). This is very similar to the 'disembodied minds' of Descartes, arguably the father of mainstream 'modern' philosophy. We shall see also that some postmodernists believe Nature is just part of culture.

The suspicion of reason and rationality clearly poses problems for a rational assessment of the value of ecosystems, and the extent of the environmental crisis. It leads to the view that all discourses are equally valid, including those that deny the environmental crisis. This aspect of postmodernism does not fight denial, it assists it. The denial of all grand narratives means that postmodernism does not supply a story or dream that would replace the 'progress' and growthism ethics of modernism. Just as evolution has been portrayed as a grand narrative (Docherty 1992), so too the environmental crisis can be seen as 'just another' grand narrative. Thus postmodernism can deny the possibility of constructing any coherent meta-narrative of the environmental crisis (Collins 2010). Cohen (2001) notes that some postmodernist statements, such as that morality and values are relativistic, culturally specific and lacking universal force, are 'simply ludicrous'. He argues that while they stayed in academia such statements were harmless fun, but when they circulate in mass culture they supplement the inventory of denials available to the powerful. The crudest deniers can exploit this intellectual malaise to claim they are 'simply offering an alternative version of history' (Cohen 2001). Cohen (2001) notes (about denial of historical atrocities) that there are not two 'points of view', as one position is 'simply a fanatical rejection of evidence and a refusal to abide by the rule of rationality and logic'. Presumably, some postmodernists would argue that the actual scientific view of the environmental crisis and the denial view are equally 'valid'. All counter-claims about the denied reality are seen as just manoeuvres in 'endless truth games' (Cohen 2001). It seems to me that this leads to more fiddling as Rome burns. The postmodernist definition of 'the other' may seem hopeful, but all too often seems to be limited to groups within the human species, rather than being applied to the rest of the 'more-than-human' world described by Abram (1996). It is time to extend our compassion *beyond* our own species.

Many of the criticisms of wild Nature thus seem to spring from an anthropocentric worldview. The 'instinctive ecological compassion' to defend the existence rights of wilderness (in precedence over human-use rights) has challenged possibly the most fundamental tenet of modern western civilization. This is 'the belief that moral standing is strictly a human quality', and that humans can behave as they wish towards the non-human world (Hay 2002). Hay goes on to note that there is currently something of a backlash within society *against* ecocentrism and in favour of anthropocentrism, with greater emphasis on social justice and emergent democracy. Humanism (and humanitarianism) have been linked to anthropocentrism, arguing that it affirms the human side of the Nature/culture pair, and that humanism must come to terms with the denied non-human side (Plumwood 2001). Humanism has arguably helped us to lose touch with ourselves as beings that are also *natural*, and have their roots in the Earth. Hence Plumwood (2001) noted that anthropocentric culture often portrays Nature as passive or dead, lacking in agency and meaning.

The issue of embedded anthropocentrism within society can be seen in other issues. 'Environmental justice' is one, where an ecocentric person would see this as justice *for* Nature. However, often the meaning is twisted to 'social justice on environmental issues'. For example, postmodernist historian Cronon (1996) speaks of 'environmental justice', but his examples are actually about problems of *human* suffering owing to environmental degradation, not destruction of the intrinsic value of the non-human world.

Questioning reality and 'Nature scepticism'

The questioning of the real serves merely to distance humanity even more from Nature. Nature is real, our ecological dependency on Nature is real, and human actions are really degrading the ecosystems that support real human societies. Postmodernists often speak of 'co-creating reality', when actually there is a real reality, which humans interpret differently. Baudrillard (1983) argued: 'all of Los Angeles and the America surrounding it are no longer real, but of the order of the hyper-real and of simulation. ... the real is no longer real.' He concluded that it is now impossible to 'prove the real'. The thrust of his argument was undoubtedly aimed at culture, but his words have been taken to include wild Nature as well. Some postmodernist academics argue that 'it is now difficult to sustain a position of "naïve realism". In scholarly circles it is difficult to suggest that the world exists outside our construction of it' (Reason and Torbert 2001).

In regard to the physical reality of the world, Massey (1994) defines 'space' in terms of the 'multiplicity of social relations', implying that human society is the key determinant. If Nature is not *real* to us however, then we are unlikely to think much about our ecological dependency on it, nor are we likely to feel a responsibility towards it. The postmodernist questioning of reality (or its definition only in relation to humanity) thus continues the anthropocentric view of the world developed by modernism. This questioning of reality has led to a significant debate within academia about the land being a 'human artefact'. A key problem here is the distinction between *influencing* the land (as all indigenous peoples did) and *creating* it (which is anthropocentric as it places all the emphasis on *human* creation). For example, it has been asserted that 'virgin forests and wilderness areas are in part artefacts of previous burns, both natural and anthropogenic ... tropical forests are "both artefact and habitat"' (Gomez-Pampa and

Kaus 1992); and that 'Wilderness has taken on connotations and mythology ... a landscape that is managed to reveal as few traces of the passage of other humans as possible ... This wilderness is a social construct' (Graber 1995). Similarly, in Australia it has been stated: 'there is no wilderness, but there are cultural landscapes ... those of Aboriginal people, present and past, whose relationships with the environment shaped even the reproductive mechanisms of forests' (Langton 1996).

So is Nature just a human artefact? Conservation biologist Michael Soulé (1995) says that the claim humans 'invented the forest' ignores that species' geographical distributions are determined largely by ecological tolerances, geological history and climate. Similarly, it has been pointed out that wilderness is not simply a cultural construct 'devised to mirror our own broken nature', but is a home to all that is wild, a blank space on the map 'that illustrates human restraint' (Tempest Williams 1999). Bryant (1995) notes that:

> If we turn our regard for nature more and more into clever philosophical word games, if we begin to think that we are intellectually creating nature rather than physically participating in it, we are in danger of losing sight of the real wolves being shot by real bullets from real aeroplanes, of real trees being clearcut, of real streams being polluted by real factories.

Philosopher Holmes Rolston (2001) argues that wilderness:

> created itself long before civilisation ... wildness a state of mind? Wildness is what there was before there were states of mind ... it seems that the main idea in nature is that the natural is not a human construct. Intentional, ideological construction is exactly what natural entities do not have: if they had it, they would be artefacts. The main idea in nature is that nature is not our idea.

Hay (2002) adds an *essential* question in regard to this debate:

> Why should it be assumed that the smallest incursion of culture into nature constitutes the end of nature? It is just as logical to argue the opposite – that because trees grow in London's parks ... London has ceased to be part of the realm of culture, and has become nature. The fact is that there are natural processes and there are cultural processes, and in any place the mix is likely to be uneven.

There is a need also to recognize how some attempts to *change* modernism have also done harm to the protection of Nature. One of these is the response to the 'humans are part of nature' debate, where some postmodernists are keen to break down the human/Nature split, a split going back at least to Descartes (Abram 1992). Given the predominance of anthropocentrism within academia, this 'breaking down' seems to have been attempted through what Plumwood (2003) has called *Nature scepticism*, by denying that 'Nature' exists. Some argue that because humans influence Nature, it thus somehow becomes *human*. Others argue the need to equate Nature with culture, where again Nature (the non-human) disappears *within* culture (the human). Thus one is left with only 'cultural landscapes' and not natural or wild areas. Wilderness, as a place where Nature comes first, has fallen foul of such approaches, being dismissed as a 'romantic legacy', or an attempt to maintain the Nature/culture dualism. The response by Gare (1995), Rolston (2001), and Plumwood (2001) to this seems useful: that humans and their culture *are* a part of Nature, but we are a 'distinctive' part. We thus need a conception of Nature that allows humans to be essentially cultural beings, while still seeing them as part of (and within) Nature (Gare 1995). By recognizing the 'other' of wildness, we bring culture and Nature together (Rolston 2001). We can thus continue to use words such as 'culture' and 'Nature', just as we can recognize that any landscape will be a result of a spectrum of natural *and* cultural influences (Hay 2002).

It would seem the failure of many scholars to acknowledge the natural/cultural mix is a key source of the confusion around this debate. Hay (2002) goes on to point out that, far-reaching though human modifications of natural areas may be, they cannot be said to be the *defining* constituents of the Earth's biophysical systems. It has also become fashionable to say that Nature has 'ended' (McKibben 2006). I understand (and share) the deep sadness that led Bill McKibben to lament the damage we are causing to Nature. However, Nature has *not* ended, if it had then so would we. To my mind, suggesting Nature has 'ended' just plays into the anthropocentric hands of those who claim everything is now 'culture'. We can still feel we are part of something larger than ourselves, *because we are*. We have an environmental crisis, but that does not mean Nature has become culture, just because we have damaged it. Hopefully, this book has made clear that humanity depends on Nature (and not the other way around). It is thus philosophically misleading to talk about humans 'constructing Nature' in any general way (Plumwood 2001). 'Construction' implies that 'what is often mere influence or impact is actually control' and suggests that because we can 'affect' the biosphere we can produce the outcomes we want. It also suggests we can reconstruct it, when 'we cannot even reconstruct a bird's feather' (Plumwood 2001). The problem with 'Nature scepticism' is that it maintains that 'everything is a human product' (Plumwood 2003). The argument that Nature is a 'human artefact' is thus a 'fashionable myth' that threatens conservation: 'people did not construct nature. They did not invent the flora and fauna of Australia, for example, although human activities such as burning and hunting may have slightly altered the genetics of some species . . .' (Soulé 2002).

There is also something happening beyond Nature scepticism, which could be called 'biophobia' or fear of life, or at least a distaste for the messy world of Nature. Part of this is the idea in Tennyson's poem that Nature is 'red in tooth and claw'. This claim that Nature is harsh, competitive and brutal ignores that Nature is also full of cooperation. That in fact our very cells are a testament of two sorts of organisms who united (the mitochondria inside our cells contain bacterial DNA). Rolston (1992) summarizes this issue as follows:

> Nature is random, contingent, blind, disastrous, wasteful, indifferent, selfish, cruel, clumsy, ugly, struggling, full of suffering, and, ultimately, death? This sees only the shadows, and there has to be light to cast shadows. Nature is orderly, prolific, efficient, selecting for adapted fit, exuberant, complex, diverse, renews life in the midst of death, struggling through to something higher . . . We miss the panoramic creativity when we restrict value to human consciousness . . .

Anthropocentrism continues in society and academia

The above underlines the importance of understanding how widely anthropocentrism is found within modern Western society. Business and government are riddled with it, so indeed is science, academia and the education network. So is the media, hence the recent documentary *The Human Planet*. Anthropocentrism is also quite subtle and insidious, and often people genuinely do not recognize their *own* anthropocentrism. Historian Donald Worster (1994) has shown that the history of ecology has been swayed at various times by prevailing paradigms within academia. A detailed study of equilibria and disequilibria theories within ecology was made by Worster (1994), who pointed out that such theories often tie in with the *worldviews* of their promoters. Using a principle of 'historicism', he argues we can 'approach recent ecological models that dramatize disturbance with a sense of scepticism and independence' (Worster 1994). He wonders if they are the 'mere reflection of global capitalism and its ideology'. In regard to Nature's dynamism, Worster (1994) concluded that:

> Nature, ecologists began to argue, is wild and unpredictable. Nature is in deep, important ways quite disorderly. Nature is a seething, teeming spectacle of diversity. Nature, for all its strange and disturbing ways, its continuing capacity to elude our understanding, still needs our love, our respect, and our help.

So why have I spent so much time here discussing whether Nature is just a human artefact? Because it underlies how academia and science view Nature *today*. One might think that natural scientists and ecologists would be *free* of anthropocentrism, that they study Nature and thus must acknowledge its intrinsic value. Sadly this is not the case. Many natural scientists reflect the dominant anthropocentric view present within Western culture. TEEB

(Kumar 2010) noted that the MEA (2005) core concept of ecosystem services emphasized an 'anthropocentric and utilitarian' approach, but that it proposed a framework centred on human dependency not only on resources, but on ecosystem functioning itself. TEEB itself is a project of the United Nations Environment Programme, yet while it mentions 'intrinsic value', it has only a half-page box on this on page 189. TEEB admits up front that its methods for determining monetary value are clearly anthropocentric and are based on 'people's willingness to pay' (see Chapter 3). On page 44 of TEEB (Elmqvist *et al.* 2010) there is a 'key message': 'All ecosystems are shaped by people, directly or indirectly and all people, rich or poor, rural or urban, depend on the capacity of ecosystems to generate essential ecosystem services. In this sense people and ecosystems are interdependent social-ecological systems.' This is a strange statement to be endorsed by TEEB and UNEP. It seems to directly reflect the postmodernist ideological argument that Nature is just a 'human artefact'. For a start, 'shaping' is an anthropocentric term and implies *knowing* what you are doing, and being in control. The environmental crisis clearly shows that we don't know what we (collectively) are doing, and environmental degradation is certainly out of control. Humans don't 'shape' Nature, they *influence* it, and that is a critical difference. For most of our human history, that influence was comparatively small. In recent times, however, that influence has become increasingly large and negative, to the point of ecological collapse.

The final sentence above is even fuller of anthropocentric 'hubris', since 'interdependence' means that Nature is also dependent on humanity. *Hubris* was a term in ancient Greece for 'Excessive pride toward or defiance of the Gods, leading to nemesis or destruction'. It is indeed excessive pride to think Nature relies on us. If we continue to think this, it will indeed lead to our nemesis. People rely on ecosystems – ecosystems *don't* rely on us. The only way one could construe that ecosystems 'rely on us' would be for us not to destroy them. Nevertheless, if humanity disappeared tomorrow, ecosystems would get on quite happily *without us* (indeed a lot happier given we are the cause of the environmental crisis). If Nature disappeared tomorrow, then humanity would quickly go extinct. Humanity and Nature are not 'interdependent social-ecological systems'. Humanity relies on Nature to survive, while Nature does not rely on us. Yet here in TEEB we have a study sponsored and endorsed by the United Nations Environment Programme, and written by many high level academics dealing with valuing ecosystem services. The study then produces a 'key message' that is clearly anthropocentric. In fact it mis-states the ecological reality of how the world works. Probably the authors did not see it as anthropocentric. Possibly they thought it might encourage a feeling of 'responsibility' through arguing that the Earth's ecosystems are dependent on us. However, what it really does is perpetuate an ecologically insane approach to living on Earth.

TEEB goes on to quote Descola (1996), who (apart from attacking the conservation movement that led and leads the campaign to protect Nature) states that Nature is 'less and less a product of an autonomous principle of development', and its 'foreseeable demise as a concept will probably close a long chapter of *our own history*' (my emphasis). Through quoting Descola (and nobody who refutes his claims), TEEB thus again nurtures the anthropocentric idea that Nature is 'less and less a product of an autonomous principle' and thus a function of humanity. Descola in fact seems to look forward to Nature's demise as the closure of a chapter in *our* history. This remark is nonsense ecologically, but also disturbingly anthropocentric. Coming from an ecocentric viewpoint, I am mystified as to how such a statement was ever included in a major report on how to protect ecosystem services? It demonstrates, however, that anthropocentrism remains quite dominant within academia and science, and this is a major problem in solving the environmental crisis.

How do we bridge the great divide?

So, bringing this together, we need to bridge this 'great divide'. We need to acknowledge that Nature has intrinsic value. We need to acknowledge we are a part of Nature, but a special part that also has culture, and the two must mesh in an ecologically sustainable way. There is thus a need to challenge the anthropocentric assumption, so as to develop an *ethic of ecological obligation*, a 'land ethic' that widens the moral community to include the land. It has been argued that a first step in recognizing an enlarged moral community is the evolution of *empathy* (Godfrey-Smith 1979). To change our culture, Taylor (1986) thought we needed an inner change in our moral beliefs, from anthropocentrism to biocentrism and respect for Nature. Hargrove (1992) argues that non-living Nature such as geodiversity should also be seen as having intrinsic value. The recognition of the rights of other species and ecosystems to exist for themselves can be seen as an acceptance of *humility* (Noss 1991), and indeed as a gesture of *planetary modesty* (Nash 2001). However, humanity has never been good at being modest.

As a society, we need to *talk* about intrinsic value. When I taught a unit 'Green Politics' at university, I asked my students: 'Does Nature have intrinsic value, a right to exist for itself, or is it just something for human use?'. There were some stunned looks. Later a student came up to me, seeming quite disturbed, and asked: 'Why have I *never* been asked this? Why have I never even thought about this?'. It was a very good question. Humans rarely talk about their self-obsession with themselves. Our education system doesn't discuss intrinsic value or environmental ethics. Nor in general do our universities. We don't talk about whether Nature has a right to exist for itself, irrespective of its use to us. *We desperately need to.* One way to do this is to rekindle our 'sense of wonder' discussed in the last chapter. Philosopher Thomas Berry (1988) suggests that there is hope in breaking free from anthropocentrism:

Yet the beginning of an intimacy can be observed. The very intensity of our inquiry into the structure and functioning of the natural world reveals an entrancement with this natural world . . . We are constantly drawn toward a reverence for the mystery and the magic of the Earth and the larger Universe with a power that is leading us away from our anthropocentrism to this larger context as our norm of reality and value.

To conclude, when I did my Ph.D. on wilderness (Washington 2006), I kept a wilderness journal (a method of research known as 'phenomenology'). I wrote about my walks through (and my interaction with) wilderness, and with what had been written about it. I recently looked up my entries on anthropocentrism. The entry below was written at my land on the edge of the Wollemi wilderness. It demonstrates my intense worry and bemusement at the hubris of anthropocentrism:

> Anthropocentrism is a form of megalomania – a literal madness. It is the idea that 'man is the measure of all things', that humans are the centre of everything. It is the bane of wilderness, as it gives it no value, no intrinsic value or right to exist. Anthropocentrism is also insidious, it creeps into philosophies. . . . If I am critical of postmodernism, it is because it is anti-modernist, but anthropocentric anti-modernism. . . . How do we break humans from their self-absorption?

If we are to rediscover our roots in the Earth and value its ecosystem services, then it is past time for our species to break free from its self-absorption. It is time to do what Thomas Berry (1988) suggests and be 'drawn toward a reverence for the mystery and the magic of the Earth'. It is time to reconnect to Nature (e.g. www.natureconnect.com.au). It is time to abandon our anthropocentrism and egocentrism. We are *not* the measure of all things. It is time to rediscover our humility, to return to our past wonder at (and respect for) the natural world. Time to become fully human in the widest, most connected and holistic sense. Time to come *home*.

7 Dealing with denial

I seek to hide,
Insist that what 'is'
Will not be.
For I am afraid,
The change scares me,
So I defy it:
I proclaim it must not be.
Am I sleep-walking,
Towards the abyss?
It is true I feel unsettled,
I can see something,
From the corner of my eye . . .
But for now,
I will pretend it is not there,
And maybe it will go away?
I really don't like to worry.
I will remain content –
Secure in my delusion.
                    ('Denial', Washington,
                                2012)

All of the environmental problems described in the preceding chapters are real. All of them have also been *denied*. Humanity is fully dependent on Nature to survive, yet this has been (and is still being) denied. Denied, not just by the odd crank, but by the majority of governments and 'we the people' over many decades. As a society we continue to act as if we are *not* dependent on Nature, no matter what the science says. How is it possible for civilizations to be blind towards the grave approaching threats to their security, even when available evidence is accumulating about these threats? Existing laws have failed to deal with climate change, loss of biodiversity, air and water pollution, soil erosion, alien species, groundwater extraction, toxic substances and overexploitation of fisheries (Brown 2008). What on Earth is going on?

We need to discuss 'denial'. Denial is as old as humanity, and possibly nobody is free from it (Zerubavel 2006). Poet T.S. Elliot in 'Burnt Norton' notes that 'Human kind ... cannot bear very much reality'. This human incapacity to hear bad news makes it hard to solve the environmental crisis (Sukhdev 2010).

Scepticism vs denial

But what is denial? Is it the same as scepticism, as some people seem to think? This is a crucial question for the whole environmental debate. The Oxford English Dictionary definition of a sceptic is: 'A seeker after truth; an inquirer who has not yet arrived at definite conclusions.' So we should *all* be sceptics in many ways, as we should all seek the truth. Scepticism is about seeking the truth and realizing the world is a complex place. Scepticism is about stepping away from superstition and dogma. Genuine scepticism in science is one of the ways that science progresses, examining assumptions and conclusions (Pittock 2009). Denial is something very different, it is a *refusal to believe something* no matter what the evidence. Those in denial demonstrate a 'wilful ignorance' and invoke logical fallacies to buttress their unshakeable beliefs (Specter 2009). In fact deniers commonly use 'Bulverism', a method of argument that avoids the need to prove that someone is wrong by first assuming they *are* wrong, then explaining why they hold such a fallacious view (Hamilton 2010). For example: 'climate scientists are just wrong', and 'they are wrong because they are too *liberal*'. Denial isn't about searching for truth, it's about the denial of a truth one doesn't like. So scepticism and denial are in some ways opposites. An objective scientist *should* be sceptical, one should not jump to conclusions or believe something simply because it is fashionable. In fact when sociologist Merton (1973) wrote about the structure of science, he stated that scientists operated by four principles: organized scepticism, universalism, communalism and disinterestedness. However, in the scientific method, true sceptics need to do three things: apply critical faculties to both sides of an argument, admit uncertainties on both sides of the argument, and accept that risk management may require appropriate policy responses *despite* the uncertainty (Pittock 2009). Deniers don't do these three things, while genuine 'sceptics' do. Scepticism is healthy in both science and society – denial is not.

It is thus important to understand the difference between scepticism and denial. Refusing to accept the overwhelming 'preponderance of evidence' is not scepticism, it is *denial* and should be called by its true name. Accordingly, here I will refer to *deniers* not sceptics. Others use the term 'denialists' but 'deniers' is more succinct and also acknowledges that almost everybody denies something. In the USA it is also common to use the term 'contrarians' for climate change deniers (Hansen 2009).

Denial is common

How common is denial? We all deny, and the ability to deny is 'an amazing human phenomenon, largely unexplained and often inexplicable ... a product of the sheer complexity of our emotional, linguistic, moral and intellectual lives' (Cohen 2001). But what is it that we deny? Many things: the things we don't want to admit exist. In our daily life most of us tend to deny *something*, whether it's our looks, age, finances, or health. We deny some things as they force us to confront change, others because they are just too painful, or make us afraid. Sometimes we can't see a solution, so they appear unsolvable. Thus many of us deny the root cause of the problem. After all, it would be much easier for us if the world would just go along in the same old comfortable way. Psychoanalysis sees denial as an 'unconscious defence mechanism for coping with guilt, anxiety or other disturbing emotions aroused by reality' (Cohen 2001). Sociologist Zerubavel (2006) in his book *The Elephant in the Room* notes that the most public form of denial is *silence*, where some things are not spoken of. The silence about the environmental crisis, the silence about the fact that humans are dependent on Nature, the silence (until recently) about our obligate dependence on ecosystem services. All these silences are part of denial.

Zerubavel (2006) cites the fable of the 'Emperor's New Clothes' as a classic example of a conspiracy of silence, a situation where everyone refuses to acknowledge an obvious truth. Zerubavel sheds light on the keeping of 'open secrets'. He shows that conspiracies of silence exist at every level of society, ranging from small groups to large corporations, from personal friendships to politics. Such conspiracies evolve through the social pressures that cause people to deny what is right before their eyes. Each conspirator's denial is complemented by the others, and the silence is usually more intense when more people conspire, and especially when there are significant power differences among them (Zerubavel 2006).

Denial is thus common, and it is important we understand this. As a form of denial, silence helps us avoid pain. When facing a frightening situation we often resort to denial. The early reports of Nazi massacres of Jews were actually dismissed by many Jews in Europe as sheer lies (Zerubavel 2006). The prospect of the 'final solution' was just too frightening to believe. Zerubavel also refers to the 'ominous silence surrounding the spectre of a nuclear war'. He notes that 'silence like a cancer grows over time', so that a society can collectively ignore 'its leader's incompetence, glaring atrocities and impending environmental disasters'. He points out that denial is inherently *delusional* and inevitably distorts one's sense of reality.

People often get upset when confronted with information challenging their self-delusional view of the world around them. Many indeed prefer such illusions to painful realities, and thus cherish their 'right to be an ostrich'. US Senator Moynihan has noted that 'everyone is entitled to his own opinion, but not to his own facts' (Gilding 2011). Tavris and Aronson (2007) point out the problem of 'cognitive dissonance', which is the rather sick feeling you get when you realize a cherished belief is not supported by the evidence. They explain that most people will go to great lengths to reduce cognitive dissonance. Quite commonly, that means denying the evidence that caused the dissonance. Hence people can deny the scientific evidence that shows there is an environmental crisis. British politician Lord Molson stated 'I will look at any additional evidence to confirm the opinion to which I have already come' (Tavris and Aronson 2007). However, Zerubavel (2006) notes that the longer we ignore 'elephants' the larger they loom in our minds, as each avoidance triggers an even greater spiral of denial. The environmental crisis has now got to the point where the elephant is all but filling the room. We may now at times talk about it, but we still deny it.

It can be seen from the above that denial is everywhere. It is thus a fundamental part of the human psyche that needs to be acknowledged. Denial is, however, a delusion, one that can become a *pathology* when it endangers the ecosystems humans rely on. So denial is an understandable and very human trait. However, that does not mean it isn't dangerous, for it sometimes is. Just as the parable from historian Pliny the Elder of the ostrich sticking its head in the sand doesn't work for the ostrich, neither does denial of something that could be life-threatening. Ignoring a serious disease can lead to one's death. Similarly, denial of serious environmental problems may lead to the collapse of ecosystems upon which humanity relies. As Catton (1982) has noted: 'But believing crash can't happen to us is one reason why it will'. Biologist Jared Diamond (2005) has shown in his book *Collapse* that societies that deny or ignore their problems tend to collapse. Denial of some problems can thus be not only life-threatening, but even society-threatening. Of course, probably the greatest denial today is climate change denial, a denial of something we find deeply worrying. The ramifications of climate change denial are very serious, including a changed climate where many species could go extinct, sea levels rise (flooding cities), worsening droughts, and a world where agriculture could be hit hard, increasing famine (Pittock 2009; Washington and Cook 2011).

Existing research in environmental sociology and social psychology has previously emphasized the notion that *information* is the limiting factor in public non-response to environmental issues such as climate change, an approach that has been characterized as the 'information deficit model' (Norgaard 2011). There is the sense that 'if people only knew' they would act differently: that is, drive less, 'rise up' and put pressure on the government (Halford and Sheehan 1991). However, other scholars believe that the 'deficit model' explanation is no longer believable. There are other barriers than lack of scientific knowledge to changing the status of climate change in the minds of the public – psychological, emotional and behavioural barriers. We need to understand the complex 'cultural circuits' of science communication in which framing, language, imagery, marketing devices, media norms and agendas all play their part (Hulme 2009).

The history of denial

Denial is as old as humanity, so we have been denying environmental problems for a long time. Paul and Anne Ehrlich (1998), in the ground-breaking book *Betrayal of Science and Reason*, tabulated the common themes of denial anti-science:

- Environmental scientists ignore the abundant good news about the environment.
- Population growth does not cause environmental damage and may even be beneficial.
- Humanity is on the verge of abolishing hunger, food scarcity is a local or regional problem and is not indicative of overpopulation.
- Natural resources are superabundant, if not infinite.
- There is no extinction crisis, so action is both uneconomic and unnecessary.
- Global warming and acid rain are not serious threats to humanity.
- Stratospheric ozone depletion is a hoax.
- The risks posed by toxic substances are vastly exaggerated.
- Regulation is wrecking the economy.

These arguments are still being made in virtually the same format (e.g. Plimer 2009). It is important to realize that today's environmental denial follows on from a long history in the denial of the environmental crisis. The campaign to deny the need to protect natural areas and wilderness was one of the first great denial issues, and continues today (Oelschlaeger 1991; Washington 2006). The organization 'Wise Use' opposes efforts to maintain environmental quality in the USA, denies the need for national parks or wilderness, opposes environmental regulation and sees no need for constraints on the exploitation of resources for short-term economic gain (Helvang 1994; Ehrlich and Ehrlich 1998). Rachel Carson's (1962) *Silent Spring* raised the problems of synthetic pesticides (especially chlorinated hydrocarbons). This generated the first great environmental denial of the twentieth century. DDT was praised by many as a saviour of humanity for reducing malarial mosquito numbers (indeed it still is by some, e.g. Plimer 2009). Carson was vilified by the pesticide industry as someone both hysterical and wrong. In fact DDT was abandoned mainly because mosquitoes *evolved resistance* against it (Oreskes and Conway 2010). History and careful biological research have shown that Rachel Carson was right (Van Emden and Peakall 1999).

The 'denial industry' for climate change (largely funded by fossil fuel companies) has also been detailed in Monbiot's (2006) book *Heat*, in Hoggan's (2009) *Climate Cover Up*, in Oreskes and Conway's (2010) *The Merchants of Doubt*, and in Washington and Cook's (2011) *Climate Change Denial: Heads in the Sand*. What is apparent when examining the history of denial is that there is far *more* involved than merely confusion about the science. There has been a deliberate attempt to muddy the waters and confuse the public, so that action on these issues is delayed or even stopped. The denial industry deliberately seeks to sow doubt and confuse the public about environmental problems. Al Gore (2006) quotes a tobacco company (Brown and Williamson) memo from the 1960s: 'Doubt is our product, since it is the best means of competing with the "body of fact" that exists in the minds of the general public. It is also the means of establishing a controversy.'

The Ehrlichs (1998) have detailed how the 'anti-science' denial movement promotes seemingly 'authoritative' opinions in books and the media that 'greatly distort what is or isn't known by environmental scientists'. The Ehrlichs note that this 'brownlash' has produced a body of 'anti-science' that is a 'twisting of the findings of empirical science – to bolster a predetermined worldview and to support a political agenda'.

Denial anti-science proponents argue that environmental regulation has gone too far, a common conservative theme (Oreskes and Conway 2010). Even in 1998, the Ehrlichs noted that denial anti-science argued that 'subtle long-term problems like global warming are nothing to worry about'. They noted that this denial anti-science interferes with and prolongs the 'already difficult search for realistic and equitable solutions to the human predicament'.

There exists also *'green-scamming'* where groups are formed that masquerade about being concerned about the environment, but actually work *against* the interests implied in their names. Hoggan (2009) calls these 'astroturf' groups, while Enting (2007) describes them simply as 'front organisations'. Green-scamming is what biologists would call 'aggressive mimicry' (Ehrlich and Ehrlich 1998). Examples of such sham green-scam groups are the National Wetland Coalition, The Sahara Club, The Alliance for Environment and Resources, The Abundant Wildlife Society of North America, The National Wilderness Institute, The American Council on Science and Health, and the Global Climate Coalition. A detailed list for climate change denial and green-scam groups can be found at the end of *Climate Change Denial* (Washington and Cook 2011). US Congressman George Miller stated that these groups were seeking to disguise their actual motives, which were driven by profits and greed (Ehrlich and Ehrlich 1998).

Denial emerges when scientific method provides information that challenges the status quo and confronts people with uncomfortable facts about the state of the Earth's environment and the impact of human activities. Evidence of severe global environment degradation is then dismissed as inconclusive and the messenger declared an 'emotive scaremonger' (Mackey 2008). Green-scam groups often use code phrases such as 'sound science' and 'balance', words that suggest objectivity, when in fact 'sound science' means science or views that are interpreted to *support* denial anti-science (Ehrlich and Ehrlich 1998). Orthodox science that proceeds by peer-review, if it disagrees with the denial anti-science, is labelled as 'junk science'. This is actually a total inversion of reality. There is a 'junk science' website (www.junkscience.com) that promotes denial anti-science. Denial anti-science (with few exceptions) does not proceed through the usual peer-review science process. In fact it is not science at all, merely unsupported statements without proven scientific evidence. PR companies have long been involved in 'spin', in seeking to modify the public's view of reality, and this is certainly the case with the denial industry (Hoggan 2009).

The Ehrlichs (1998) document many of the then denial authors in the US, whose views were also quoted around the world. It is important to reiterate that climate change denial is merely the last in a long line of denial anti-science campaigns. This started with DDT, then continued with nuclear winter, tobacco, acid rain and the ozone hole. Today almost everyone (but not some deniers) accepts that CFCs are responsible for the hole in the ozone layer, yet only 10 years ago this was a hot topic of denial. The reason why denial over this is no longer strongly promoted may be that there is no powerful industry currently funding such denial. The refrigeration industry found economic alternatives to CFCs and the world has moved on, and the ozone hole is now starting to close (Hulme 2009).

Denial books on the environmental crisis continue to emerge. Jacques *et al.* (2008) explain that between 1972 and 2005 there were some 141 denial books published, of which 130 came from conservative 'think tanks'. In the 1990s, 56 denial books came out, 92 per cent linked to right-wing foundations or think tanks (Oreskes and Conway 2010). Probably the best known denial book is that by Lomborg (2001) *The Skeptical Environmentalist*. The Danish Committee for Scientific Dishonesty concluded this book had fabricated data, selectively discarded results and misused statistical methods. It concluded that Lomborg was 'out of his depth' in the field of science (Hoggan 2009).

When considering the history of denial, we should remember that science (as in all fields) has a broad selection of people: radical, conservative, rational and irrational. Remember also how widespread denial is in the human psyche. There will always be *someone* with a science degree somewhere who will champion almost any cause, and sometimes they will have Ph.D.s and can even be Professors (we have a couple in Australia). Just because there is a Professor of something denying the environmental crisis does not mean it is not true, it just means that particular Professor is in denial. This is why one must make use of the *preponderance of evidence* in science, the collective view. It should also be remembered that having a degree (or several degrees) in another field of science does *not* make one an expert in (for example) climate change. Despite this, it is common practice for denial organizations to quote one particular scientist who is in denial.

Monbiot (2006) concludes about the climate change denial industry that:

> By dominating the media debate on climate change during seven or eight critical years in which urgent international talks should have been taking place, by constantly seeding doubt about the science just as it should have been most persuasive, they have justified the money their sponsors

spent on them many times over. I think it is fair to say that the professional denial industry has delayed effective global action on climate change by several years.

Hoggan (2009) describes the denial industry as:

> A story of betrayal, a story of selfishness, greed and irresponsibility on an epic scale. In its darkest chapters it's a story of deceit, of poisoning public judgement – of an anti-democratic attack on our political structures and a strategic undermining of the journalistic watchdogs who keep our social institutions honest.

Ideological basis for denial

The organized denial industry has thus played a major part in slowing or stopping action on environmental problems. Oreskes and Conway (2010) detail the support that conservative think tanks have given to denial and ask 'what is going on?'. The link that united the tobacco industry, conservative think tanks and a group of denial scientists is that they were *implacably opposed to regulation*. They saw regulation as the slippery slope to socialism. They felt that concern about environmental problems was questioning the ideology of laissez-faire economics and free market fundamentalism. These conservative bodies equate the free market with liberty, so for them:

> Accepting that by-products of industrial civilization were irreparably damaging the global environment was to accept the reality of market failure. It was to acknowledge the limits of free market capitalism ... science was starting to show that certain kinds of liberties are not sustainable – like the liberty to pollute.
>
> (Oreskes and Conway 2010)

So if science impacts on their view of 'liberty', if it shows that regulation of pollution is needed, then science had to be opposed and *denied*. The basis for much denial is thus *ideological*, where science and the environmental crisis are denied owing to a conservative ideological hatred of regulation affecting the free market. It is of interest that sociology until recently has overlooked the organized conservative opposition to climate change action (McCright and Dunlap 2000). Sociology and society as a whole can no longer afford to do this.

Psychological types of denial

However, there is more involved than just the denial industry. Cohen (2001) describes three varieties of denial:

Literal denial – the assertion that something did not happen or is not true. For global warming, this form of denial is akin to the generation of counter-claims by oil companies that climate change is not happening (Gelbspan 1997; McCright and Dunlap 2000).

Interpretive denial – in which the facts themselves are not denied, but they are given a different interpretation. Euphemisms and technical jargon are used to dispute the meanings of events. For example, military generals speak of 'collateral damage' rather than the killing of citizens. Interpretive denial is what we commonly call 'spin'.

Implicatory denial – where what is denied are 'the psychological, political or moral implications . . . Unlike literal or interpretive denial, knowledge itself is not at issue, but doing the "right" thing with the knowledge' (Cohen, 2001). This is not negation of information per se, rather a failure to incorporate this knowledge into everyday life or transform it into social action. People have access to information, accept this information as true, yet, for a variety of reasons, *choose to ignore it* (Norgaard 2011).

Categorization of the three types of denial is useful when considering the broad range of denial overall. The first, *literal denial* is a key strategy of the denial industry. The second type, *interpretive denial* is generally what we see from government and business. This is what Fromm (1976) described as the way governments do things that 'give the impression that the problems are recognized and something is being done to resolve them. Yet nothing of real importance happens'. The third type of denial, *implicatory denial*, is the type of denial most common in the public. Implicatory denial is about 'bridging the moral and psychic gap between what you know and what you do' (Cohen 2001). Much of the knowledge about an environmental problem is accepted, but fails to be *converted into action*. We are vaguely aware of choosing not to look at the facts, but not quite conscious of just what it is we are evading (Cohen 2001). For example, the people in a study done in Norway believed in climate change, expressed concern about it, yet lived their lives as though they did not know (Norgaard 2011). Many of us could in fact be described as 'status apes', so that if something is likely to threaten our status, we ignore or deny it.

'Distraction' is also an everyday form of denial. If we are worried about something we tend to 'switch off' about the information and shift our attention to something else. We can also tend to 'de-problematize' it by rationalizing that 'humanity has solved these sort of problems before' (Hamilton 2010). We can also 'distance ourselves' from the problem by rationalizing that 'it's a long way off'. There is also 'hairy-chested denial', where people deny climate change, as it will impact on pleasures such as big, fast cars (Hamilton 2010). Blame-shifting is another part of implicatory denial, where we shift the blame onto others, such as the US, China, captains of industry, or the Developing World.

'Not knowing' certain things can be strategic (Norgaard 2011). To 'not know' too much about climate change maintains the notion of the innocence of those involved, and the sense that if one did know one would have acted more responsibly. As Jensen (2000) observed 'for us to maintain our way of living we must . . . tell lies to each other, and especially to ourselves'. In 2004, a large survey of American citizens was carried out regarding climate change. They found that 'more scientifically informed' respondents not only felt less personally responsible for global warming, but also showed less concern about it (Kellstedt *et al.* 2008). The 'information deficit model' is thus inadequate to understand how people respond to scientific controversies. Much more is involved in people's personal denial.

Zerubavel (2002) outlined the social dimension of 'ignoring' as the 'sociology of denial', where many people in society take part in co-denial. Norgaard (2003) noted that denial involves self-censoring or 'knowing what not to know'. Denial is the elephant in the room that we don't see. By avoiding it we thus do nothing to solve the problems it represents. However, Zerubavel (2006) notes:

> 'Elephants' rarely go away just because we pretend not to notice them. Although 'everyone hopes that if we pretend not to acknowledge their existence, maybe . . . they will go away' even the proverbial ostrich that sticks its head in the sand does not really make problems disappear by simply wishing them away. Fundamentally delusional, denial may help keep us unaware of unpleasant things around us but it cannot ever actually make them go away.

The reason it is so difficult to talk about the elephant in the room is that 'not only does no one want to listen, but no one wants to talk about not listening' (Zerubavel 2006). We thus *deny our denial*. This is a particular form of self-deception made famous by Orwell (1949) in his novel *Nineteen Eighty Four* as 'double-thinking'. Zerubavel (2006) notes that the longer we pretend not to notice the elephants, the larger they loom in our minds. However, one can break the silence of denial, and our strong need to deny things is counterbalanced by our equally strong need to expose denial. As soon as we acknowledge the elephant, it starts to shrink. Zerubavel (2006) explains that breaking conspiracies of silence implies 'foregrounding' the elephant in the room and 'calling a spade a spade'. Denial can have its own tipping point where 'increasing social pressure on the remaining conspirators to also acknowledge the elephant's presence eventually overrides the social pressure to keep denying it' (Zerubavel 2006). This is one tipping point we *do* need, to get society to acknowledge its denial about the environmental crisis.

Norgaard (2011) concludes that denial of the issue of climate change serves not only to manage negative emotions and preserve our sense of self-identity, but to maintain global economic interests and perpetuate global environmental inequalities. It is thus easier for many of us to slip into implicatory denial, rather than face the need for change. So why do we deny reality? Rees (2008) argues that in times of stress the brain's 'reptilian brain stem' (amygdala) will override the rational cortex, so we do stupid things. Thus our dedication to growth comes from these survival instincts. Rees (2008) concludes that if we are to survive today, we must assert our capacity for 'consciousness, reasoned deliberation and willpower' to 're-write the "myths we live by" and articulate the necessary conditions for sustainability'. Interestingly, a recent paper by Kanai *et al.* (2011) provides some evidence in support for Rees' conjecture about the amygdala. It found that greater political liberalism was associated with increased grey matter volume in the anterior cingulate cortex, whereas greater conservatism was associated with increased volume of the right amygdala. They note that the amygdala has many functions, including fear processing, and individuals with a large amygdala are more sensitive to fear. They note also that one of the functions of the anterior cingulated cortex is to monitor uncertainty, and this may help people deal with an uncertain world.

Ways we let denial prosper

Finally, we should ask 'Do we let denial prosper'? There are a number of aspects involved in this.

Fear of change: Of course many of us are not in denial, but it seems that many people, organizations and governments *are*. Why has there been a failure to feel an urgency to solving the environmental crisis? One reason why many of us don't take action is the *fear of change*. When struggling with the trauma of change, segments of society can turn away from reality 'in favour of a more comfortable lie' (Specter 2009). Even in 1969, C.P. Snow noted that many people felt anxious about the future, acting like they were 'under siege'. The fear of change is related to denial, and is a strong trait in humanity, indeed it is the hallmark of conservatism (though some prefer to call this neoliberalism or radical liberalism, Giddens 1994). Many conservatives just don't *trust* scientists (and certainly not environmentalists) as they think they are too 'liberal' (and hence suspect). This was the conclusion of the website www.skepticalscience.com that examines climate change denial arguments. One climate change denier stated 'the cheerleaders for doing something about global warming seem to be largely the cheerleaders for many causes of which I disapprove' (Orthodoxnet 2007). Studies have consistently found conservatism to be negatively related to pro-environmental attitudes, especially among political elites (McCright and Dunlap 2000).

Conservatives see environmental regulation as threatening core elements of conservatism such as the primacy of individual freedom, private property rights, laissez-faire government and promotion of free enterprise (McCright and Dunlap 2000). For example, a binding treaty and carbon price are seen as a direct threat to sustained economic growth, the free market, national security and sovereignty, and the continued abolition of government regulations – key conservative goals. Hoggan (2009) points out that in the US, among highly educated people, 75 per cent of Democrats believe humans are causing climate change, but among Republicans it is only 19 per cent. McCright and Dunlap (2000) point out that conservatives also tend to believe that 'radical environmentalists' are socialists 'who want to take over the world'.

Failure in values: Another reason why denial prospers is a *failure in values*. There is little discussion of ethics or values in modern society, and we discussed this in Chapter 5. It is a truism that if you don't know where you are coming from you don't know where you are going. If we don't actually strongly *value* the natural world that is in crisis and threatened, then we probably won't feel the urgency to save it.

Fixation on economics and society: Another reason we fail to act on the environmental crisis is to do with our *fixation on economics and society*. Our society looks first to economics and second to social issues. It is resourcist, modernist (or sometimes postmodernist), consumerist, utilitarian and anthropocentric (Oelschlaeger 1991; Washington 2006). Hulme (2009) suggests that a confident belief in the human ability to control Nature is a dominant, if often subliminal, attribute of the international diplomacy that engages climate change. The intelligentsia in our society has mainly focused on social justice, and *environmental justice* is rarely given equal time or prominence (Washington 2006). Under these circumstances it is hard for many people to feel a sense of urgency, as ecological degradation is just not *real* to them. This is partly owing to the fact that our society in the West is now more isolated from the natural world than ever before.

Our society is also fixated on growth economics, to the extent that there is rarely any discussion of a future 'steady state' economy (Daly 1991). We discuss this further in Chapter 9. If you don't put ecological sustainability first, and instead just focus on economy and society, you are not going to feel a great sense of urgency regarding the environmental crisis.

Ignorance of ecology and exponential growth: Another key reason why we let denial prosper is our lack of an *'ecological grounding'*. Most people don't understand how the world works in terms of ecosystems. Responding to this has been the key driver of this book. The ecological grounding of our society has improved over the last 30 years, but many decision-makers are still woefully ignorant. Some of them still think environmental issues are just about 'tree hugging'. For this reason they feel no urgency to act on environmental issues.

Another reason why people don't feel an urgency to act is our inability to really understand 'exponential growth' (Brown 1978). Part of the urgency of the environmental crisis is that there are so many environmental problems escalating at exponential rates, yet humans generally do not *think* exponentially. This is highlighted by the French riddle about a water lily in a pond, where the lilies double in size every day. On the thirtieth day the pond is full, so when is it half full? When asked, many people reply 'the fifteenth day', when of course the answer is the twenty-ninth day (Brown 1978). Many environmental problems are getting worse exponentially. Failure to understand exponential growth leads to a failure to act urgently on environmental problems, and aids denial.

Gambling on the future: Another aspect that delays us taking action is *gambling on the future*. Many of us are gamblers at heart. Some people are willing to accept a staggeringly high percentage of risk. Climatologist Stephen Schneider (2009) noted that the public does not understand probability, whereas scientists do. This is a serious problem, for some people are happy to *gamble* on their children's and the planet's future. Schneider at a talk asked who in the room had fire insurance and everyone put up their hand. He then said that the risk of your house burning down was far *less* than the risks inherent with climate change. If people were willing to act on the risk of fire, then why were they not willing to act on climate change risk? Hulme (2009) points out that scientists and campaigners get frustrated when the public does not seem to respond to their scientific assessment of risk. As a result, risk communicators tend to 'shout louder', and the public is faced with an increasingly distraught alarm call. This in itself can put off those who respond negatively to perceived 'alarmist' statements (whether they are true or not). However, if you are a gambler then you may not feel any sense of urgency, as you will always be gambling that things will turn out fine, or as we say in Australia: 'she'll be right mate!'.

The media: Another aspect that assists denial to prosper is *the media*, which Ehrlich and Ornstein (2010) note has largely become a *disinformation* service. The media has poorly communicated environmental science. Hoggan (2009) explains that in Canada in 2006 the majority of people blamed global warming on the ozone hole. Hansen (2009) notes that 'scientific reticence' may hinder communication with the public. Scientists may be more worried about being accused of 'crying wolf' than they are about being accused of 'fiddling while Rome burns'. To put it another way, scientists are in a double-bind, for the demands of objectivity suggest that they should keep aloof from contested issues, but if they do then the public will not know what an objective view looks like (Oreskes and Conway 2010). Hansen (2009) asks whether future generations might not wonder how we today could have been so stupid as to do nothing. He suggests that this would include scientists who did not adequately communicate the danger.

The media also loves *controversy*, and will seek to provoke argument. This is often justified as being 'balanced' reporting, when in fact it shows major bias. A situation where the judgement of the vast majority of the scientific community is given equal space with denial advocates is anything but 'balanced'. In fact 'balance' has become a form of bias in favour of extreme minority views (Oreskes and Conway 2010). If one examines newspapers one could be forgiven for thinking that science is split evenly about whether human-caused climate change is real, rather than more than 95 per cent of climate scientists saying this. Hoggan (2009) also notes that often people from green-scam organizations (or think tanks) will be invited to write articles in newspapers, *without* acknowledging their organizations' links and funding. They are often presented as 'independent' scientists when in fact often they are either not scientists, or come with a strong bias.

The media rarely checks factual accuracy. In 2007, the purported results of an 'important new scientific paper' were reported on the internet. It claimed that under-sea bacteria were responsible for the build-up of CO_2 in the atmosphere. Within hours this supposed study was reported on denial blogs and circulating around the world through the media as evidence to show that humanity did not cause climate change. Of course, it was a hoax created by journalist David Thorpe (see Hulme 2009). Thorpe did this to show that some people will use *anything* that supports their argument, whether it's true or not, and whether they had checked its accuracy. These factors in the media make it easier for people to deny the environmental crisis, or at least ignore it. In fact, Oreskes and Conway (2010) argue it has made it easier for our governments to do almost nothing about climate change.

Conclusion

So clearly we *do* let denial prosper. Rees (2008) concludes that on the dark side of myth, our shared illusions converge on deep denial. Our best science may tell us that the consumer society is on a self-destructive path, but we successfully deflect the evidence by repeating in unison the mantra of perpetual growth (Rees 2008). Westra (2008) believes the instrumental rationality of neoliberals (conservatives) is attuned to goals, not the concrete qualitative sustaining of life on Earth. What neoliberal policy has accomplished is a widening global inequality that exacerbates neglect of both population health and the global environment. Indeed, inequality fuels denial of environment concerns, as beneficiaries of neoliberal policy are protective and defensive of their gains (Westra 2008). Avoidance is sweet temptation notes Wackernagel and Rees (1996), but denial leads to 'greater pain tomorrow'. They conclude that the first step towards a more sustainable world is to accept ecological reality and the socio-economic challenges it implies.

This chapter has covered a lot of ground on denial, and I refer those interested in digging deeper to read *Climate Change Denial: Heads in the Sand* (Washington and Cook 2011). To conclude, denial is part of humanity, it has probably been with us since humans first evolved. There are those who operate from greed and deliberately create a denial industry to confuse people. This is immoral and destructive. Similarly, there are the denial spin-doctors in government who seek to use 'weasel words' and fool the public that they are taking meaningful action, when often they are not. However, when it gets down to it, there is also denial in 'we the people'. We let ourselves be duped and conned, we let our consciences be massaged, and we let our desire for the safe and easy life blot out unpleasant realities. We delude *ourselves*. However, if a large part of the public abandons denial, they can fairly quickly turn around corporate denial, especially if it costs the corporations profits. If a large part of the community tells our politicians that they want real action, not weasel words, then politicians will actually *act*. We are not powerless drones who cannot change things. En masse, if we accept the 'Great Work' (Berry 1999) of repairing the Earth, we have the vision, the creativity and the power to solve the environmental crisis, and at the same time make the world a better place. That nobody should deny.

8   Do we have a problem?

An endless sadness
As each wonder leaves us.
Do you then feel
The death of a forest?
Or another extinction?
Our heritage passing
In our childish spite?
For we are the Masters,
Controllers of chaos.
So please will you tell me
The GNP value
Of a world fast fading?
Or would you rather complain
Of the price of salvation?
(From 'Passing',
Washington 2010)

Having covered a lot of ground in the previous chapters, I would like to consolidate things and check whether we really *do* have a problem? Do we have an environmental crisis, and is this because we don't understand our roots are in the Earth? Some years ago I worked for local government as Director of Sustainability. At a seminar with councillors I mentioned the need to 'solve the environmental crisis'. One councillor replied 'What crisis? It is news to me!'. Thankfully, at that time others spoke up, saying 'Where have you been the last thirty years?'. However, the question is still out there, the question of whether we *really* have a problem? The problem of 'shifting baselines' has been noted by Pauly (1995), where successive generations adjust to the state of the environment they find, so a degraded ecosystem may be accepted as 'normal'. If people don't visit wilderness and natural ecosystems they may not realize just how degraded other ecosystems have become. Many people seem to think that those who talk about an environmental crisis are just on about 'tree hugging' and that the consequences of how we have treated the Earth are being alarmingly *overstated*. So, is there really an environmental crisis? Are we close to environmental catastrophe? Are humans really dependent on Nature? Do we have a crisis *because* we refuse to accept that we are dependent on Nature to survive?

Ecocide?

In regard to an 'environmental crisis', what do we mean by this? The terms 'crisis' and 'catastrophe' are deemed 'emotive' terms by some. What constitutes a crisis or a catastrophe? Just as genocide is wiping out human populations, are we conducting 'ecocide', a wiping out of the ecosystems upon which we ourselves depend? How should we speak about reality in an honest way, without being 'alarmist' or stretching the truth? Well, first, what do we 'know' about the actual ecological state of the world? Not the pretend world of governments, business, shares and sport, but the *actual* living world we are part of. We know from the Millennium Ecosystem Assessment (MEA 2005) that '60 per cent (15 of 24) of ecosystem services are being degraded or used unsustainably'. That should sound a warning, but some people don't seem to think this really conveys any sense of urgency. The MEA also tells us that species numbers are in steep decline, and that over the past few hundred years humans have increased the species extinction rate at least a *thousand times* over the background rate. As a result, 10–30 per cent of mammal, bird and amphibian species are currently threatened with extinction (MEA 2005). Freshwater ecosystems have the highest proportion of species threatened with extinction.

Now some in denial will inevitably cast doubt on the MEA, just as they have on the other major international scientific assessment, the International Panel on Climate Change or IPCC (e.g. Plimer 2009). This is despite the fact that 1,360 experts from 95 countries wrote the MEA, overseen by the UN, especially its Environment Programme (UNEP), with involvement by the International Union for the Conservation of Nature (IUCN), the World Bank and many others. While those in denial will seek to portray such overwhelmingly broad scientific studies as a grand *conspiracy* (as explained in Washington and Cook 2011), this is clearly a denial of reality. The fact that 1,360 experts in the field (many of them quite cautious and conservative) have agreed on these figures means they are the best understanding of the situation we have. I shall thus accept their honesty, integrity and most importantly – their *veracity*. There is no credible doubt about the seriousness of the data coming in about the reality and gravity of our environmental problems.

Sukhdev (2010) in *The Economics of Ecosystems and Biodiversity* (TEEB) notes that humanity has not widely understood that our survival depends on *coexistence*, on living in harmony with Nature. This would seem to be self-evident, yet sadly this appears not to be the case. So 60 per cent of ecosystem services are being used unsustainably and degrading, and the extinction rate is 1,000 times the rate recorded in the fossil record.

Actually, rather than being 'over-exaggerated', these figures are probably an *underestimate*. The 'father' of biodiversity, Professor E. O. Wilson of Harvard University, believes the extinction rate is 1,000 to 10,000 times greater than normal, so that something like three species go extinct each and every hour (Wilson 2002). The MEA figure may thus underestimate the extinction rate by a factor of 10.

Professor Wilson believes that without action (and this is an essential point to remember), by 2100 *half* of the world's species will be extinct (Wilson 2003). Half the world's species, but only if we keep going the way we are, *if we do nothing*. This estimate was made before the full extent of the impact of climate change was understood, which on its own may send 18–35 per cent of species extinct (Thomas *et al.* 2004). Taken together, this is why many scientists argue the Earth has entered its sixth period of mass extinction (Leakey and Lewin 1998). There have been five other mass extinctions, the last was when the dinosaurs went extinct 65 million years ago (see Figure 8.1). These other extinctions wiped out 25 per cent, 19 per cent, 54 per cent, 23 per cent and 17 per cent of families (Eldredge 2001).

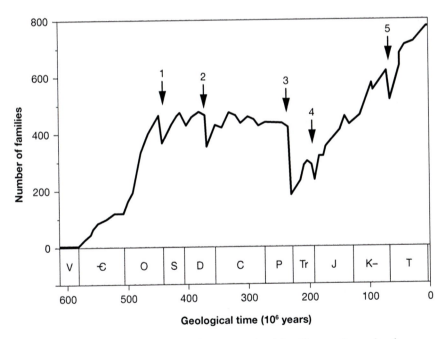

Figure 8.1 History of the diversity of marine animal families, as shown by the fossil record over time. The curve connects 77 discrete data points, each giving the total number of well-skeletonized families from a particular stratigraphic stage. Arrows indicate the Big Five episodes of mass extinction.

Source: May (2002, Figure 1).

We can see that what humanity is now doing would rival the other great extinction 245 million years ago in the Permian. We are well on the way already to passing the last mass extinction when the dinosaurs went extinct 65 million years ago. Yet now *we* (not an asteroid) are the prime cause of another mass extinction, and this is not something to be proud of. But how many of us know this? When I mentioned this recently to my co-author of *Climate Change Denial* he looked shocked and said 'people don't know this, and they need to!'. Indeed they do. Perhaps nothing highlights the problem as well as the fact that most of the public do not know that human action may destroy half the living world remaining on Earth. The living world that nurtured us, and from which we evolved: our brothers, sisters and cousins.

Is this a crisis? Well, ask your children or your relatives' children. I have talked to primary school children in the Australian bush and told them the extinction figures. I didn't preach to them or tell them what to think, I asked them what *they* thought. They were horrified. When I asked 'why?', they told me 'It's just wrong!'. They were right. Of course, some adults in denial say that extinction doesn't matter, that it is 'normal' (e.g. Plimer 2009), without acknowledging the hugely accelerated rate of extinction we are causing, or the fact that by century's end human action could lead to the loss of half of the world's species. If this loss happens, it will close off the evolutionary potential of half of the life on Earth, an incredibly damning indictment on humanity. As Soulé and Wilcox (1980) have said: 'Death is one thing – an end to birth is something else.'

But is it *really* a problem?

But to play Devil's Advocate, is this *really* a problem? Ecologists and evolutionary biologists know it is, but most of the public does not seem to know. Most of the species going extinct are not cute and cuddly animals such as koalas or pandas (mind you, both of those are now threatened). So if one was selfish, and interested only in yourself and humanity, one could still ask '*why* exactly does it matter'? Well the MEA (2005) notes that: 'Everyone in the world depends completely on Earth's ecosystem and the services they provide such as food, water, disease management, climate regulation, spiritual fulfilment and aesthetic enjoyment.'

This study notes that the structure of the world's ecosystem changed more rapidly in the second half of the twentieth century than at any time in recorded human history. Virtually all of the Earth's ecosystems have now been significantly transformed through human actions. Most significant are changes such as the transformation of approximately one quarter (24 per cent) of Earth's terrestrial surface to cultivated systems (MEA 2005). More land was converted to cropland from 1950 to 1980 than in the 150 years between 1700 and 1850 (MEA 2005). The result is that now 38 per cent of global ecosystems are transformed (MEA 2005). In fact the UNEP study TEEB (Elmqvist *et al.* 2010) states that 35 per cent of Earth's surface is used just for crops and livestock. Grazing alone accounts for 26 per cent of the land surface. There are then all the other actions that transform ecosystems, such as logging, fragmentation of habitat, pollution by toxins, pest invasion, overfishing, etc. Rees (2008) notes that, overall, humans have transformed half of the land area of Earth, and use more than half of the planet's accessible freshwater.

The crux of *why* it matters is twofold. The first is ethical, that Nature has 'intrinsic value' and a right to survive, even if it is of no use to humans (see Chapter 6). The second is pragmatic and selfish and considers only our own interests: because humanity *relies* on the ecosystem services that Nature provides to us. We discussed ecosystem services in Chapter 3, and showed that ecosystem services are essential to our survival. However, they are so often overlooked, and almost never factored into economic indicators or calculations. As long ago as 1970, Paul and Anne Ehrlich (1970). noted: 'the most subtle and dangerous threat to man's existence is the potential destruction of those ecological systems upon which the very existence of the human species depends.'

This has proved to be prophetic in nature. This is also why the Union of Concerned Scientists (UCS 1992) warned of the need for a change in our *stewardship* of the planet. This is why Wackernagel and Rees (1996) noted that despite our increasing technological sophistication, humans remain in a state of *obligate dependence* on the productivity and life-support services of the ecosphere. That means there is no alternative, we *depend* on these. Looking at the situation from a purely anthropocentric and utilitarian basis (i.e. what is useful to us), we thus should be concerned, and we should admit that we *do* indeed have a problem. Looking at the situation from an ecocentric or altruistic perspective, one can only be horrified at what we are doing to the fellow species we share this world with, and to future generations who will inherit an impoverished Earth. Either way we have a huge problem.

It is not just a problem of species extinction either. The MEA (2005) also summarized that human activity is putting such a strain on Nature that the ability of the planet's ecosystems to sustain future generations can no longer be taken for granted. Rees (2008) summarizes the situation by explaining that during the twentieth century:

- human population quadrupled to 6.4 billion;
- industrial pollution went up 40-fold;
- energy use increased 16-fold and CO_2 emissions 17-fold;
- fish catches expanded by a factor of 35;
- water use increased ninefold.

To this one can add that one quarter of coral reefs are destroyed and another 20 per cent are degraded, and 35 per cent of mangroves were lost in two decades (MEA 2005); 30 million hectares of tropical forest are cleared yearly

(Daily and Ellison 2002). Half the world's people live in countries where water tables are falling as aquifers are depleted (Brown 2011). On a finite world, clearly something has got to give. You cannot keep increasing the stresses on Nature without something going wrong, without what Winston Churchill called 'a period of consequences'. Indeed, something *is* going wrong. All forms of biodiversity are generated and maintained by natural ecosystems. Axiomatic as this may seem, we need to remind ourselves that no one can exist without the life support basis supplied by natural ecosystems. But the world overall is run by the *wisdom of the marketplace*. Despite this: 'from morning coffee to evening nightcap we benefit from our fellow species, without recognising it we utilize hundreds of products each day that owe their origin to wild plants and animals' (Daily 1997).

Our welfare is intimately tied up with the welfare of biodiversity. Ecosystems both mediate and respond to climate systems, through a variety of physical, biological and chemical feedback cycles. The uncertainty of resulting synergisms and potential global effects demonstrates the challenge, as exemplified in the Amazon basin (Daily 1997). With synergisms (separate problems that interact to increase overall impact), you don't just add the impacts, you *multiply*. Meanwhile, humanity continues to perform the 'potentially trillion dollar unnatural experiment on Laboratory Earth' (Schneider 1997). Indeed, given human society and our economy are *fully dependent on ecosystem services*, this experiment is worth far more than a trillion dollars, it is worth no less than the survival of our societies.

Other scholars put the matter more baldly than the scientists and scholars who wrote the MEA or TEEB, as these are by nature cautious. Rees (2008) states that human activity has become the most significant geological force altering the face of the planet. He calls humanity *Homo sapiens var economicus* and says we have become a 'renegade species' whose activities threaten our own long-term security by wreaking havoc on the natural world. He goes on to say that many (if not most) of the problems societies face in creating sound environment policies stem quite simply from the lack of recognition of the crucial roles natural ecosystems play in maintaining society's health and happiness. In terms of energy and material flow there is simply no 'out there' anymore. Once we dumped wastes to 'out there' in the belief that there were no limits, and this could not hurt us. However, the 'out there' is actually the ecosystems that support us. The premise that human beings are 'embedded in Nature' is so simple that it is generally overlooked or dismissed as 'too obvious'. However, if humans are part of Nature's fabric, the environment is no mere 'scenic backdrop' but *becomes the play itself* (Wackernagel and Rees 1996). The ecosphere is where we live, humanity is dependent on Nature, not the reverse. Sustainability requires that our emphasis shift from 'managing resources' to managing *ourselves,* that we learn to live as part of Nature. If we did this, then 'economics at last becomes human ecology' (Wackernagel and Rees 1996).

Crisis or catastrophe?

So, as to the terms 'crisis' and 'catastrophe', are these valid words to use? The Oxford English dictionary defines *crisis* as: 'A time of intense difficulty or danger; a time when a difficult or important decision must be made.'

Given the summary above, today is clearly a time of intense difficulty in terms of the natural world and the ecosystem services it supplies us. It is also a time when a difficult and important decision (or series of decisions) must be made to maintain the ecosystems that maintain our societies. In 1982 it was argued humanity is in a 'predicament' not a crisis, since the conditions we face are not of recent origin and will not soon abate (Catton 1982). However, since then things have got worse, and the term environmental 'crisis' is *exactly* the right word to use when half the world's species are at risk and ecosystems are being degraded and collapsing. The Oxford dictionary defines 'catastrophe' as 'an event causing great and usually sudden damage or suffering; a disaster'. It then gives an example, being 'an environmental catastrophe'. Given the extent of mass extinction, soil erosion, industrial pollution, growing population and consumption, and growing and unsustainable water use, again one can validly call this a *catastrophe*, or at least a catastrophe in the making.

Every ecosystem collapse (see Chapter 4) is of course a catastrophe for that particular ecosystem. It may not be a catastrophe for humanity in every case, but taken together it is building up to this. It is most significant also that many scholars note that the environmental crisis will impact most strongly on the poor. They are the ones who rely directly on ecosystem services and who will suffer most (Gowdy *et al.* 2010). The idea that 'trickle down' from the consumer economy will help the poor has clearly failed (Layard 2005; Sneddon *et al.* 2006). Rather, the consumer society is a direct threat to the well-being of the world's poorest. Our unsustainable use of the world's ecosystems, our failure to believe in and acknowledge *limits* (Meadows *et al.* 1972), has led to an environmental crisis, one on the way to becoming a catastrophe for both Nature and human civilization (Rees 2008). Peter Goldmark, former Rockefeller Foundation president concludes that the death of our civilization is 'no longer a theory or academic possibility; it is the road we're on' (Brown 2011). Some of us may be uncomfortable and squirm at the words 'crisis' and 'catastrophe'. However, if we want to accept reality and not slip into the delusion of denial, then we need to acknowledge these words are *entirely appropriate* to the predicament we face. A predicament we created.

A deeper problem?

But is there a deeper problem at work? Philosopher Thomas Berry (1988) states:

We can break the mountains apart; we can drain the rivers and flood the valleys. We can turn the most luxuriant forests into throwaway paper products. We can tear apart the great grass cover of the western plains, and pour toxic chemicals into the soil and pesticides onto the fields until the soil is dead and blows away in the wind. We can pollute the air with acids, the rivers with sewage, the seas with oil – all this in a kind of intoxication with our power for devastation. . . . We can invent computers capable of processing ten million calculations per second. And why? To increase the volume and speed with which we move natural resources through the consumer economy to the junk pile or the waste heap. Our managerial skills are measured by our ability to accelerate this process. If in these activities the topography of the planet is damaged, if the environment is made inhospitable for a multitude of living species, then so be it. We are supposedly, creating a technological wonderworld . . . But our supposed progress toward an ever-improving human situation is bringing us to a wasteworld instead of a wonderworld.

Accelerating climate change, accelerating deforestation, soil erosion, fisheries collapse and species extinction all tell us our current demands on Nature are impoverishing the Earth and compromising humanity's future well-being. In spite of these trends, society operates as if Nature were an 'expendable' part of our economy, just an 'externality' (Wackernagel and Rees 1996). It is clear that underlying forces driving destruction of ecosystem services include unsustainable growth, overconsumption, overpopulation and environmentally destructive technologies. Even in 1982 it was apparent that humanity had become 'locked into stealing ravenously from the future' (Catton 1982). An important stress is also the pattern of gross inequity within and between nations (Daily 1997).

Miller (1990) believes we have a 'throwaway' worldview, based on the following beliefs:

- We are apart from Nature.
- We are superior to other species.
- Our role is to conquer and subdue wild Nature to further our goals by humanizing the Earth's surface.
- Resources are unlimited because of our ingenuity in making them available, or in finding substitutes – there is always 'more'.
- The more we produce and consume, the better off we are.
- The most important nation is the one that can command and use the largest fraction of the world's resources.
- The ideal person is the self-made individualist who does his or her own thing and hurts no one.

Miller concludes our current worldview is 'the supreme pathology of all history'. Sekine (1992) argues industrialization led to dis-embedding of human beings from their natural environment, of technology from ecology, of science from knowledge, to yield the one-sided society of capitalism. Clearly we have a *problem*, but what caused the problem? Rees (2008) notes that:

> The world presently has the wealth, human capital and natural resource to execute a smooth transition to global sustainability out of mutual self interest, yet we do not act. . . . Despite forty years of organised environmentalism, two world summits on environment and development, repeated warnings by scientists and the emergence of 'sustainable development' as a mainstream mantra, global society continues its drive toward ecological disaster and geopolitical chaos.

To avoid the descent into chaos, Rees (2008) argues the world community must 'acknowledge the true human nature of our collective dilemma and act consciously to override the innate socio-behavioural predispositions that block collective action'. Rees (2008) notes that humanity got to this point through unconscious expansionist tendencies, reinforced by the social construction of both a *perpetual growth myth* and increasingly a *global consumer myth*. Those who would guide humanity to sustainability are therefore pitted against formidable biological and cultural imperatives. In the early twenty-first century Nature and nurture have converged in a dangerous liaison that has 'rendered modern Homo sapiens fundamentally unsustainable' (Rees 2008). Greer (2009) concludes that civilization is sleepwalking towards the abyss, as we fail to grasp the most basic elements of ecological reality.

In the best of all possible worlds, love of Nature, compassion for the less well off in the human family and mutual self-interest would be reasons enough for the global community to act assuredly *now*. But sadly this is not the best of all possible worlds. 'Biophilia' is the term coined by Professor Wilson (1984) for the 'love of life', of Nature, but it has been said that love of Nature has never been a significant political force. It has also been noted that humans are not notably 'moved by compassion' (Rees 2008). This is confirmed by Ehrlich and Ornstein (2010) in *Humanity on a Tightrope* in their discussion of the problem of the human tendency to put people into 'them and us' boxes. Even mutual self-interest holds no ground if there are risks, and when exclusive self-interest promises a 'bigger pay off' (Rees 2008). As Caldwell (1984) notes: 'Individual self-interest alone will never save the world. Safeguarding the Biosphere requires a social commitment of a moral, quasi-religious character'.

Rees (2008) goes on to say that most of Nature's services are derived free from ecosystems and thus remain unpriced, so people tend to mistakenly assume natural resources are *unlimited*. This permits the idea of perpetual material growth to 'remain unquestioned yet unsustainable', at the expense of ecosystems and life support. In effect, the markets are blind to the harmful ecological consequences of growth. The relentless pursuit of economic efficiency and material wealth has *no moral or ethical compass*, so we 'continue to erode natural systems that demand consideration of time horizons far beyond shareholder reports and election cycles' (Soskolne *et al.* 2008).

Catton (1982) notes that the stakes have become phenomenally high and include equity, democracy, human tolerance and peaceful coexistence. All are in jeopardy owing to the environmental crisis. Daily (1997) argues that civilization is on a dangerous course but its fate is not yet sealed. Our decision-making frameworks need to ensure protection of humanity's most fundamental source of well-being: Earth's life support systems. Yet this has not been effectively conveyed to decision-makers or the public. As Chapter 3 explains, mostly the benefits provided by ecosystems are *not traded* in formal markets and do not send price signals that can lead to change to unsustainable activities. This is a major factor driving the conversion of ecosystems to human-dominated systems. As an example of the dominance of the 'free market' idea, it has been pointed out that the benefits from mining the metal molybdenum are easier to measure than the ecosystem services benefits that derive from leaving land un-mined and natural (Daily 1997).

Daily (1997) says that making economic institutions sensitive and responsive to natural constraints, and dealing with the limitations of such institutions, are requisites for effective Earth management. Failure to foster the continued delivery of ecosystem services undermines economic prosperity, forecloses options, and diminishes other aspects of well-being. It also threatens the very persistence of civilization (Daily 1997). While academia is a long way from fully understanding ecosystem services, the accelerating rate of disruption of the biosphere makes imperative the incorporation of current knowledge into the policymaking process. It has also been argued that *capitalism itself* is the problem. Paradoxically, while unimpeded, abstract market calculations are the taproot of capitalism's economic viability, they are *also* the source of capitalism 'profaning of the world' (Westra 2008). Capitalism is thus seen as an inverted social order that conflicts fundamentally with concrete human needs and goals (Westra 2008). Of course by now, deniers will be claiming that this is a 'Marxist conspiracy', without realizing that Marx himself thought Nature was just a resource for human use (Eckersley 1992; Hay 2002). I doubt any of the above environmental scientists and scholars are Marxists. For that matter, nor am I. However, one does not have to be a Marxist to note that capitalism (and the idea that free markets *must* rule) is a major contributor to the mess we are in. Scholar after scholar has noted that our economic system, (and the belief that free markets are infallible) does not let us see the damage this system is causing the life support systems that *actually* underpin our societies, and hence our economy.

It has been argued that the transition towards 'ecological disintegrity' is characterized by a fundamental imbalance in 'pluralistic governance' leading to:

1) obsessive focus on growth in productivity, and irrational use of non-renewable resources;
2) disinvestment from public infrastructure and changes in social policy to maintain class structures;
3) little consideration of the *ecological and social consequences* associated with the processes of production and conspicuous consumption.

(Rainham et al. 2008, emphasis added)

Clearly, the idea of endless growth and increasing consumption is unsustainable on a finite Earth. Conflicting interests, opposing worldviews, incompatible analyses, rising material expectations and fear of change have led to a disorienting mass of interpretations of 'sustainability' and how to achieve it (Wackernagel and Rees 1996). From an ecological perspective, adequate land and associated productive natural capital are *fundamental* to the prospects for continued human existence on Earth. Both human population and average consumption are increasing, yet the total area of productive land and natural capital stocks are fixed or in decline (Wackernagel and Rees 1996). This cannot go on, and ecosystems are telling us this is not sustainable – by degrading and collapsing. Of course, we would not adopt any such damaging behaviours if our relationship with Nature were one of coexistence and responsible stewardship (Sukhdev 2010). I would add that if we believed in the intrinsic value of Nature we would not be able *ethically* to adopt such a system, or to continue its use.

Conclusion

So what *is* the deeper problem? Well actually there are multiple deeper problems that underlie the environmental crisis, and underlie the reasons why we don't take action. As Chapter 6 discussed, we cannot consider root causes without looking at our society's worldview, ethics, values and ideologies. The dominant modernist worldview sees Nature as just a resource for human use (utilitarianism), is anthropocentric and does not see Nature as having intrinsic value. Modernism believes in 'progress' based on the mastery of Nature. Both capitalism and Marxism are based on the utilitarian and resourcist view of Nature. They are also based on 'growthism' and an endlessly growing economy. This ideology of endless growth has been called 'ever-moreism' (Boyden 2004). This has been allied with the mantra of the 'free market', which has become a God, but a free market that is 'free' of any relation to ecological reality.

So do we have a problem? Do we have a crisis? Do we have a burgeoning catastrophe? The answer is *yes to all three*. So, what do we do about it? The next chapter deals with this. Certainly the point of this chapter was not to suggest 'doom and gloom'. Fear tends to paralyse people (Hulme 2009;

Norgaard 2011) and those in despair tend to be like those in denial: they do nothing. Accepting the reality of a problem does not mean 'giving up', it means *finding solutions*. However, to frame the following discussion, it is worth pondering a quote by Albert Einstein (Daily and Ellison 2002):

No problem can be solved from the same consciousness that created it.

9 Solutions to keep our roots in the Earth

I hearing get, who had but ears,
And sight, who had but eyes before;
I moments live, who lived but years,
And truth discern, who knew but learning's lore.
I will not doubt the love untold
Which not my worth or want hath bought,
Which wooed me young, and woos me old,
And to this evening hath me brought.
(From 'Inspiration', Henry David Thoreau,
as quoted by Emerson 1862)

Scale of the problem

The previous chapters have clearly shown that humanity *needs* Nature to survive, always has, always will. Statements about the 'end of Nature' are just hubris. If Nature ends then so do we. To think otherwise is to deny the ecological reality of how the world works. Humanity is nurtured by the Web of Life, yet we are degrading that web, and threaten half the life we share this world with. We cannot send half the life on Earth extinct (and cause ecosystem collapse), without it rebounding on *us*. It already is, which is why we have an environmental crisis. Hopefully, that is no longer news to you. Hopefully you also see that we have to *accept reality* and solve our problems.

Ecologist Peter Vitousek and colleagues (1997) have noted that: 'We are the first generation with tools to understand the changes in the Earth's systems caused by human activity and the last with the opportunity to influence the course of many of the changes now rapidly under way.' It is thus time to use those tools to make that change. It is time to grow up and drop our delusions, our megalomaniac fantasy of being 'masters of Nature'. We never 'conquered' Nature, we just raided fossil carbon deposits to cause the environmental crisis (Greer 2009). We have stolen fossil energy from the past, and owing to the impacts this causes, we are robbing the future, making it less than it could have been. It is time to rediscover our connection to Nature, and re-establish our roots in the Earth. Environmentalism has now become the 'most significant human, moral and theological problem confronting the contemporary world' (Collins 2010). If we don't face up to the ecological crisis 'we will have no future as sane, ethical and spiritual beings' (Swimme and Berry 1992). It is time to move into what Swimme and Berry call the *Ecozoic* period of human history, when humans move from being a 'seriously dumb species' (Soskolne 2008) and realize their profound unity and connection with the whole of creation.

So ... how do we do this? How do we *solve* the environmental crisis? How do we turn things around and move towards ecological sustainability in the long term? How do we rediscover our roots in the Earth? There is no shortage of sustainable strategies, but what society lacks is the intellectual and emotional acceptance of the fact that humanity is materially dependent on Nature, and that Nature's productive capacity is limited (Wackernagel and Rees 1996). We need to relearn the truth that our roots lie in the Earth. So how do we turn things around? Well, first, it is essential to say it is not hopeless! There is *always hope*, provided that it is tied into being rational and facing reality. Second, it will not be *easy*, as we need to directly challenge the dominant worldview, power structures, economic system, and cultural and religious underpinnings of our society. It would have been far easier 30 years ago when William Catton (1982) wrote his visionary book *Overshoot*, but we deluded ourselves, went into denial, and failed to take significant action. No generation has faced a challenge with the complexity, scale and urgency of the one we face (Brown 2011). Now we need to act quickly. There can now be no doubt about the critical *urgency* to solving the environmental crisis. Whether we solve this or not will be played out this century, almost certainly before mid-century. Third, this means that we cannot continue 'business-as-usual', we have to stop and take a serious look at ourselves, our worldview, our ethics, our values, our ideologies, our societies, our economy, our technologies and our denial. The MEA (2005) noted that significant changes to policies, institutions and practices *can* mitigate many of our negative consequences on ecosystems. However, they also noted that the changes required are large and *not currently under way*.

When faced with the possibility of climate catastrophe, climate scientist Barrie Pittock (2009) argues there are three broad psychological reactions: *nihilism* (it's hopeless so let's enjoy ourselves), *fundamentalism* (God or the 'market' will save us) or *activism* (we can solve this). I espouse the latter, as together we can indeed solve the environmental crisis. Humans are intelligent, and when committed can (and have) solved huge problems. The Second World War, the Marshall Plan to rebuild Europe after that war, and the Space Race are excellent examples of successful major actions that some would have said were 'impossible'. Atlee (2003) describes 'co-intelligence' as the human capacity to generate creative responses, and it is this we need to foster. The situation we face is a huge problem, but it is also a major *opportunity*, an opportunity to build a truly sustainable future. Even in narrow economic terms it is a major opportunity (McNeil 2009). The actions that are needed to solve a given environmental problem (e.g. climate change) are often the actions we need to take to solve other environmental problems. Thus, while the problems may be synergistic, *so are the solutions*. We should be doing these things for many reasons. For example, we need to stabilize population for reasons of food, biodiversity protection and water supply, yet this also reduces carbon emissions. By acting on climate change, we solve the imminent crisis of energy insecurity resulting from the peak in global oil production, and we also take a big step towards stopping the biodiversity extinction crisis. We need to stop burning polluting coal and oil for health reasons as well as climate. The climate crisis is a key problem we must solve, but in fact it is a *symptom* of an unsustainable worldview and an unsustainable society. Through the process of solving climate change, we will thus also improve many other urgent environmental problems, if we do it the *appropriate* way.

Hulme (2009) refers to what have been called 'wicked' problems, a term deriving from cultural theory. Wicked problems have no one simple solution. Rather than just one 'silver bullet' to solve the problem, he suggests *silver buckshot*, the multiple solutions one applies to the problem. Solving the underlying environmental crisis will require several different approaches, a number of 'silver buckshot'. Given that I am seeking to cover solutions to the environmental crisis in just one chapter, it could validly be asked whether I have fallen into hubris *myself* in attempting this? So much is involved, and many books have been written on this. Some notable books are Catton (1982) *Overshoot*, Ehrlich and Ehrlich (1991) *Healing the Planet*, Berry (1999) *The Great Work*, Soskolne (2008) *Sustaining Life on Earth* and Brown (2011) *World on the Edge*. Indeed, I wrote my own book *Ecosolutions* in 1991 (Washington 1991). It is notable how much agreement there is in such books as to the problems *and* the solutions. To be realistic, the most I can do here is cover the broad structure of what the solutions will involve. This will cover worldview, economy and consumerism, population, poverty, education and communication, ecological sustainability, technology, and the 'Great Work'. Given that people get bogged down in the detail, I will also conclude each section with a short 'What you can do!' paragraph.

Worldview, ethics, values and ideologies

Bandaid solutions will not work. We need to change society's **worldview**, the way we see the world, and move to an ecological worldview (Catton 1982), or what has been called *ecosophy*, a philosophy of ecological harmony (Naess 1989), or a 'biosensitive' society with a 'biounderstanding' worldview (Boyden 2004). The term 'ecological civilization' has been coined in China for this idea, even by the General Secretary of the Communist Party (ChinaDaily 2007). As Oreskes and Conway (2010) conclude, 'science has shown us that contemporary industrial civilization is not sustainable'. Biologist E. O. Wilson (2002) is brutally honest, pointing out that humanity has become a 'serial killer of the biosphere'. This human-centred worldview has been called the 'Dominant Social Paradigm', 'Manifest Destiny' (McCright and Dunlap 2000) and 'defiance' where we defy and deny evidence of the environmental crisis (McKibben 2006). It sees Nature just as a group of resources that only have value for human use. But why is a new worldview so essential? Because without it we will not remove the Cornucopian cataracts from our eyes, and we will remain blind to the underlying real causes of the environmental crisis (Catton 1982).

The alternative is to adopt an ecocentric approach. To value Nature for *itself* and see the natural world as something sacred. Are we ego-centric or ecocentric? Is the Universe just about *us* and our consumption, or is it about sharing our planet with the wondrous evolved diversity of life? Over the past 200 years, Western consumerism and resourcism have impoverished the natural world we share, and brought us to the brink of tremendous further loss. This is the elephant in the room we can no longer afford to ignore. We now have to be realists. Thirty years ago, William Catton (1982) argued there are five ways to approach 'ecologically inexorable change'. These were based on whether people accepted the 'circumstances' of environmental impact, but also the 'consequences' of the need to change. These were *realism* (we accept the circumstances and consequences); *cargoism* (accept circumstances but disregard consequences); *cosmeticism* (disregard circumstances but partially accept consequences); *cynicism* (disregard both circumstances and consequences); and *ostrichism* (circumstances and consequences denied). It is time to be a realist, and that means thinking about how we view the world.

Ethics are related to values, and Zerubavel (2006) speaks about the silence of denial about ethics:

> 'The best way to disrupt moral behaviour' notes political theorist C. Fred Alford 'is not to discuss it and not to discuss not discussing it'. 'Don't talk about ethical issues' he facetiously proposes 'and don't talk about our not talking about ethical issues'. As moral beings we cannot keep non-discussing 'undiscussables'. Breaking this insidious cycle of denial calls for an open discussion of the very phenomenon of undiscussability.

The ethical dimensions of climate change are starting to be recognized. Anglican Bishop David Atkinson (2008) argued:

> Climate change is . . . opening up for us . . . questions about human life and destiny, about our relationship to the planet and to each other, about altruism and selfishness, about the place of a technological mindset in our attitude to the world, about our values, hope and goals,

and about our obligations for the present and for the future. These are moral and spiritual questions.

So people are acknowledging the fundamental *ethical* questions involved in what we are doing to the world. Indeed, people are reconsidering their worldview, and have been revolting against the narrow focus of modernism for decades. People also tend to be more altruistic than the economic model predicts (Brondizio *et al.* 2010). Paul Collins (2010) argues that discussion now *has* to move to the moral sphere, that we face a massive, overarching moral problem, bigger than war, more serious than financial meltdowns. We have to talk in a language that shows what we are doing to Nature is *evil*, that we are committing biocide and ecocide. We now need to adopt a fundamental moral principle that the good of the planet must come *before* everything else (Collins 2010). As Thomas Berry (1994) has noted 'the ecological imperative is not derivative from human ethics' but the other way around.

One insight sees humanity as divided into three 'personal identities'. These are the 'independent self-construal' identity or Western individualist, the 'interdependent self-construal' who define themselves through connections to other humans (e.g. family, society) and the 'meta-personal self-construal' (Hamilton 2010). The last one is self-connected to all living things and the cosmos. The first two focus on either ourselves or other humans, while the third approach extends our focus *outside* humanity to the rest of the world. It is this concept of an expanded self that underpins Buddhism (and some indigenous cultures) (Hamilton 2010). However, Western society tends to encourage the first two approaches (primarily the first) but not the third. It is for this reason that it is so essential that we change our modernist worldview. There are many practical and useful things that can be done without changing our worldview (e.g. as discussed by McNeil 2009), but if we don't also change our worldview, we are likely to get ourselves re-entangled in the same mess we are in now. Fundamentally, we need to tackle the 'isms' of modernism, industrialism and consumerism.

Can we change our worldview? Some people feel threatened by this question. However, things are happening, and a clean industrial revolution *is* on the way (Diesendorf 2007; McNeil 2009). Similarly, people's views of how humans relate to Nature are changing. Many people may not put it into words, but they *care* about the Earth. This is where the conservation and environment movements came from, this is where the desire to buy 'green' products comes from. This is where the drive to sustainability that has swept across the community (and some businesses and governments) comes from. This is why international lawyer Polly Higgins (2009) calls for an International Declaration of Planetary Rights, and 72 nations mention environmental rights in their constitutions (Engel 2008). This is why there is a move towards 'Earth jurisprudence' (Flavin 2010). The shift to sustainability will depend on powerful networks of pioneers and champions.

Assadourian (2010) suggests the change can be made by six powerful institutions: education, business, government, the media, social movements and sustainable traditions. Of course, much work remains to be done. The education system by and large has failed to educate us about human dependence on Nature. Business and government have largely treated Nature as an 'externality' they can ignore. The media only deals with the issue spasmodically with each new environmental disaster. Social movements for change have not grown as fast as they need to.

However, a groundswell for change *is* there, though it will take decades to make the change to a new worldview (Assadourian 2010). It's a question of whether people can abandon denial and use their new worldview to *force* action. Now, deniers hate the idea of changing our worldview. They espouse the same modernist and consumerist worldview that got us into this mess. They see any call for a change of worldview as a Marxist conspiracy, even though an ecocentric approach does not sit well with *either* traditional capitalism or Marxism, for Marxists don't generally relate to an ecocentric worldview either. What we are talking about goes *beyond* these limited political ideologies. And in some ways that is the rub, as neither capitalists nor Marxists 'get it'. They can only espouse more consumption, more growth, *forever*. McCright and Dunlap (2010) note that society needs 'reflexivity', a form of critical self-evaluation, a 'self-confrontation with the unintended and unanticipated consequences of modernity's industrial capitalist order'. This would be a first step to changing our worldview.

To solve the environmental crisis we need to accept reality. So what impedes us from accepting reality? We have seen that worldview, ethics and values can do this. *Ideologies* or 'isms' also stop us from accepting reality. These can be capitalism, socialism, resourcism, consumerism, industrialism – they are all based on the idea of Nature being just a resource for human use. Together you could lump them as 'modernism' (Oelschlaeger 1991) or 'modernity' (Hamilton 2010), as discussed in Chapter 6. Calls to delay action on the environmental crisis because it will have a 'negative effect on the economy' show just how powerfully the modernist ideology can drown out reality. You can't have an economy *without* functioning ecosystems, yet those who are wedded to the ideological view of eternal growth and exploiting Nature are blind to the realities of ecosystem limits and carrying capacity. We have come to the end of the time where it didn't seem to matter that almost no one saw the difference between ways of enlarging human carrying capacity and exceeding it (Catton 1982). They simultaneously don't understand – and are not listening to or learning from – the mistakes of the past. When ideology blinds you to a dangerous reality, surely it is time to abandon that ideology?

One prevalent ideology that developed in response to modernism was *postmodernism*, which we discussed in Chapter 6. I am treading on some sacred cows here, as postmodernism (and the related post-structuralism) are often a dominant ideology within academia. However, action on the environmental crisis is too important to shy away from discussing any ideology that may foster denial or inaction. Postmodernism en masse seems to remain as anthropocentric as its predecessor, modernism. I truly hope, however, that it might evolve to become ecocentric. Gare (1995) has observed that postmodernism has demonstrated many problems with modernism, while it has been *powerless to oppose them*. Postmodernism is thus good at analysing the problems modernism has caused, but very poor at finding solutions to them. As an ideology it (like its predecessor modernism) is thus not aiding us to roll back denial and solve the environmental crisis. We need something *more*. We need a grand narrative and dream of repairing the Earth (Berry 1999).

To recap, we need to change our worldview, ethics, values and ideologies. Humanity is thus faced with a complex problem of *conscious evolution* (Ehrlich and Ornstein 2010) or cultural evolution to create a thoughtful, ecologically literate human, motivated by a sense of responsibility to the planet (Soskolne *et al.* 2008). The change in worldview is unlikely to come from governments and business. It certainly won't come from a media owned by conservative corporate interests. It has been concluded sadly that it is also unlikely to come from the education system (Ehrlich and Ornstein 2010). That leaves *us* – 'we the people'. This is not as hopeless as some might think. Ecologist Paul Ehrlich notes that there are thresholds in human behaviour when cultural evolution moves rapidly, so that: 'When the time is ripe, society can be transformed virtually overnight' (in Daily and Ellison 2002). When enough of us change our worldview then governments, business and the education system will follow. To quote Gandhi: 'We must become the change we want to see in the world'.

What you can do!

Talk about this! Become a champion for changing society's worldview. Talk about intrinsic value, environmental ethics and environmental justice. Don't shy away from the issue, raise it with friends and family. *Argue the need for change.* You may find more allies than you thought?

The growth economy and consumerism

Changing society's worldview means changing our economy also. It has become a truism for most political parties to support a *growth economy* based on consumerism and a growing population. Ecological economist Herman Daly (Daly and Cobb 1989) has noted 'there is something wrong in treating the Earth as if it were a business in liquidation'. Growth has become a fetish, even a God for both the Left and the Right. Daly (1999) notes we have in fact achieved 'uneconomic growth', in terms of its impact on the planet. There has been an almost total victory of growthism and free-market economics, far more of a victory than economists such as John Maynard Keynes, John Stuart Mill or even Adam Smith ever originally intended (Hamilton 2010; Gilding 2011). In recent years, the vast majority of economists have actively promoted materially wasteful economic growth or quietly tolerated it (Czech 2000). However, the market is not telling us the truth, by omitting indirect environmental 'externalities', we all end up paying for these (Brown 2011). However, growth for growth's sake is in the end *meaningless* and destructive. Loss of species, coral reefs or glaciers, and inundation of coastlines cannot be compensated for by growth in consumption or by monetary transfers (Hulme 2009). Neumayer (2007) argues that a utilitarian approach that assumes we can degrade natural capital is a problem as 'Climate change, at least above a certain temperature, violates fundamental principles of sustainable development, intergenerational stewardship and fairness and therefore violates the inalienable rights of future generations'.

Growth economics also violates the fundamental ecological reality of the Earth. Hulme (2009) notes there is a paradox at the heart of economic analyses of climate change: the presumption of growth. Is the presumption of endless growth compatible with plans to solve the environmental crisis? Why do future analyses make growth a cardinal assumption? Ecological economist Spash (2007) argues: 'Traditional pro-growth policies fail to address the problems humanity faces, the necessary transition or the nature of widespread environmental change we are undertaking. All these realisations raise the question of economic activity "for what"?'

Many believe that the fixation on growth and the assumption that increasing consumption is the path to well-being is *precisely* why we have an environmental crisis. Economist Richard Layard (2005) notes:

> Economic growth is indeed triumphant, but to no point. For material prosperity does not make humans happier: the 'triumph of economic growth' is not a triumph of humanity over material wants; rather it is the triumph of material wants over humanity.

Sukhdev (2010) says the root causes of biodiversity loss lie in the nature of the human relations with Nature. He sees the root cause of the problem as being our dominant economic model, which:

> promotes and rewards more versus better consumption, private versus public wealth creation, human-made capital versus natural capital. This is the 'triple whammy' of self-reinforcing biases that leads us to uphold and promote an economic model in which we tend to extract without fear of limits, consume without awareness of consequences and produce without responsibility for third party costs, the so-called 'externalities' of business.

Usually, the rationale for growth and development is that it helps people such as the poor (even if it is only as a result of the 'trickle down' effect). Some even argue that 'green fatalism' holds back improving the lot of the poor (Fox in Hulme 2009), and that growth is the solution to environmental decline. However, Sneddon *et al.* (2006) note that the primary drivers of environmental degradation, energy and material use, have increased hugely, yet inequalities in access to economic opportunities have also dramatically increased within and between most societies. The UN report 'Rethinking Poverty' (UN DESA 2009) notes that while there has been a reduction in overall poverty, the inequality of income has increased. The mantra of development and growth is thus not helping the poor. Growth is continuing, but the poor get fewer and fewer of the benefits (Layard 2005).

A 'steady state' economy was proposed by Georgescu-Roegen (1971) and Daly (1973, 1980) that operates on the basis of:

- constant human population;
- constant stock of artefacts or goods;
- levels of these goods sufficient for a 'good life';
- the throughput of matter and energy (to maintain artefacts and population) being kept as low as feasible. Products must be long-lasting.

Such a steady-state economy makes sense in today's world. Our economy is fundamentally broken, and we need to move to prosperity *without* growth. Prosperity for the few founded on ecological destruction and persistent social injustice is no foundation for a civilized world (Jackson 2009). We also need to integrate the disciplines of ecology (literally the 'study of the home') and economy (literally the 'management of the home'). There are now professional societies of 'ecological economics', and many top-class economists now accept that economics *relies* on maintaining ecosystems and the services they provide us. The report 'Growth Isn't Possible' (Simms *et al.* 2010) by the New Economics Foundation has summarized in detail *why* endless growth not only will not continue to bring us benefits, but just isn't possible if we are to maintain the ecosystem services on which humanity relies. There are also 'degrowth' movements, most notably in France (Latouche 2010), and recently the 'Occupy Wall Street' citizens protest sprang up, and soon spread around the world.

Is it 'economic' to solve the environmental crisis? This has the question back to front. We should ask whether it is economic *not* to solve it. It may indeed cost a lot of money to take strong action to solve it, just as it cost a lot to finance the Space Race. It won't cost more than we already spend on the military, however (Pittock 2009). Brown (2011) in fact estimates it will cost *about one eighth* of the world's military budget. Arguments of false economic expediency also need to be refuted. The UK Stern Review (Stern 2006) showed that failing to act on climate change would end up costing us *more* than acting now. The same applies to other environmental problems. Professor Garnaut (2008) of the Australian Garnaut Climate Review argued that 'Prudent risk management would suggest that it is worth the sacrifice of a significant amount of current income to avoid a small chance of a catastrophic outcome'.

Lester Brown (2006) concludes that we face two overriding challenges: restructuring taxes and reordering fiscal priorities. Saving civilization means restructuring the economy, and at wartime speed. It also means restructuring taxes to get the market to tell the *ecological truth* (Brown 2011).

The key problem of our growth economy is *consumerism*. After all, environmental impact comes from population *times* consumption. Even in the 1950s, retail analyst Victor Lebow (1955) concluded:

> Our enormously productive economy demands that we make consumption our way of life, that we convert the buying and use of goods into rituals, that we seek our spiritual satisfaction and our ego satisfaction in consumption. . . . We need things consumed, burned up, worn out, replaced and discarded at an ever-increasing rate.

Today, for some people, consumption has become the meaning of life, the 'chief sacred', the point of morality, the criterion of existence, the 'mystery before which one bows' (Ellul 1975). It is no small irony that the same consumption that has lately become the 'meaning of life' has now also emerged as the greatest hazard to life. Ultimately, we cannot roll back denial of the environmental crisis unless we roll back our consumer worldview (Starke and Mastny 2010). The 2010 State of the World Report examines our addiction to consumerism, explaining how consumer cultures exaggerate the forces that have allowed human societies to outgrow their environmental support systems (Assadourian 2010). Hamilton (2010) argues that many of us have constructed a personal identity through shopping and consumerism. We have substituted consumerism for meaning (Collins 2010). Asking people embedded in the consumer myth to change their consumerism may thus be like asking them to change their identity, *yet this is what we must do.*

Sukhdev (2010) notes we have become attuned to giving 'yes' answers for trade-off choices that result in more consumption, more private wealth, more physical capital – as against *better* consumption, more public wealth, more natural capital. Society extends that false logic implicitly when we ignore the depletion of forests, fisheries and so on. This is part of a perverted logic of 'promoting growth' or 'promoting development', without defining these terms in holistic or equitable ways from either an intra- or inter-generational perspective (Sukhdev 2010). Thus, while we promote endless growth on a finite planet, we don't think about whether this is fair to future generations, or indeed fair to the rest of life we share the planet with. Growth and development have thus become 'given truths' we must uphold without thought. They are virtual Gods. This ideology ignores or denies human ecological dependency on Nature, ignores the environmental crisis, and even ignores the well-being of future generations.

Assadourian (2010) shows that the consumer ethic, seen as 'natural' by consumers, is actually a *cultural teaching*, a purposeful social construct. Following the Second World War, the USA was 'blessed' with great industrial capacity and large numbers of underemployed workers (returned soldiers). To take advantage of labour and break people out of their wartime habit of thriftiness, industry organized to legitimize profligate consumption, to make it a *spiritual activity* (Rees 2008). Tacey (2000) points out that consumers in Western society are spiritually empty, so that shopping temporarily fills this void. Mass consumption requires that consumer demand remains insatiable (Westra 2008). However, preventing the collapse of human civilization requires nothing less than a *wholesale transformation* of dominant consumer culture (Flavin 2010). Consumption has gone up sixfold since 1960, but numbers have only grown by a factor of 2.2. Consumption expenditure per person has almost tripled (Assadourian 2010). According to the Global Footprint Network, humanity now uses the resources and services of 1.5 Earths (GFN 2011), an unsustainable situation. If all the world were to adopt American lifestyles we would need *at least four more planets* to supply them (Graff 2010). Assadourian (2010) suggests three goals to tackle consumerism. First, consumption that undermines well-being has to be discouraged. Second, we need to replace private consumption of goods with public consumption of services (e.g. libraries, public transport). Third, necessary goods must be designed to last and be 'cradle to cradle' recyclable.

So, how do we change our economy and break our culturally maladaptive consumerism? 'The Economics of Ecosystems and Biodiversity' study (Kumar *et al.* 2010) concluded that greater economic and ecological rationality in addressing natural capital is not only necessary but possible. Many leading-edge economists now accept environmental science and accept the need for change to ecological economics and a steady state economy. One urgent need is for 'tax shifting' and 'subsidy shifting' (Brown 2006). We need environmental taxes to send the message that things need to change, the most obvious being a carbon tax (or ETS), but also a landfill tax so that those generating garbage pay for it (Brown 2006). We need to remove subsidies from things that promote the environmental crisis (such as fossil fuels) to things that help solve it (such as renewable energy). Way back in 1997, 2,500 economists (including six Nobel Prize winners) endorsed the concept of tax shifts for climate change (Klugman 1997), so the recognition of the need is not new. Globally, $700 billion in subsidies goes to environmentally destructive activities (fossil fuels, pumping out aquifers, clearing forests and overfishing) (Brown 2006). So we need to remove the many subsidies that accelerate the environmental crisis. The next step is to move to a 'Green GNP' and drop the existing GNP and GDP indicators that take no cognizance of environmental reality. Many economists now agree that instead of measuring GDP (a flow concept), a better measure is the stock of wealth that includes natural capital (Kumar *et al.* 2010).

E. F. Schumacher wrote his seminal book 'Small is Beautiful' way back in 1973, pointing out the problem of consumerism. It is thus finally time for us to come to grips with and reject this created ideology. It is critical that we now plan for products 'cradle to cradle', and that we see pollution as a 'symbol of design failure' (McDonagh and Braungart 2002). We need to reject throwaway products, and we need to plan for reuse *before* recycling. After all, a refillable glass bottle used repeatedly requires only a tenth as much energy per use as an aluminium can that is recycled (Brown 2006). Groups such as www.noimpactproject.org and www.sfcompact.blogspot. com are citizen movements that reject consumerism. The New Economics Foundation is another resource (NEF 2012).

What you can do!

Challenge the mantra of endless economic growth. Talk about the need for a steady state economy. Argue for tax and subsidy shifts, and for a Green GDP. Argue for an 'honest market' that factors in environmental costs. Reuse and recycle, and grow your own food. Argue against rampant consumerism and consume less, shop less, and *live more!*

Population

In terms of solving the environmental crisis, three of the biggest elephants that we don't see standing in the room are climate change, population and consumerism. I have discussed climate change denial elsewhere (Washington and Cook 2011) and we discussed consumerism above, but population is an equally difficult elephant for us to see. Perhaps the only problem more 'wicked' than climate change is population. Nothing else seems to raise such passion. Into it comes issues such as religion, racism, social and environmental justice, equity and poverty. There is also no more taboo issue *politically* than population. Collectively, the public and governments have been shying away from facing up to it for decades. Yet Hulme (2009) asks, if there is a 'safe' level of greenhouse gases to avoid runaway climate change, then 'is there not also a desirable world population?'.

The knee-jerk reaction to raising the issue of population is to call one 'anti-human' or a 'racist' (Collins 2010). In fact I do not believe in the dubious concept of 'race', and the ethnic origin of people is not the point. The total numbers and distribution of people and their impact on the Earth's carrying capacity *is* the point. Unsustainable population growth pushes the world beyond its carrying capacity (Catton 1982). The world is finite. We know that human numbers have grown exponentially and that they are now larger than ever before, having just reached 7 billion people. Various projections indicate that by 2050 the population will grow to between 8 and 10.5 billion people (UN 2009). So . . . what is an ecologically sustainable population? Biocapacity data suggest that if we made no change at all to consumption patterns, we could currently sustain a population of 4 to 5 billion. If everybody on Earth shared a modest standard of living, midway between the richest and the poorest, that figure would fall to around 3 billion (PM 2010). Collins (2010) concludes that human population numbers are now so far beyond sustainability as to render the concept irrelevant. At current levels of consumption, global food production will need to increase 50 per cent in the next four decades to meet growing population (Kumar 2010). It is hard to see how this is possible given the many accelerating and interconnected environmental problems food production now faces (Brown 2011).

In 1968 Paul Ehrlich published 'The Population Bomb', which alerted the world to the dangers of exponentially growing population. He was later central (Ehrlich, Ehrlich and Holdren 1977) in coining the equation:

$$I = PAT$$

Environmental impact equals population × affluence × technology. Our impact on the Earth is thus the number of people times their affluence (per capita consumption of resources) times the technology we use. Of course I accept that most of the impact from pollution and carbon emissions are *currently* coming from the consumers in the developed world (Monbiot 2009). However, the developing world is rapidly seeking to catch up. If this is done using traditional carbon-polluting industry then the result will be steeply accelerating global carbon emissions, resource consumption, and other pollution. The technology used to 'catch up' will thus be the critical factor, as will the question of whether they seek to catch up to the incredibly wasteful American (or Australian) level. However, improving technology or reducing affluence can only reduce our impact so far. In the end the numbers of people themselves count. A big population has a big impact, especially as the developing world expands its economy. Despite a 30 per cent increase in resource efficiency, global resource use has expanded by 50 per cent over 30 years (Flavin 2010). This is mainly a consequence of the increasing affluence of the large populations in the developing world. This is why China is now the world's biggest carbon polluter, while India now ranks sixth (Assadourian 2010). Accordingly, we need to target *all three* components of I = PAT if we seek to reduce human impact: containing population, limiting affluence and cleaning technology.

Why is population such a diabolical policy issue? Because it cuts at the heart of the received wisdom of two million years of human evolution, where *more* people was always better (Washington 1991). 'More' meant we could gather more food, cut down more forest, hunt more animals, defend ourselves better, and ostensibly gather more taxes for the State (though of course more money needs to be spent also!). 'More people' as a concept until the last 100 years has always been seen as a good thing for society. Collins (2010) believes that at the core of the population problem is a conflict of rights: the right of the individual to reproduce, and the right of other species to continue to exist. It is very hard for us to understand in our hearts that now 'more' is no longer better. Add to this the religious bans against birth control methods (e.g. the Catholic Church). Add to that the fundamental desire of governments to have more citizens and greater power. Population ecologist Meyerson (see Hartmann *et al.* 2008) notes:

> Conservatives are often against sex education, contraception and abortion and they like growth – both in population and in the economy. Liberals usually support individual human rights above all else and fear the coercion label and therefore avoid discussion of population growth and stabilisation. The combination is a tragic stalemate that leads to more population growth.

Population exacerbates all the other environmental problems, including climate change. It means cutting more forest for farmland, over-farming land so that it erodes, killing more 'bush meat' (wild animals) for food, overfishing the rivers and seas. It means burning more fossil fuels as a way of fuelling development. As Chris Rapley, the Director of London's Science Museum notes about population:

> So controversial is the subject that it has become the 'Cinderella' of the great sustainability debate – rarely visible in public, or even in private. In inter-disciplinary meetings addressing how the planet functions as an integrated whole, demographers and population specialists are usually notable by their absence.
>
> (BBC 2006)

If we are going to accept reality then *we need to accept all of it.* Population growth is a key contributor to the on-going environmental crisis. We need to stop denying this and develop rational, ecologically based, population policies. Education and family planning are the key, and by doing this, Iran was able to halve its population growth rate from 1987 to 1994 (Brown 2011). 'More people' is no longer 'better'. To deny this just exacerbates denial of the causes of the environmental crisis (O'Connor and Lines 2008).

> **What you can do!**
>
> Dare to talk about the double whammy of growing population and consumption per person on a finite world, that the two together multiply to cause unsustainable impact. Argue for an ecologically sustainable population target for your nation. Have no more than two children. Talk about how our ecological footprint is at least 1.5 Earths. Explain that we need action on *both* population and consumption.

Reducing poverty

Rather than ending poverty, modernism has led to the environmental crisis, and this is now impacting strongly on the poor, who rely on ecosystem services. The 'trickle down' approach has proven to be cynical spin on the part of the consumer economy. Inequity in income distribution has increased within OECD countries but also in major emerging economies such as China and India (OECD 2011). However, poverty exacerbates environmental problems, which in turn exacerbate poverty. An increasing population in poverty means they push ecosystem services *beyond* their sustainable level, so they degrade. Less available (free) ecosystem services means the poor have less with which to live. We are in danger of going into a downward reinforcing spiral (MEA 2005). Despite this, major reports on poverty such as the UN's 'Rethinking Poverty' (UN DESA 2009) do not actually mention the key aspect of environmental degradation.

Brown (2006, 2011) notes that in an increasingly integrated world, eradicating poverty and stabilizing population have become national security issues. In fact eradicating poverty is one of the four components of 'Plan B' of the Earth Policy Institute (Brown 2011). Slowing population growth helps eradicate poverty (and its distressing symptoms), and conversely, eradicating poverty helps slow population growth (Brown 2006). With time running out, the urgency of doing both simultaneously is clear. One way of narrowing the gap between rich and poor is by ensuring *universal education*, and universal primary education by 2015 is one of the Millennium Development Goals. The World Bank estimates that $12 billion a year could achieve this for 80 of the world's poorest countries. An important incentive is to get children into 'school lunch programs'. Girls especially benefit, as they stay in school longer, marry later, and have fewer children (thus easing population pressures). Carrying this out in the 44 lowest income countries would cost an estimated extra $6 billion a year (Brown 2006).

Another means of reducing poverty is for developed countries to forgive some of the huge debt owed by developing nations. Servicing such debt (some of it decades old) means poor nations cannot address either poverty or environmental problems. We have seen above that if the developing world uses old carbon-polluting and resource-wasteful technology to grow its economy, the environmental crisis will worsen markedly. They thus need assistance to develop in smarter ways, and rich nations should be spending 1–2 per cent of their GDP on environmental aid to the developing world *in all our interests*. It has been estimated that additional funding to reach basic social goals to break out of the poverty trap would cost $68 billion a year (Brown 2006). There is also a growing movement towards 'fair trade' with the developing world, which for too long has been forced to sell their products too cheaply. To summarize the importance of this issue, the Worldwatch Institute way back in 1992 noted: 'The fate of the fortunate is immutably bonded to the fate of the dispossessed through the land, water, and air: in an ecologically endangered world, poverty is a luxury we can no longer afford' (Durning 1992).

What you can do!

Support fair trade products. Support 1–2 per cent of GDP going in environmental aid to the developing world. Support the forgiving of much of the old debt owed by developing nations.

Education and communication

Part of the background of the environmental crisis also lies in a failure (at many levels) to educate and communicate. George Perkin Marsh was a diplomat interested in Nature, who wrote the book *Man and Nature* in 1864. However, he almost certainly had a more *accurate* view of humanity's role in the natural world than that possessed by the average decision-maker today (Daily 1997). Possibly even the Greek philosopher Plato had a more accurate understanding of the consequences of deforestation when he wrote about a deforested area, where the formerly rich forest land had become 'only food for bees' (Daily 1997). More than 130 years after Marsh's book, most 'educated' people still remain sadly *unaware* of its basic message: that humans are part of Nature and reliant upon it. The fact that they are ignorant that the economy is a wholly owned subsidiary of the ecosystem amounts to a condemnation of schools, colleges, universities and the media. It also highlights the failure of professional ecologists to communicate their findings to the public (Daily 1997). Many of us in cities typically forget that Nature works in closed loops. Nothing in Nature grows *forever*, indeed Edward Abbey (1977) noted that 'growth is the ideology of the cancer cell'. Big-city life breaks down understanding of natural material cycles and provides little sense of our intimate connection with Nature. Despite this estrangement, we are not just 'connected' to Nature, the reality is we *are* Nature (Wackernagel and Rees 1996).

A key problem is that school curricula almost never cover ecology in the detail needed to get across human ecological dependence on Nature. The problem extends even to universities, which Ehrlich and Ornstein (2010) observe are full of conservatism, entrenched interests, and 'frequent sloppy thought'. There is also the problem of narrow disciplinary courses failing to address big interdisciplinary issues. The issue is not just education, it is about *empowerment* to take action. Plenty of facts about environmental degradation have been around for decades. The trouble is finding how you empower people to think about them and take meaningful action. Often such action may just be through 'small meaningful local actions that individuals or small groups can guarantee to carry through to completion' (Hill 1998). However, we need collective action as well, as we discuss later under 'politics'.

What you can do!

If you have children at school, speak to the school about discussing the environmental crisis and human ecological dependency on Nature. If you are at university, promote these ideas there. Work to empower your local groups to take action. Support the creation of 'Life Centres' to discuss environmental issues.

Ecological sustainability – the key focus

Clearly, solving the environmental crisis means becoming ecologically sustainable in the long term. 'Sustainability' has become something of a buzz word, and some question whether it has retained any meaning, given it is often left undefined. However, as for contestable concepts such as democracy, justice, peace and freedom, the ideas behind it remain *essential*. Sustainability and sustainable development are terms that arose from the 'Our Common Future' report (WCED 1987). The terms reflect the growing groundswell of concern about what is happening to the world (Soskolne *et al.* 2008). Sustainability is a word that can encompass many meanings. One description is that it is an attempt to provide the best outcomes for the human and natural worlds into the future. At the heart of the concept of sustainability is a vision of achieving human and ecosystem well-being *together*. Sustainability is generally considered to be made up of three strands: social, economic and ecological (sometimes called environmental). All three of these are necessary. Think of sustainability as being a three-legged stool, with each strand being a leg. For the stool to function, *all* three legs must be in place. Sustainability and its three strands are often not defined, but should be. I was involved in an attempt to define them (WCC 2008), as shown below:

Social sustainability is often confused with social justice or social respons-ibility, but while these are part of it, social sustainability has a broader focus.

Social sustainability aims for a society that can live in a long-term balance with the world and its ecosystems. In other words, this would be a world at peace, both among people and *between* people and Nature. A sustainable society will require fairness (equity) and justice, locally and globally, within this generation, between our generation and future generations, and between humanity and Nature. It will require that social justice *and* environmental justice work hand in hand, where environmental justice is justice for the non-human world (see Chapter 6).

Economic sustainability is about creating an economy that is sustainable over the long term, not just a short-term growth economy. This means it will be a *steady state* economy that does not rely on eternal growth and damage the ecosystem services that underpin our society (as discussed earlier). Ecological economics seeks to integrate ecology and economics through understanding we must protect and maintain our natural capital.

Ecological sustainability is about taking action to solve the Earth's environmental crisis by monitoring, restoring and supporting the biodiversity and ecosystems that support us. It means that we ensure we do not exceed the Earth's carrying capacity. It means greatly reducing our carbon footprint by controlling our greenhouse gas emissions. It means changing our worldview.

However, people historically have tended to devote the majority of their time to their society and their economy. This is not to say that governments have focused on social justice and social sustainability, merely to point out that, owing to the anthropocentrism discussed in Chapter 6, humanity has focused on *itself*, its society and economy. To return to the 'three-legged stool' analogy, it is the third leg, ecological sustainability, that has received less attention, and thus may collapse (hence the need for this book).

Certain interests worldwide seek to shift the focus of 'sustainability' primarily to an economic or social focus, so that they can continue business-as-usual, which may not be *ecologically* sustainable. Social and economic factors must remain a key part of the decision-making process, but in order to respond to the urgency of the environmental crisis, extra weight needs to be given to restoring the balance, by focusing on the long-overlooked side: *ecological sustainability*. Spratt and Sutton (2008) note that because of climate change, sustainability is now not so much a 'radical idea as simply an indispensable course of action if we are to return to a safe-climate planet'. Without a stable climate we cannot reach ecological sustainability (Pittock 2009). However, without ecological sustainability, we are unlikely to return to a stable climate. Assadourian (2010) explains that institutions now will have to be fundamentally oriented to sustainability. Aronson *et al.* (2010) argue that the disconnection between our knowledge and our actions is largely caused by three 'great divides': an ideological divide between economists and ecologists; an economic development divide between the rich and the poor; and an information divide, which obstructs communications between scientists, public opinion and policymakers. These divides prevent our economies from responding effectively to urgent signals of environmental and ecological stress. Equally they stop our societies responding to continuing poverty and exploitation.

One aspect of ecological sustainability is the aspect of how we produce food. Crop yields in organic farming may be 20 per cent lower, but inputs of fertilizer and energy are reduced by 30–50 per cent and pesticide use by 90 per cent (Kumar 2010). Another interesting practical way to support ecological sustainability as been the idea of creating 'Life Centres' (Boyden 2004). They would be new public institutions that focus on the processes of life, and the well-being of people *and* Nature. Such networks of Life Centres would focus on the idea of 'healthy people on a healthy planet'. They would play a direct educational role, act as forums for discussion and as a clearing house of information. They would thus fill a serious gap in the institutional structure of society and would help us rediscover our roots in the Earth. They would help to counteract the tokenism that is rife within organizations when discussing 'sustainability', which is so often 'more talk than action' (Sukhdev 2010). Deniers of course hate both the term 'sustainability' itself and the philosophy behind it. They mostly deny that there are *any* environmental problems, and thus any need for a sustainability philosophy to solve them.

What you can do!

Talk about sustainability, especially *ecological* sustainability. Don't put up with tokenism, but argue for serious action in *your* community. Support the idea of 'Life Centres' and environmental education programs in your community, and lobby your Council to set these up.

Technology – a renewable future

Given the environmental crisis, we should question the unbridled scientific 'can do' optimism that argues that humans are 'masters of Nature' and can do anything, as this is 'progress'. This belief is 'Cornucopianism', the idea that technology can solve everything (Oreskes and Conway 2010) and is one reason why some are suspicious of science, not because of the data discovered, or even the process. We should indeed question the outdated modernist philosophy of domination of Nature (Hulme 2009). It is thus not science *as a whole* that people should be suspicious of, just the 'domination of Nature' worldview within our society (including *some* scientists). So the problem has not been science or even technology per se: it has been that they have not been *appropriate*.

Appropriate to what? Appropriate to the reality we face. Appropriate to the fact that humanity faces an environmental crisis. Appropriate to the rapidly reducing time frame over which we need solutions. I would never say 'if it's not done in 10 years it will be too late', because effective action using appropriate technology is *never too late*. It is unlikely our civilization will collapse in one huge step, rather it may be in a series of steps that allows us to learn and find solutions (Greer 2009). However, accepting reality shows us there is an *urgency* to solving the environmental crisis. We need an environmental revolution, but unlike the Industrial Revolution, this one will make use of appropriate technology, but will also be driven by our need to make peace with Nature (Brown 2006).

So, in terms of appropriate technology – are there solutions? *Yes.* This is one of the most frustrating aspects of the whole debate, the denial of real and workable solutions. There are many solutions out there to roll back environmental problems. Amory Lovins of the Rocky Mountain Institute details how we can transform industrial production so as to use less resources and energy (see www.natcap.org). The environmental crisis is not an irrevocable decree of fate to which we must submit. It is a human-caused problem and has human-invented solutions, *provided we act.* As research and demonstration continue, technologies are becoming cheaper. One of the most frustrating aspects is that appropriate technology such as renewable energy will create a large number of green jobs, more jobs than the fossil fuel and mining industries combined (McNeil 2009). Yet many who supposedly support 'job creation' will (in the same breath) oppose renewable energy.

Key among these appropriate technologies is renewable energy. The Sun radiates to Earth each year something of the order of 7,500 times (EPI 2008) to 10,000 times (Pittock 2009) as much energy as humans consume. There is thus no problem with there being enough renewable energy available. The issue has always been harnessing this effectively and economically. The renewable energy sources available are all available essentially forever (in human history terms). Why then has there been a history of ignoring or even *repressing* renewable energy? The answer is simple: oil and coal. Society went down the coal path in the industrial revolution, and became addicted to coal for stationary energy use and steam trains. Then oil was discovered, and provided an easy liquid fuel for transport. We became addicted to both. They make great wealth for corporations, who will fight to continue this until they are stopped in the public interest. We need alternatives to both.

And the alternatives exist, both in terms of technologies and the scenarios and policies for implementing them. I will not list them in great detail, as others such as Diesendorf (2007) have already done this. Before discussing renewable technologies, however, it is important to discuss the issue of 'baseload' power, as this is a common criticism of renewable energy. A common claim is 'the Sun doesn't shine at night!', when in fact concentrated solar thermal with a heat sink can run at night, as do other renewables such as wind and geothermal. These all have high reliability. In fact coal power stations are quite inflexible, they take time to start and stop. It is this very inflexibility that the coal industry has sought to turn into a virtue under the title 'baseload' power. What we should be considering is the actual *reliability* of the system overall, rather than whether each renewable technology is 'baseload' (AWEA 2012). The mix of renewables overall discussed below can be just as reliable as current coal-fired generation (Elliston *et al.* 2012), in fact its flexibility means it may be more reliable. The concept of 'baseload' thus becomes redundant.

Renewable energy supplied an estimated 16 per cent of global final energy consumption at the end of 2010 (REN21 2011). In regard to electricity, renewables produced 1,320 GW (312 GW excluding hydroelectricity) of electricity in 2010. By early 2011, renewables comprised 25 per cent of electricity capacity from all sources. They accounted for approximately half of the estimated 194 GW of *new* electric capacity added globally during 2010. By early 2011, at least 118 countries had some type of policy target or renewable support policy at the national level, up from 55 countries in early 2005. Total investment in renewable energy reached $211 billion in 2010, up from $160 billion in 2009 (REN21 2011). Civilization can reach a 95 per cent sustainably sourced energy supply by 2050. There are up-front investments required to make this transition in the coming decades (1–2 per cent of global GDP), but they will turn into a positive cash flow after 2035, leading to a positive annual result of 2 per cent of GDP in 2050 (WWF 2011). A large-scale wind, water and solar energy system can reliably supply all of the world's energy needs, with significant benefit to climate, air quality, water quality, ecological systems and energy security, at reasonable cost (Delucchi and Jacobson 2011). However, energy efficiency and conservation must play a key role also in any sustainable energy future (WWF 2011). Also, our energy demand cannot keep on growing. If we halve our energy use through energy conservation, then it is feasible to supply this through renewable energy. Rather than continuing to grow each year, however, it then needs to decline in line with reducing our unsustainable human population. Renewable energy technologies are summarized below:

- **Windpower.** The cost of wind energy has come down hugely over the last 30 years. It is already cheaper than nuclear electricity and should soon rival coal-fired electricity in cost (Diesendorf 2009). Over the past 10 years, global wind power capacity has continued to grow at an average cumulative rate of over 30 per cent, with a total installed capacity of some 200 GW, and forecast to reach 450 GW by 2015 (GWEC 2010). By 2020, Germany should produce 25 per cent of overall electricity from wind (GWEC 2010). The wind doesn't always blow in any one spot, but it does blow *somewhere* all the time. A widely distributed wind power network will thus form part of a reliable renewable system (Diesendorf 2007). Several countries met high shares of their electricity demand with wind power in 2010, including Denmark (22 per cent), Portugal (21 per cent), Spain (15.4 per cent), and Ireland (10.1 per cent) (REN21 2011). Noise and bird death are over-rated problems with wind power. Bird deaths caused by wind turbines are a minute fraction of the total human-caused bird deaths: less than 0.003 per cent in 2003 (NRC 2007). Each year in the US, collisions with buildings kill 97 to 976 million birds; collisions with high-tension lines kill at least 130 million birds; collisions with cars kill around 80 million birds; while collisions with wind turbines killed an estimated 20,000 to 37,000 birds (NRC 2007).

- **Solar.** Solar thermal is ideal for water heating and can make a significant contribution to space heating and cooling. Electricity can be produced either by concentrated solar thermal (CST) (also called concentrated solar power, CSP) or by photovoltaic (PV). As of 2011 there were 1.1 GW of CST installed worldwide (REN21 2011), and 15 GW are under development or construction (IEA 2009). Recently, growth appears to be slowing as the cost of PV decreases (REN21 2011). A proposal is under consideration for a vast solar thermal installation in the Sahara that could provide a sixth of Europe's electricity needs (Kanter 2009). Solar thermal storage systems (such as molten salts of sodium and potassium nitrate) can also store solar energy for many hours for later use at night. In this way solar thermal can add to the reliability of renewable systems. Estimates indicate CST could reach 6,000 GW by 2050 (WWF 2011). By 2050, with appropriate support, CST could provide 11.3 per cent of global electricity, with 9.6 per cent from solar power and 1.7 per cent from backup fuels (fossil fuels or biomass) (IEA 2010).

  At the end of 2011 there was 40 GW of PV installed globally (REN21 2011) with annual growth rates of 25–30 per cent (WWF 2011). Together the prospects for rapid growth of solar (thermal and PV) are excellent. This is contrary to the views expressed by nuclear and denial advocates. The two main central problems of solar – remoteness from markets and the need for storage to counter its intermittent nature – have now been largely solved (Delucchi and Jacobson 2011).

- **Geothermal and hot rocks.** Geothermal traditionally harnesses the steam produced naturally by the Earth's heat. Global generating capacity in 2011 was 11 GW (REN21 2011), almost all being conventional geothermal in which hot water reaches the Earth's surface in volcanic regions. However, conventional geothermal is limited to just a few regions of the world. There is far more potential energy stored in hot rocks 3–5 km below the surface in non-volcanic regions. Such 'hot rocks' can be used to produce steam if water is injected, which is then run through a steam turbine. Hot rock geothermal technology is on the brink of medium-scale demonstration in Australia (Geodynamics 2011).

- **Hydroelectricity.** Hydroelectricity is currently the most developed form of renewable electricity, producing 1,010 GW at the end of 2010

(REN21 2011). This still has large potential in Africa and parts of Asia. However, large hydroelectricity dams (such as the Three Gorges in China and Sardar Sarova in India) generally have major adverse environmental and social impacts (IR 1996). Small- and medium-scale hydro projects in widely distributed areas are thus better options.

- **Wave and tidal power (and ocean currents).** The power of the tides has been harnessed in various places in the world (e.g. the Rance Estuary in France) with around 0.5 GW in operation (REN21 2011). However, conventional tidal power is limited to a few regions of the world where very high tides prevail. Wave power has been harder to harness, but there are demonstration plants in Portugal, the US, Germany, Scotland and Australia (REN21 2011).
- **Bioenergy.** Plants store solar energy in wood, fibre and oils. These can be burned to produce energy for both stationary sources and transport. Wood and plant oils are the oldest form of renewable energy. Unless there is major transport involved (using fossil fuels), or inputs of fertilizers produced with fossil fuels, then such bioenergy comes close to being carbon neutral. Plants take up CO_2, which is then released when they are burnt. Diesendorf (2007) notes that bioenergy offers both threats and opportunities. If poorly implemented it could result in soil depletion, consumption of scarce water resources and loss of biodiversity. If implemented appropriately, it could have very low environmental impacts, could help restore degraded land, and could play an important part in a sustainable renewable future (WWF 2011). Biofuels are much discussed and confusion is rife. They can be useful in reducing carbon emissions (especially regionally), if sourced from plantations or agricultural residues. They can be harmful if you clear existing rainforest to grow oil palms (as in Indonesia), or if you clear old growth forest. Bioenergy must demonstrate a significant *net* carbon reduction over its whole life cycle. It should not come from native forests but from mixed species plantations or agricultural and sawmill wastes. Bioenergy electricity plants could be used to provide peak load demand in an integrated renewable energy system (Elliston *et al.* 2012).

Bioenergy is thus a significant but overlooked source of renewable energy. Biomass is also important in terms of replacing 'energy-dense' construction materials. Wood has an energy density of 1–3 MJ/kg whereas steel is 34 and aluminium is 170 (Pittock 2009). Bioenergy can also be obtained from the production of *biochar* (charcoal), where this is then used as an agricultural product that sequesters carbon into soil, and also improves water and nutrient retention. Biochar is thus not just carbon neutral, it is *carbon-negative*, removing carbon from the atmosphere and putting it in soils (Lehmann *et al.* 2006; Taylor 2010). This is one of the most important carbon-negative technologies available, given that climatically we have already overshot the 'safe' level of CO_2 in the atmosphere (Washington and Cook 2011). Estimates vary of how much carbon biochar can sequester in soils. The International Biochar Initiative (IBI 2012) estimates that we could achieve 1 Gt of carbon sequestered annually before 2050. Lehmann *et al.* (2006) argue that by 2100 we could achieve 5.5–9.5 Gt/yr carbon sequestered. However, the most rigorous estimate is that biochar could sequester up to 1.8 Gt/yr, 12 per cent of human CO_2 emissions (Woolf *et al.* 2010). The potential of biochar to lower atmospheric CO_2 is thus significant. It is thus a pity that it has not received the urgency from governments that it deserves.

The use of all these technologies (often suited to remote locations) has been improved by the ability to use high-voltage DC transmission cables with emission losses of less than 3 per cent over 1,000 km, compared to 30–40 per cent for normal AC transmission lines (Siemens 2010). To solve climate change will require a rapid and major conversion to energy efficiency and renewable energy, as we have delayed for so long. We need an urgent large-scale programme. This major effort in renewable energy would be a key part of the 'Great Work' I discuss later. To put the economics of this in perspective, it has been pointed out that the money needed would be much less than what we already spend on the military (Pittock 2009). A recent study by engineers and scientists in Australia has estimated that Australia could in fact become renewable-powered in 10 years at a cost of 3 per cent of GDP a year (Wright and Hearps 2010). The assumptions used in this study, the energy source split, the modelling and the feasible time span of 10 years have been questioned (Diesendorf 2011), though not the fact that a shift to 100 per cent renewables *can* in fact be done.

Renewable energy is thus *entirely feasible*. However, unless we reduce consumerism, the sheer scale of renewables required to supply an increasingly affluent world in the time required would be mind-boggling (Assadourian 2010). We thus need a renewable conversion that goes hand in hand with a reduction in energy demand, at least in developed countries, and a reduction in consumerism everywhere. For years we buried our heads in the sand and denied the potential of renewable energy. However, the technologies exist, are feasible and affordable – all we need is the *political will*.

One **inappropriate** technology needs brief discussion: *nuclear power*. It is not the answer because you don't solve one serious problem with another. Energy expert Amory Lovins (2006) notes:

> So the big question about nuclear 'revival' isn't just who'd pay for such a turkey, but also . . . why bother? Why keep on distorting markets and biasing choices to divert scarce resources from the winners to the loser – a far slower, costlier, harder, and riskier niche product – and paying a premium to incur its many problems?

So why is society debating its merits? The reason is owing to the powerful nuclear and uranium mining lobbies, which (owing to concern over climate change) see a chance to resurrect their nuclear fantasy. Nuclear power is not a viable solution for the following reasons:

- It's not carbon neutral anyway, and can produce 10–40 per cent as much CO_2 as a coal-fired power station, depending on the ore grade (Mudd and Diesendorf 2008). Nuclear energy results in 9–25 times more carbon emissions than wind energy (Jacobson and Delucchi 2011).
- Nuclear energy is too slow to deploy. It takes many years to build and commission a nuclear power station. The overall historic and present range of nuclear planning-to-operation times for new nuclear plants has been 11–19 years, compared with an average of 2–5 years for wind and solar installations (Jacobson and Delucchi 2011). Wind farms could generate the same power for 60 per cent of the construction costs, and are much cheaper to run (Lovins and Sheikh 2008).
- Nuclear power is not cheap. The current cost of nuclear is estimated to be 8–12 cents/kWh (Jacobson and Delucchi 2011) while wind energy is around 4–7 cents/kWh and solar CST is 11–15 cents/kWh and should drop to 8 cents by 2020 (Delucchi and Jacobson 2011). If the huge subsidies to nuclear power are taken into account (Diesendorf 2012) and the hidden external costs (Sovacool 2010), nuclear is even more expensive than solar electricity.
- Conventional nuclear fission relies on finite stores of uranium. A large-scale nuclear programme with a 'once through' fuel cycle would exhaust these in roughly a century (Jacobson and Delucchi 2011). There are thus not enough total uranium reserves to provide a low-carbon future anyway, *unless* we move to fast breeder reactors. These have major safety problems and there is potential for a large (non-nuclear) explosion that might rupture the reactor vessel and disperse radioactive material into the environment (Kumar and Ramana 2009). They also increase the risk of nuclear proliferation (Jacobson and Delucchi 2011). Few fast breeder reactors are currently producing electricity, and none are doing so on a commercial basis (Diesendorf 2007).
- The nuclear energy fuel cycle produces uranium and plutonium that, with minor modifications, can be used in nuclear weapons. It thus increases the risk of nuclear proliferation (Jacobson and Delucchi 2011) where fissionable material may fall into the hands of terrorists.
- Nuclear power stations produce highly radioactive waste that must be separated from the environment for at least a hundred thousand years.
- Nuclear power stations cannot blow up like a bomb, but *can* melt down like Chernobyl and Fukushima and release large amounts of dangerous radioactivity.
- When nuclear power stations reach the end of their design life, they are so radioactive that dismantling them is a problem. Demolition waste must be stored for thousands of years (Wald 2009).

These considerations suggest that nuclear fission reactors are unlikely to play a major role in replacing fossil fuels and reducing total emissions by 2050 (Jacobson and Delucchi 2011). Given the above, why would we rush into a nuclear future? Nuclear power is a false solution. It offers little, it offers late, and, in the near future when high-grade uranium ore is used up, it doesn't offer a big cut in the carbon footprint. It is very expensive and provides its own high risk to future generations. We should not reject denial about the environmental crisis overall, but then deny the serious problems around nuclear power.

What you can do!

Demand a 100 per cent renewable energy future from your governments *within 20 years*, with immediate strong Mandatory Renewable Energy Targets and feed in tariffs for renewable energy of all types. Oppose further fossil fuel power plants. Oppose the mirage of nuclear energy. Install renewable energy yourself (e.g. solar hot water, PV). Get a sustainability audit of your home showing how you can cut energy and water use.

The politics of it all!

Many of us shy away from politics. However, in reality this is just a form of denial. It is pure laziness, a way of abrogating any responsibility to do anything about the world's problems. If we all do this then nothing will happen, and the above solutions will not take place. 'Business as usual' would continue and the world would move that much closer to ecological (and social) disaster. Disdain for politics is in fact really 'giving up'. Many politicians would *like* to act on the environmental crisis, but need to know they have the community's support. That means *you* need to tell them! *You* need to be politically active, to write letters to the paper and your local representatives. Your effectiveness and enjoyment of activism will be enhanced by joining an environmental or climate action group (Diesendorf 2009). We know change is unlikely to come from the business community en masse (though some may have seen the light). We know the change we need is currently unlikely to come from the education system (but hopefully this will change). It is also unlikely that it will come from governments – unless *we* make it happen.

So don't switch off and ignore politics. As Edmund Burke noted: 'All that is needed for evil to triumph is for good men to do nothing.' This could be modified to say: 'All that is needed to ensure environmental disaster is that good people do nothing.' The only way that we have to make the changes needed to solve the environmental crisis is to create the change needed. That means *activism*. That means political action and political lobbying. The political maxim is 'one letter equals a hundred votes'. So if they get 1,000 letters, it seriously worries them. Hence your contribution really *does* count. Solutions exist to the environmental crisis, as detailed here. It is not impossible or hopeless. We have noted the problems of the denial industry, and of denial that we ourselves foster. We have discussed denial of solutions such as renewable energy. However, when it comes down to it, one of our major problems is *lack of political will*. It is no good just sitting back and blaming this on 'politicians'. We elect them, they are *our* representatives. If they are not taking action it is because we are not telling them to take action. I have argued in this book for the critical need to accept ecological reality, that we are dependent on Nature. However, here I point out the essential need for *political reality*. If we want to solve the environmental crisis then we need to be active in environmental politics. I am not advocating you vote for any particular political party. Whatever party you vote for will need people inside it who tell them about the environmental crisis and the need for effective policies to solve it. This too is a key part of the 'Great Work'.

What you can do!

Be politically active (in whatever party). Join an environmental or climate action group. Write a letter, or even better, *go and see* your local member. Demand he/she supports change for ecological sustainability. Demand he/she supports strong climate change action.

The 'Great Work'

So the modernist and consumerist approach of Western society has failed, in fact it has caused the environmental crisis. Philosopher Thomas Berry (1999) argues that contemporary history has shown three things: 1) the devastation of the Earth; 2) the incompetence of religion and cultural traditions to deal with this devastation; 3) the rise of a new ecological vision of the Universe. We now need an ecocentric ethic, an ethic not based just on enlightened self-interest, but one that considers the rest of Nature too (Assadourian 2010). We need a 'biosensitive' society with a *biounderstanding* worldview (Boyden 2004). Berry argues our task is to undertake 'The Great Work' (1999), and he provides an ecocentric vision for this work of Earth repair. Berry notes that every culture produces a 'Great Work', an overarching vision that 'gives shape and meaning to life by relating the human venture to the larger destinies of the Universe'. This is in fact a very necessary 'grand narrative'. It is an over-arching worldview, a narrative that provides meaning at a time when we desperately need *meaning* to foster the deep beliefs that will allow us to solve these problems. It is a dream that people can believe in. It is a dream that can inspire young and old. It is a dream that can lead to a sustainable future. Martin Luther King inspired people because of his statement 'I have a dream!'. He would not have inspired them if he had said 'I have a catastrophe!'. *People need hope*, they need a dream to work towards. Hope is linked to imagination and this allows us to conceive the world differently and create a sustainable future (Collins 2010). Change comes from necessity, hope, realizable aspirations and joy, not shame and blame (Wackernagel and Rees 1996). Given the urgency involved in our predicament, this grand narrative, this Great Work of repairing the Earth is *precisely* the dream we need, precisely what we need to move forward to an ecologically sustainable future. There will be many parts to the Great Work and they will change over time. However, the big shift is accepting this new worldview: this Great Work of Earth Repair.

Conclusion – regrowing our roots in the Earth

The environmental crisis is telling us we need to change the way we view the world, that we need to move *beyond* modernism and consumerism and move to an ecocentric worldview (Assadourian 2010). It is a major, inconvenient and unpalatable truth for a modernist and consumerist society. It is a major reality check. On the other hand, I agree with Hulme (2009) and Pittock (2009) that climate change (and the environmental crisis overall) really is an *opportunity to get things right*. However, as Lester Brown (2006) notes, the scarcest of all resources is *time*. We cannot just reset the clock, for Nature is the timekeeper. If someone erects a tombstone for our civilization, it cannot say we did not understand, for we do. It cannot say we did not have the resources, for we do. It could only say we were too slow to act, and that time ran out (Brown 2006).

The reality of the environmental crisis is a wake-up call that forces us to acknowledge that all is not well with the world, and our custodianship of it. It is a wake-up call that denial of our roots in the Earth is a dangerous element in the human psyche that can become a pathology. Lester Brown (2006) asks whether the future world will be a world of decline and collapse or a world of environmental restoration. Can the world mobilize quickly enough? Where will the wake-up calls come from? What form will they take? Will we hear them? (Brown 2006). However, we still have an opportunity to get it right, to heal the damage our society, our numbers, our growth economy, our consumerism, our inappropriate technologies and our carbon fuels have done to the world. It is the chance to abandon denial and accept reality, ethics and responsibility. We can no longer say it's not 'economic' to solve the environmental crisis and protect Nature. We have to, and thus we can *make it economic*. It certainly won't cost more than the $1,531 billion a year we spend on the military (SIPRI 2010). In fact, Brown (2011) estimates it will cost $185 billion a year, or just 12 per cent of the world's yearly military budget. We need to use the 'silver buckshot' solutions to halt the environmental crisis. Silver buckshot means you *use what works*.

If we have the vision, the dream of Earth repair, the faith and hope that we can solve the environmental crisis, then 'yes we can'. If we believe we can make a difference then we *will*. If we despair, give up our hope of solving these issues, if we abdicate our choice to act, then we will fail. We either choose to act for an ecologically sustainable future or we contribute to a growing environmental disaster (Pittock 2009). However, the situation is not all about doom and gloom, it's about a new future, new technologies, new government policies, new markets, new opportunities, and a new worldview of how we live on Earth. It won't be simple or easy, but if we can face and conquer our denial, then our future is exciting as we make a better world. Can we solve the environmental crisis? *We can if we choose to.*

By way of concluding, each of us needs to pause and think. We need to return to the basics, and ask ourselves some deep, soul-searching questions:

- Does Nature have *intrinsic value*, a right to exist for itself?
- Are we part of Nature, and if we are, then does it not deserve our respect and love?
- Do we depend on Nature to survive, and rely on its ecosystem services? If we do, then is it not time we stopped denying this reality?
- What do we value? If we value the diversity of life we share this world with, if we value the rights of future generations, then we need to stop denying the problems we face.
- What do we believe in? If we believe in the *reason* that underpins science, then we need to accept what the peer-reviewed mainstream science tells us.
- What do we fear? Personally, my greatest fear is that humanity's lack of action will leave a vastly impoverished world to the future.
- Do we accept a responsibility to others and the future? If we do then *it's up to us to act, not 'others'*. Saving our civilization is not a spectator sport (Brown 2006). It is time for us *together* to change the world for the better.

We evolved as part of Nature, and we remain fully dependent on Nature to survive. Our current worldview, economics and actions are not rooted in the Earth, but in an idea that we can be 'masters' of Nature. Yet this is an ecological absurdity, one that has caused great grief to the world, and also to the human poor. It is time to wake up, to accept that Nature has intrinsic value, to accept we have come close to a disaster that would impoverish the Earth and future generations. Our roots have *always* been in the Earth. This is not something to be ashamed of, or something to hide or to deny. It is something to celebrate, to honour and to value. We should feel wonder at Nature, we should feel responsibility to our brother and sister species we share this planet with. It makes good sense on many levels. It is pragmatic, scientific *and* ethical. Through rediscovering our roots in the Earth, we become fully human. Now, more than ever, it is a time to *care*.

References

Abbey, E. (1977) *The Journey Home*, New York: Dutton.

Abelson, P. (1999) 'A potential phosphate crisis', *Science*, vol. 283, no. 5410, p. 2015.

Abram, D. (1992) 'The mechanical and the organic: On the impact of metaphor in science', *Wild Earth*, vol. 2, no. 2, pp. 70–75.

Abram, D. (1996) *The Spell of the Sensuous*, New York: Vintage Books (Random House).

Alexander, A., List, J., Margolis, M. and D'Arge, R. (1998) 'A method for valuing global ecosystem services', *Ecological Economics*, vol. 27, no. 2, pp. 161–170.

Amsel, S. (2007) '"Environmental Issues": Keystone Species – the American Alligator', Exploring Nature Educational Resource, 5 November, 2011, see: www.exploringnature.org/db/detail.php?dbID=7&detID=67 (accessed 19/11/11).

Aronson, J., Blignaut, J., De Groot, R., Clewell, A., Lowry II, P., Woodworth, P., Cowling, R., Renison, D., Farley, J., Fontaine, C., Tongway, D., Levy, S., Milton, S., Rangel, O., Debrincat, B. and Birkinshaw, C. (2010) 'The road to sustainability must bridge three great divides', *Ann. N.Y. Acad. Sci.*, vol. 1185, pp. 225–236.

Assadourian, E. (2010) 'The rise and fall of consumer cultures', in *2010 State of the World: Transforming Cultures from Consumerism to Sustainability*, eds L. Starke and L. Mastny, London: Earthscan.

Atkinson, D. (2008) *Renewing the Face of the Earth: A Theological and Pastoral Response to Climate Change*, London: Canterbury Press.

Atlee, T. (2003) *The Tao of Democracy: Using Co-Intelligence to Create a World that Works for All*, Manitoba, Canada: The Writers Collective.

AWEA (2012) 'Windpower and reliability: The roles of baseload and variable resources. American Wind Energy Association', see: www.awea.org/learnabout/publications/upload/Baseload_Factsheet.pdf (accessed 11/2/12).

Baudrillard, J. (1983) 'Simulacra and Simulations', in *Jean Baudrillard, Selected Writings*, ed. M. Poster (1988), Stanford: Stanford University Press.

BBC (2006) 'Earth is too crowded for Utopia', *BBC News online*, 6 January 2006, see: http://news.bbc.co.uk/2/hi/science/nature/4584572.stm (accessed 5/6/12).

Berry, T. (1988) *The Dream of the Earth*, San Francisco: Sierra Club Books.

Berry, T. (1994) quoted by McDonagh, S. (1994) *Passion for the Earth: Christian Vocation to Promote Justice, Peace and the Integrity of Creation*, London: Geoffrey Chapman.

Berry, T. (1999) *The Great Work: Our Way into the Future*, New York: Bell Tower.

Berry, T. (2000) 'Thomas Berry – Wild earth Interview', *Wild Earth*, vol. 10, no. 2, pp. 93–97.

Boyden, S. (2004) *The Biology of Civilisation: Understanding Human Culture as a Force in Nature*, Sydney: UNSW Press.

Brondizio, E., Gatzweiler, F, Zografos, C. and Kumar, M. (2010) 'The Socio-cultural Context of Ecosystem and Biodiversity Valuation', in *The Economics of Ecosystems and Biodiversity: Ecological and Economic Foundations*, ed. P. Kumar, London: Earthscan.

Brown, A. J. (1992) *Keeping the Land Alive: Aboriginal People and Wilderness Protection in Australia*, Sydney: Environmental Defender's Office.

Brown, D. (2008) 'The ominous rise of ideological think tanks in environmental policy-making', in *Sustaining Life on Earth: Environmental and Human Health through Global Governance*, ed. C. Soskolne, New York: Rowman & Littlefield Publishers.

Brown, L. (1978) *The 29th Day*, Washington: Norton & Co.

Brown, L. (2006) *Plan B 2.0: Rescuing a Planet under Stress and a Civilization in Trouble*, New York: W. W. Norton & Co.

Brown, L. (2011) *World on the Edge: How to Prevent Environmental and Economic Collapse*, New York: W.W. Norton & Co.

Bryant, P. (1995) 'Constructing nature again (Australian Society of Literature on the Environment Network)', in *Main Currents in Western Environmental Thought*, ed. P. Hay (2002), Sydney: UNSW Press, pp. 24–25.

Butler, C. (2002) *Postmodernism: A Very Short Introduction*, Oxford/New York: Oxford University Press.

Cain, M., Bowman, W. and Hacker, S. (2008) *Ecology*, Sunderland, MA: Sinauer Associates.

Caldwell, L. (1984) 'Political aspects of ecologically sustainable development', *Environmental Conservation*, vol. 11, pp. 299–308.

Caldwell, L. (1990) *Between Two Worlds: Science, the Environmental Movement and Policy Choice*, Cambridge: Cambridge University Press.

Cameron, J. (2003) *Changing Places: Re-imagining Australia*, Double Bay, NSW: Longueville Books.

Carson, R. (1962) *Silent Spring*, Boston, MA: Houghton Mifflin.

Catton, W. (1982) *Overshoot: The Ecological Basis of Revolutionary Change*, Chicago, IL: University of Illinois Press.

ChinaDaily (2007) 'Ecological civilization', *China Daily Newspaper*, see: www. chinadaily.com.cn/opinion/2007–10/24/content_6201964.htm (accessed 28/2/12).

Cohen, S. (2001) *States of Denial: Knowing about Atrocities and Suffering*, New York: Polity Press.

Collins, P. (2010) *Judgment Day: The Struggle for Life on Earth*, Sydney: UNSW Press.

Cordell, D. (2010) 'The story of phosphorus: Sustainability implications of global phosphorus scarcity for food security', Doctoral thesis. Collaborative Ph.D. between the University of Technology, Sydney (UTS) and Linköping University, Sweden. Linköping University Press, ISBN 978–91–7393–440–4, Linköping, see: http://urn.kb.se/resolve?urn=urn:nbn:se:liu:diva-53430 (accessed 19/11/11).

Cordell, D., Drangert, J. and White, S. (2009) 'The story of phosphorus: Global food security and food for thought', *Global Environmental Change*, vol. 19, no. 2, pp. 292–305.

Costanza, R. and Daly, H. (1992) 'Natural capital and sustainable development', *Conservation Biology*, vol. 6, pp. 37–46.

Costanza, R. and Hannon, B. M. (1989) 'Dealing with the mixed units problem in ecosystem network analysis', in *Network Analysis of Marine Ecosystems: Methods and Applications*, eds F. Wulff, J. G. Field and K. H. Mann, Heidelberg: Springer-Verlag.

Costanza, R. and Neil, C. (1981) 'The energy embodied in the products of the biosphere', in *Energy and Ecological Modelling*, eds W. J. Mitsch, R. W. Bosserman and J. M. Klopatek, New York: Elsevier.

Costanza, R., D'Arge, R., De Groot, R., Farberk, S., Grasso, M., Hannon, B., Limburg, K., Naeem, S., O'Neill, R., Paruelo, J., Raskin, R., Suttonkk, P. and Van den Belt, M. (1997) 'The value of the world's ecosystem services and natural capital', *Nature*, vol. 387, pp. 253–260.

Crabbe, P. (2008) 'The Copenhagen consensus: A global public-good perspective comparing the Earth Charter with other recent declarations', in *Sustaining Life on Earth: Environmental and Human Health through Global Governance*, ed. C. Soskolne, New York: Lexington Books.

Cronon, W. (1996) 'The trouble with wilderness: Or getting back to the wrong nature', in *Uncommon Ground: Rethinking the Human Place in* Nature, ed. W. Cronon, New York: W. W. Norton & Co.

Crotty, M. (1998) *Foundations of Social Research: Meaning and Perspective in Research Process*, Sydney: Allen & Unwin.

Crutzen, P. (2006) 'Albedo enhancement by stratospheric sulphur injections: A contribution to resolve a policy dilemma', *Climatic Change*, vol. 77, no. 3–4, pp. 211–220.

Czech, B. (2000) *Shoveling Fuel for a Runaway Train: Errant Economists, Shameful Spenders, and a Plant to Stop Them All*, Berkeley, CA: University of California Press.

Daily, G. (1997) *Natures Services: Societal Dependence on Natural Ecosystems*, Washington, DC: Island Press.

Daily, G. and Ellison, K. (2002) *The New Economy of Nature: The Quest to make Conservation Profitable*, Washington, DC: Island Press.

Daly, H. (1973) 'The steady state economy', in *Toward a Steady State Economy*, ed. H. Daly, New York: Freeman & Co.

Daly, H. (1980) *Economics, Ecology, Ethics: Essays Towards a Steady State Economy*, New York: Freeman & Co.

Daly, H. (1991) *Steady-State Economics: Second Edition with New Essays*, Washington, DC: Island Press.

Daly, H. (1999) 'Uneconomic growth and the built environment: In theory and in fact', in *Reshaping the Built Environment: Ecology, Ethics, and Economics*, ed. C. J. Kibert, Washington, DC: Island Press.

Daly, H. and Cobb, J. (1989) *For the Common Good: Redirecting the Economy Toward Community, the Environment, and a Sustainable Future*, Boston, MA: Beacon Press.

Dasmann, R. (1966) *The Destruction of California*, New York: Macmillan.

De Groot, R., Fisher, B. and Christie, M. (2010) 'Integrating the Ecological and Economic Dimensions in Biodiversity and Ecosystem Service Valuation', in *The Economics of Ecosystems and Biodiversity: Ecological and Economic Foundations*, ed. P. Kumar, London: Earthscan.

Delucchi, M and Jacobson, M. (2011) 'Providing all global energy with wind, water, and solar power, Part II: Reliability, system and transmission costs, and policies', *Energy Policy*, vol. 39, pp. 1170–1190.

Derrida, J. (1966) 'Structure, sign and play in the discourse of the human sciences', in *Critical Theory Since Plato*, ed. H. Adams, New York: Harcourt Brace Jovanovich.

Descola, P. (1996) 'Constructing natures: symbolic ecology and social practice', in *Nature and Society: Anthropological Perspectives*, eds P. Descola, and G. Palsson, New York: Routledge.

Diamond, J. (1993) *The Third Chimpanzee: The Evolution and Future of the Human Animal*, New York: Harper Perennial.

Diamond, J. (2005) *Collapse: How Societies Choose to Fail or Succeed*, New York: Viking Press.

Diesendorf, M. (1997) 'Ecologically sustainable development principles', in *Human Ecology, Human Economy: Ideas for an ecologically sustainable future*, eds M. Diesendorf and C. Hamilton, Sydney: Allen & Unwin.

Diesendorf, M. (2007) *Greenhouse Solutions with Sustainable Energy*, Sydney: UNSW Press.

Diesendorf, M. (2009) *Climate Action: A Campaign Manual for Greenhouse Solutions*, Sydney: UNSW Press.

Diesendorf, M. (2011) 'A cheaper path to 100 renewables', *Climate Spectator*, 21 Oct, 2011, see: www.climatespectator.com.au/commentary/cheaper-path-100-renewables (accessed 15/11/11).

Diesendorf, M. (2012). 'Economics of nuclear electricity', in *Nuclear Energy and Human Security: Critical Debates*, eds M. Cabellero-Anthony, R.M. Basrur and C. Koh, London: Routledge.

Docherty, T. (1992) *Postmodernism: A Reader*, New York: Harvester Wheatsheaf.

DPWH (1991) *Tasmanian Wilderness World Heritage Area Draft Plan of Management*, Hobart: Tasmanian Dept of Parks, Wildlife and Heritage.

Duncan, G. (1998) 'The psychological benefits of wilderness', *Ecopsychology on line*, vol. 6, (e-journal), see: http://ecopsychology.athabascau.ca/Final/duncan.htm (accessed 5/6/12).

Durning A. T. (1992) *How much is Enough: The Consumer Society and the Future of the Earth*, New York: Norton Books/The Worldwatch Institute.

Eckersley, R. (1992) *Environmentalism and Political Theory: Toward an Ecocentric Approach*, London: UCL Press.

Ehrlich, P. (1968) *The Population Bomb*, New York: Buccaneer Books.

Ehrlich, P. (2011) Jack Beale Lecture by Professor Paul Ehrlich, University of NSW, Sydney, Australia, 31/10/2011.

Ehrlich, P. and Ehrlich, A. (1970) *Population, Resources, Environment: Issues in Human Ecology*, San Francisco, CA: W. H. Freeman.

Ehrlich, P. and Ehrlich, A. (1981) *Extinction: The Causes and Consequences of the Disappearance of Species*, New York: Random House.

Ehrlich, P. and Ehrlich, A. (1991) *Healing the Planet: Strategies for Resolving the Environmental Crisis*, New York: Addison-Wesley Publishing Company.

Ehrlich, P. and Ehrlich, A. (1998) *Betrayal of Science and Reason: How Anti-environmental Rhetoric Threatens Our Future*, New York: Island Press.

Ehrlich, P. and Ornstein, R. (2010) *Humanity on a Tightrope: Thoughts on Empathy, Family and Big Changes for a Viable Future*, New York: Rowman & Littlefield.

Ehrlich, P., Ehrlich, A. and Holdren, J. (1977) *Ecoscience: Population, Resources, Environment*, San Francisco, CA: W. H. Freeman.

Eldredge, N. (2001) 'The sixth extinction', *ActionBioscience* article, see: www.actionbioscience.org/newfrontiers/eldredge2.html (accessed 26/11/11).

Elliston, B., Diesendorf, M. and MacGill, I. (2012) 'Simulations of scenarios with 100% renewable electricity in the Australian National Electricity Market'. *Energy Policy*, vol. 45, pp. 606–613, doi:10.1016/j.enpol.2012.03.011.

Ellul, J. (1975) *The New Demons*, New York: Seabury Press.

Elmqvist, T., Maltby, E., Barker, T., Mortimer, M. and Perrings, C. (2010) 'Biodiversity, ecosystems and ecosystem services', in *The Economics of Ecosystems and Biodiversity: Ecological and Economic Foundations*, ed. P. Kumar, London: Earthscan.

Elton, C. S. (1958) *Ecology of Invasions by Animals and Plants*, London: Chapman & Hall.

Emerson, R. W. (1862) 'Thoreau (a testimonial)', in *The Portable Emerson*, eds C. Bode and M. Cowley, New York: Penguin Books.

Engel, J. (2008) 'A covenant of covenants: A federal vision of global governance for the twenty-first century', in *Sustaining Life on Earth: Environmental and Human Health through Global Governance*, ed. C. Soskolne, New York: Lexington Books.

Enting, I. (2007) *Twisted: The Distorted Mathematics of Greenhouse Denial*, Melbourne: Australasian Mathematical Sciences Institute.

EPA (2011) 'Effects of acid rain', see: www.epa.gov/acidrain/effects/surface_water.html (accessed 8/11/11).

EPI (2008) 'Solar thermal power coming to a boil', Earth Policy Institute, see: www.earth-policy.org/index.php?/plan_b_updates/2008/update73 (accessed 4/3/12).

Esbjornson, C. (1999) 'In defence of anthropocentrism: A wilderness proposal', *Wild Earth*, Spring, pp. 28–31.

Evernden, N. (1992) *The Social Creation of Nature*, London: John Hopkins University Press.

Ewert, A. and Shellman, A. (2003) 'The role of higher education in wilderness for the 21st century', *Jour. Phys. Ed. Rec. Dance*. vol. 74, pp. 28–32.

FAO (2008) *Current World Fertilizer Trends and Outlook to 2011/12*, Rome: Food and Agriculture Organization of the United Nations.

Flanders, M. and Swann, D. (1963) 'First & Second Law' song from 'At the Drop of Another Hat' by Flanders & Swann (copyright 1963), by permission of the Estates of Michael Flanders & Donald Swann, Administrator Leon Berger: leonberger@donaldswann.co.uk, see: www.nyanko.pwp.blueyonder.co.uk/fas/hatintro.html (accessed 5/11/11).

Flavin, C. (2010) 'Preface' to *State of the World 2010: Transforming Cultures from Consumerism to Sustainability*, eds L. Starke and L. Mastny, New York: Worldwatch Institute/Earthscan.

Fowler, C. and Hobbs, L. (2003) 'Is humanity sustainable?', Proc. Royal Soc. London, Series B: *Biological Sciences*, vol. 270, pp. 2579–2583.

Fox, S. (1981) *John Muir and his Legacy: The American Conservation Movement*, Boston, MA: Little Brown & Co, p. 43.

Fox, W. (1990) *Toward a Transpersonal Ecology: Developing New Foundations for Environmentalism*, Boston, MA: Shambhala.

Fromm, E. (1976) *To Have or to Be*, New York: Abacus Books.

Gare, A. (1995) *Postmodernism and the Environmental Crisis*, London/New York: Routledge.

Garnaut, R. (2008) *The Garnaut Climate Change Review*, Garnaut Climate Change Review Australia, see: www.garnautreview.org.au (accessed 7/3/12).

Gelbspan, R. (1997) *The Heat is On: The High Stakes Battle Over Earth's Threatened Climate*, Reading, MA: Addison-Wesley Publishing Company.

Geodynamics (2011) 'Geodynamics power from the Earth Annual Report 2010–2011', see: www.geodynamics.com.au/IRM/content/PDF/Geodynamics_AnnualReport_2011_Web.pdf (accessed 22/11/11).

Georgescu-Roegen, N. (1971) *The Entropy Law and the Economic Process*, Harvard: Harvard University Press.

GFN (2011) 'World footprint: Do we fit on the planet?', Global Footprint Network, see: www.footprintnetwork.org/en/index.php/GFN/page/world_footprint/ (accessed 19/11/11).

Giddens, A. (1994) *Beyond Left and Right: The Future of Radical Politics*, Palo Alto, CA: Stanford University Press.

Gilbert, N. (2008) 'A quarter of mammals face extinction', *Nature*, vol. 455, p. 717.

Gilding, P. (2011) *The Great Disruption: How the Climate Crisis Will Transform the Global Economy*, London: Bloomsbury.

Godfrey-Smith, W. (1979) 'The value of wilderness', *Environmental Ethics*, vol. 1, pp. 309–319.

Gomez-Pampa, A. and Kaus, A. (1992) 'Taming the wilderness myth', *Bioscience*, vol. 42, no. 4, pp. 271–279.

Gore, A. (2006) *An Inconvenient Truth*, New York: Bloomsbury Publishing.

Gorke, M. (2003) *The Death of our Planet's Species,* Washington, DC: Island Press.

Gowdy, J., Howarth, R. and Tisdell, C. (2010) 'Discounting ethics and options for maintaining biodiversity and ecosystem integrity', in *The Economics of Ecosystems and Biodiversity: Ecological and Economic Foundations*, ed. P. Kumar, London: Earthscan.

Graber, D. (1995) 'Resolute biocentrism: The dilemma of wilderness in national parks', in *Reinventing Nature? Responses to Postmodern Deconstruction*, eds M. Soulé and G. Lease, Washington, DC: Island Press.

Graff, J. (2010) 'Reducing work time as a path to sustainability', in *State of the World 2010: Transforming Cultures from Consumerism to Sustainability*, eds L. Starke and L. Mastny, New York: Worldwatch Institute/Earthscan.

Greer, J. M. (2008) *The Long Descent: A User's Guide to the End of the Industrial Age*, Canada: New Society Publishers.

Greer, J. M. (2009) *The Ecotechnic Future: Envisioning a Post-peak World*, Canada: New Society Publishers.

Gunderson, L. and Holling, C. (2002) *Panarchy: Understanding Transformations in Human and Natural Systems*, Washington, DC: Island Press.

GWEC (2010) *Global Wind Report: Annual Market Update 2010*, Global Wind Energy Council, see: www.gwec.net/fileadmin/images/Publications/GWEC_annual_market_update_2010_-_2nd_edition_April_2011.pdf.

Haberl, H., Erb, K., Krausmann, F., Gaube, V., Bondeau, A., Plutzar, C., Gingrich, S., Lucht, W. and Fischer-Kowalski, M. (2007) 'Quantifying and mapping the human appropriation of net primary production in earth's terrestrial ecosystems', *Proceedings of the National Academy of Sciences of the USA*, vol. 104, pp. 12942–12947.

Halford, G. and Sheehan, P. (1991) 'Human responses to environmental changes', *International Journal of Psychology*, vol. 269, no. 5, pp. 599–611.

Hall, D. O. and Rao, K. (1999) *Photosynthesis*, Sixth Edition, Cambridge, UK: Cambridge University Press.

Hamilton, C. (2010) *Requiem for a Species: Why We Resist the Truth about Climate Change*, Australia: Allen & Unwin.

Hansen, J. (2009) *Storms of my Grandchildren: The Truth about the Coming Climate Catastrophe and our Last Chance to Save Humanity*, London: Bloomsbury.

Hansen, J., Sato, M., Ruedy, R., Kharecha, P., Lacis, A., Miller, R., Nazarenko, L., Lo, K., Schmidt, G. A., Russell, G., Aleinov, I., Bauer, S., Baum, E., Cairns, B., Canuto, V., Chandler, M., Cheng, Y., Cohen, A., Del Genio, A., Faluvegi, G., Fleming, E., Friend, A., Hall, T., Jackman, C., Jonas, J., Kelley, M., Kiang, N. Y., Koch, D., Labow, G., Lerner, J., Menon, S., Novakov, T., Oinas, V., Ja, J., Rind, D., Romanou, A., Schmunk, R., Shindell, D., Stone, P., Sun, S., Streets, D., Tausnev, N., Thresher, D., Unger, N., Yao, M. and Zhang, S. (2007) 'Dangerous human-made interference with climate: A GISS model E study', *Atmos. Chem. Phys.*, vol. 7, pp. 2287–2312.

Hargrove, E. (1992) 'Weak anthropocentric intrinsic value', *The Monist*, vol. 75, no. 2, pp. 208–226.

Harper, S. (1995) 'The way of wilderness', in *Ecopsychology: Restoring the Earth, Healing the Mind*, eds T. Roszak, M. Gomes and A. Kanner, San Francisco, CA: Sierra Books.

Hartmann, B., Meyerson, F., Guillebaud, J., Chamie, J. and Desvaux, M. (2008) 'Population and climate change', *Bulletin of Atomic Scientists*, 16th April 2008, see: www.thebulletin.org/web-edition/roundtables/population-and-climate-change.

Hay, P. (2002) *Main Currents in Western Environmental Thought*, Sydney: UNSW Press.

Heidegger, M. (1977) *The Questions Concerning Technology and Other Essays*, New York: Harper Torchbooks.

Helvang, D. (1994) *The War Against the Greens: The 'Wise Use' Movement, the New Right, and Anti-environmental Violence*, San Francisco, CA: Sierra Club Books.

Hendee, J., Stankey, G. and Lucas, R. (1978) *Wilderness Management*, Forest Service, US Dept of Agriculture Miscellaneous Publication No. 1365, Washington, DC: USDA.

Higgins, P. (2009) 'Trees have rights too: ecological justice for all', see: http://treeshaverightstoo.com/ (accessed 14/11/11).

Hill, S. B. (1998) 'Redesigning agroecosystems for environmental sustainability: A deep systems approach', *Systems Research and Behavioural Science*, vol. 15, pp. 391–402.

Hoggan, J. (2009) *Climate Cover Up: The Crusade to Deny Global Warming*, Vancouver: Greystone Books.

Holdren, J. and Ehrlich, P. (1974) 'Human population and the global environment', *American Scientist*, vol. 62, pp. 282–292.

Holling, C., Gunderson, L. and Ludwig, D. (2002) 'In quest of a theory of adaptive change', in *Panarchy: Understanding Transformations in Human and Natural Systems*, eds L. Gunderson and C.Holling, Washington, DC: Island Press.

Hooper, D., Chapin, F., Ewel, J., Hector, A., Inchausti., Lavore, S., Lawton, J., Lodge, D., Loreau, M., Naeem, S., Schmid., Setala, H., Symstad, A., Vandermeer, J. and Wardle, D. (2005) 'Effects of biodiversity on ecosystem functioning: A consensus of current knowledge', *Ecological Monographs*, vol. 75, no. 1, pp. 3–35.

Hulme, M. (2009) *Why We Disagree about Climate Change: Understanding Controversy, Inaction and Opportunity*, Cambridge: Cambridge University Press.

IBI (2012) 'How much carbon can biochar remove from the atmosphere?

IEA (2010) 'Technology roadmap: Concentrating solar power', International Energy Agency, see: www.iea.org/papers/2010/csp_roadmap.pdf (accessed 5/2/12).

IPSO (2012) Ocean solutions: 2012 international earth systems expert workshop, International Programme in the State of the Ocean, see: www.stateoftheocean.org (accessed 22/3/12).

IR (1996) 'Environmental impacts of large dams: African examples', International Rivers website, see: www.internationalrivers.org/africa/environmental-impacts-large-dams-african-examples (accessed 3/2/12).

IUCN (1980) World Conservation Strategy: Living Resource Conservation for Sustainable Development, Switzerland: International Union for Conservation of Nature and Natural Resources.

Jackson, T. (2009) *Prosperity Without Growth: Economics for a Finite Planet*, London: Earthscan.

Jacobson, M. and Delucchi, M. (2011) 'Providing all global energy with wind, water, and solar power, Part I: Technologies, energy resources, quantities and areas of infrastructure, and materials', *Energy Policy*, vol. 39, pp. 1154–1169.

Jacques, P., Dunlap, R. and Freeman, M. (2008) 'The organisation of denial: Conservative think tanks and environmental scepticism', *Environmental Politics*, vol. 17, no. 3, pp. 349–385.

Jensen, D. (2000) *A Language Older than Words*, New York: Context Books.

Johnson, C. (2007) 'Rebalancing Australia's Ecology', *Science Alert*, 2 October 2007, see: www.sciencealert.com.au/opinions/20070310–16405.html (accessed 12/11/11).

Kanai, R., Feilden, T., Firth, C. and Rees, G. (2011) 'Political orientations are correlated with brain structure in young adults', *Current Biology*, vol. 21, pp. 677–680.

Kanter, J. (2009) 'European solar power from African deserts?', *New York Times*, 18 June 2009.

Kellstedt, P., Zahran, S. and Vedlitz, A. (2008) 'Personal efficacy, the information environment, and attitudes towards global warming and climate change in the United States', *Risk Analysis*, vol. 28, no. 1, pp. 113–126.

Klugman, P. (1997) 'Earth in the balance sheet: Economists go for green', see: http://web.mit.edu/krugman/www/green.html and http://dieoff.org/page105.htm (accessed 2/2/12).

Knudtson, P. and Suzuki, D. (1992) *Wisdom of the Elders*, Sydney: Allen & Unwin.

Kristeva, K. (1992) 'The other of language', in *The Judgement of Paris: Recent French Theory in a Local Context*, ed. K. Murray, Sydney: Allen & Unwin.

Kumar, A. and Ramana, M. (2009) 'The safety inadequacies of India's fast breeder reactor', *Bulletin of the Atomic Scientists*, 21 July 2009, (e-journal), see: http://thebulletin.org/web-edition/features/the-safety-inadequacies-of-indias-fast-breeder-reactor (accessed 5/6/12).

Kumar, P. (2010) *The Economics of Ecosystems and Biodiversity: Ecological and Economic Foundations*, London: Earthscan.

Kumar, P., Brondizio, E., Elmqvist, T., Gatzweiler, F., Gowdy, J., De Groot, R., Muradian, R., Pascual, U., Reyers, B., Smith, R. and Sukhdev, P. (2010) 'Lessons learned and linkages with national policies', in *The Economics of Ecosystems and Biodiversity: Ecological and Economic Foundations*, ed. P. Kumar, London: Earthscan.

Langton, M. (1996) 'The European construction of wilderness', *Wilderness News* (Australia), vol. 143, pp. 16–17.

Latouche, S. (2010) 'Growing a degrowth movement', in *State of the World 2010: Transforming Cultures from Consumerism to Sustainability*, eds L. Starke and L. Mastny, New York: Worldwatch Institute/Earthscan, Box 22 (p. 181).

Layard, R. (2005) 'The national income: A sorry tale', in *Growth Triumphant: The 21st Century in Historical Perspective*, ed. R. Easterlin, Ann Arbor, MI: University of Michigan Press.

Leakey, R. and Lewin, R. (1998) *The Sixth Extinction: Biodiversity and its Survival*, London: Phoenix.

Lebow, V. (1955) 'Price competition in 1955', *Journal of Retailing*, Spring, 1955, see: http://classroom.sdmesa.edu/pjacoby/journal-of-retailing.pdf (accessed 9/3/12).

Lehmann, J., Gaunt, J. and Rondon, M. (2006) 'Bio-char sequestration in terrestrial ecosystems – a review', *Mitigation and Adaptation Strategies for Global Change*, vol. 11, pp. 403–427.

Leopold, A. (1949) *A Sand Country Almanac, with Essays on Conservation from Round River*, New York: Random House (1970 printing).

Liu, Y., Villalba, G., Ayres, R, and Schroder, H. (2008) 'Global phosphorus flows and environmental impacts from a consumption perspective', *Journal of Industrial Ecology*, vol. 12, no. 2, pp. 229–247.

Lomborg, B. (2001) *The Skeptical Environmentalist: Measuring the Real State of the World*, Cambridge: Cambridge University Press.

Lopez, B. (1986) *Arctic Dreams*, New York: Scribners, pp. 277–278.

Lopez, B. (1988) 'Landscape and narrative', in *Crossing Open Ground*, ed. B. Lopez, New York: Scribners, p. 5.

Lovins, A. (2006) Quoted in WADE (2006) *World Survey of Decentralised Energy 2006*, Washington, DC: World Alliance for Decentralised Energy, see: www.localpower.org/nar_publications.html (accessed 5/6/12).

Lovins, A. and Sheikh, I. (2008) *The Nuclear Illusion*, Colorado: Rocky Mountain Institute, see: www.rmi.org/Knowledge-Center/Library/E08-01_NuclearIllusion (accessed 5/6/12).

Lowenthal, D. (1964) 'Is wilderness "paradise enow"?: Images of nature in America', *Columbian University Forum*, vol. 7, pp. 34–40.

Lyotard, J. R. (1992) 'Answering the question: What is postmodernism?', in *Postmodernism: A Reader*, ed. T. Docherty, New York: Harvester Wheatsheaf, p. 46.

Mackey, B. (2008) 'The Earth Charter, ethics and global governance', in *Sustaining Life on Earth: Environmental and Human Health through Global Governance*, ed. C. Soskolne, New York: Rowman & Littlefield Publishers.

Marsh, G. P. (1864) *Man and Nature: Or, Physical Geography as Modified by Human Action*, New York: Scribner.

Marshall, P. (1996) *Nature's Web: Rethinking our Place on Earth*, Armonk, New York: ME Sharpe Inc.

Marshall, R. (1930) 'The Problem of the Wilderness', *Scientific Monthly*, vol. 30, no. 2, pp. 141–148.

Massey, D. (1994) *Space, Place, and Gender*, Minneapolis, MN: University of Minnesota Press.

May, R. (1973) *Stability and Complexity in Model Ecosystems*, Princeton, NJ: Princeton University Press.

May, R. (2002) 'The future of biological diversity in a crowded world', *Current Science*, vol. 82, no. 11, pp. 1325–1331.

McCann, K. (2000) 'The diversity–stability debate', *Nature*, vol. 405, pp. 228–233.

McCright, A. and Dunlap, R. (2000) 'Challenging global warming as a social problem: An analysis of the conservative movement's counter-claims', *Social Problems*, vol. 47, no. 4, pp. 499–522.

McCright, A. and Dunlap, R. (2010) 'Anti-reflexivity: The American conservative movement's success in undermining climate science and policy', *Theory, Culture and Society*, vol. 27, no. 2–3, pp.100–133.

McDonagh, W. and Braungart, M. (2002) *Cradle to Cradle: Remaking the Way We Make Things*, New York: North Point Press.

McKibben, B. (2006) *The End of Nature*, New York: Random House.

McNeil, B. (2009) *The Clean Industrial Revolution: Growing Australian Prosperity in the Greenhouse Age*, Sydney: Allen & Unwin.

MEA (2005) *Living Beyond Our Means: Natural Assets and Human Wellbeing, Statement from the Board, Millennium Ecosystem Assessment*. UNEP (available www.millenniumassessment.org).

Meadows, D., Meadows, D., Randers, J. and Behrens, W. (1972) *The Limits to Growth*, Washington, DC: Universe Books.

Merton, R. (1973) *The Sociology of Science: Theoretical and Empirical Investigations*, New York: University of Chicago Press.

Miller, B., Reading, R., Hoogland, J., Clark, T., Ceballos, G., List, R., Forrest, S., Hanebury, L., Manzano, P., Pacheco, J. and Uresk, D. (2000) 'The role of Prairie Dogs as keystone species: Response to Stapp', *Conservation Biology*, vol. 14, no. 1, pp. 318–321.

Miller G. T. (1990) *Living in the Environment*, Belmont, CA: Wadsworth.

Monbiot, G. (2006) *Heat: How to Stop the Planet Burning*, London: Penguin Books.

Monbiot, G. (2009) 'The population myth', see: www.monbiot.com/archives/2009/09/29/the-population-myth/ (accessed 19/11/11).

Monist (1992) 'The Intrinsic Value of Nature, Special Edition', *The Monist*, vol. 75, no. 2, pp. 119–137.

Mudd, G. and Diesendorf, M. (2008) 'Sustainability of uranium mining and milling: Toward quantifying resources and eco-efficiency', *Environmental Science & Technology*, vol. 42, no. 7, pp. 2624–2630.

Muir, J. (1916) *A Thousand Mile Walk to the Gulf*, Boston, MA: Houghton Mifflin, pp. 211–212.

Naess, A. (1973) 'The shallow and the deep, long-range ecology movement: A summary', *Inquiry*, vol. 16, pp. 95–100.

Naess, A. (1984) 'A defence of the deep ecology movement', *Environmental Ethics*, vol. 6, p. 266.

Naess, A. (1989) *Ecology, Community and Lifestyle*, Cambridge: Cambridge University Press.

Nash, R. (1967) *Wilderness and the American Mind*, First Edition, New Haven/London: Yale University Press.

Nash, R. (2001) *Wilderness and the American Mind*, Fourth Edition, New Haven/London: Yale Nota Bene.

NAU (2011) 'Atmospheric reactions of sulphur and nitrogen', Northern Arizona University, see: www2.nau.edu/~doetqp-p/courses/env440/env440_2/lectures/lec37/lec37.htm (accessed 6/3/12).

NEF (2012) See: www.neweconomics.org/publications/five-ways-well-being-postcards (accessed 20/3/12).

Nelson, M. (2003) 'An amalgamation of wilderness preservation arguments', in *Environmental Ethics: An Anthology'*, eds A. Light and H. Rolston, Oxford: Blackwell.

Neumayer, E. (2007) 'A missed opportunity: The Stern Review on climate change fails to tackle the issue of non-substitutable loss of natural capital', *Global Environmental Change*, vol. 17, no. 3–4, pp. 297–301.

NGP (2011) 'Prairie dogs wildlife species guide', Nebraska Game Parks, see: http://outdoornebraska.ne.gov/wildlife/wildlife_species_guide/prairiedogs.asp (accessed 5/6/12).

Nietzsche, F. (1871) 'The birth of tragedy from the spirit of music', in *Critical Theory Since Plato*, ed. H. Adams (1992), Fort Worth: Harcourt Brace Jovanovich.

Norgaard, K. (2003) 'Denial, privilege and global environmental justice: The case of global climate change'. Paper presented at the annual meeting of the American Sociological Association, Atlanta Hilton Hotel, Atlanta. Available from www.allacademic.com.

Norgaard, K. (2011) *Living in Denial: Climate Change, Emotions, and Everyday Life*, Cambridge, MA: MIT Press.

Norton, B. (1995) 'Ecological integrity and social values: At what scale', *Ecosystem Health*, vol. 1, no. 4, pp. 228–241.

Noss, R. (1991) 'Sustainability and wilderness', *Conservation Biology*, vol. 5, pp. 120–123.

Nowell, K. and Jackson, P. (1996) *Wild Cats, Status Survey and Conservation Action Plan*, Gland, Switzerland: IUCN/SSC Cat Specialist Group, IUCN.

NRC (2007) *Environmental Impacts of Wind-Energy Projects*, Washington, DC: National Research Council of the US National Academy of Science, see: https://download.nap.edu/catalog.php?record_id=11935 (accessed 5/2/12).

O'Connor, M. And Lines, W. (2008) *Overloading Australia: How Governments and Media Dither and Deny on Population*, Sydney: Envirobook.

Odum, E. P. (1953) *Fundamentals of Ecology*, Philadelphia, PA: W. B. Saunders.

Odum, H. and Odum, E. (2001) *A Prosperous Way Down: Principles and Policies*, Boulder, CO: University Press of Colorado.

OECD (2011) *Divided We Stand: Why Inequality Keeps Rising*, Paris: Organisation for Economic Cooperation and Development, see: www.oecd.org/document/51/0,3746,en_2649_33933_49147827_1_1_1_1,00.html (accessed 2/2/12).

Oelschlaeger, M. (1991) *The Idea of Wilderness: From Prehistory to the Age of Ecology*, New Haven/London: Yale University Press.

Oreskes, N. and Conway, M. (2010) *Merchants of Doubt: How a Handful of Scientists Obscured the Truth on Issues from Tobacco Smoke to Global Warming*, New York: Bloomsbury Press.

Orthodoxnet (2007) Post 14 by 'Augie' on 10 June 2007 at Orthodoxnet website, see: www.orthodoxytoday.org/blog/2007/06/03/they-call-this-a-consensus/#comment-95231 (accessed 5/6/12).

Orwell, G. (1949) *Nineteen Eighty Four*, London: Secker and Warburg.

Outwater, A. (1996) *Water: A Natural History*, New York: BasicBooks.

Paine, R. T. (1966) 'Food web complexity and species diversity', *The American Naturalist*, vol. 100, no. 910, pp. 65–75.

Pascual, U., Muradian, R., Brander, L., Gomex-Baggethun, E., Martin-Lopex, B. and Verma, M. (2010) 'The economics of valuing ecosystem services and biodiversity', in *The Economics of Ecosystems and Biodiversity: Ecological and Economic Foundations*, ed. P. Kumar, London: Earthscan.

Pauly, D. (1995) 'Anecdotes and the shifting baseline syndrome of fisheries', *Trends in Ecology and Evolution*, vol. 10, no. 10, p.430.

Pittock, A. B. (2009) *Climate Change: the Science, Impacts and Solutions*, London: CSIRO Publishing/Earthscan.

Plimer, I. (2009) *Heaven and Earth: Global Warming: The Missing Science*, Ballan, Vic: Connorcourt Publishing.

Plumwood, V. (2001) 'Towards a progressive naturalism', *Capitalism, Nature, Socialism*, vol. 12, no. 4, pp. 3–32.

Plumwood, V. (2003) 'New nature or no nature?', unpublished paper provided by the author, 14/8/03. This paper has since been incorporated in Plumwood, V. (2006) 'The concept of a cultural landscape: Nature, culture and agency in the land', *Ethics and the Environment*, vol. 11, no. 2, pp. 115–150.

PM (2010) 'Capacity population', Population Matters leaflet, see: http://population matters.org/documents/capacity_leaflet.pdf (accessed 15/11/11).

Prineas, P. and Gold, H. (1983, 1997) *Wild Places: Wilderness in Eastern New South Wales*, Sydney: Colong Foundation for Wilderness.

Purcell, B. (2010) *Dingo*, Canberra: CSIRO Publishing.

Rainham, D., McDowell, I. and Krewski, D. (2008) 'A sense of possibility: What does governance for health and ecological sustainability look like?', in *Sustaining Life on Earth: Environmental and Human Health through Global Governance*, ed. C. Soskolne, New York: Lexington Books.

Reason, P. and Bradbury, H. (2001) *Handbook of Action Research: Participative Inquiry and Practice*, London: Sage Publications.

Reason, P. and Torbert, W. (2001) 'Toward a transformational social science: A further look at the scientific merits of action research', *Concepts and Transformations*, vol. 6, no. 1, pp. 1–37.

Rees, W. (2008) 'Toward sustainability with justice: Are human nature and history on side?', in *Sustaining Life on Earth: Environmental and Human Health through Global Governance*, ed. C. Soskolne, New York: Lexington Books.

Reimchen, T. (2001) 'Salmon nutrients, nitrogen isotopes and coastal forest', *Ecoforestry*, Fall, 2001, pp. 13–15, see: http://web.uvic.ca/~reimlab/reimchen_ecoforestry.pdf (accessed 5/11/11).

REN21 (2011) *Renewables 2011 Global Status Report*, Paris: Renewable Energy Policy Network for the 21st Century, see: www.ren21.net/Portals/97/documents/GSR/REN21_GSR2011.pdf (accessed 3/2/12).

Rigby, K. (2003) 'Tuning in to spirit of place', in *Changing places: Re-imagining Australia*, ed. J. Cameron, Double Bay, NSW: Longueville Books.

Robertson, M., Brown, A. and Vang, K. (1992) *Wilderness in Australia: Issues and Options*, Canberra: Australian Heritage Commission.

Rojstaczer, S., Sterling S. and Moore, N. (2001) 'Human appropriation of photosynthesis products', *Science*, vol. 294, no. 5551, pp. 2549–2552.

Rolston, H. (1985) 'Valuing wildlands', *Environmental Ethics*, vol. 7, pp. 23–48.

Rolston, H. (1992) 'Disvalues in nature', *The Monist*, vol. 75, no. 2, pp. 250–280.

Rolston, H. (2001) 'Natural and unnatural: Wild and cultural', *Western North Amer. Nat.*, vol. 61, no. 3, pp. 267–276.

Roszak, T. (2002) 'Ecopsychology since 1992', *Wild Earth*, vol. 12, no. 2, pp. 38–43.

SCEP (1970) *Man's Impact on the Global Environment: Report of the Study of Critical Environmental Problems*, California: MIT Press.

Schneider, S. (1997) *Laboratory Earth: The Planetary Gamble we can't Afford to Lose*, New York: Basic Books.

Schneider, S. (2009) 'Mitigation and Adaptation to Climate Change', UNSW Institute of Environmental Studies (IES) Seminar by Professor Stephen Schneider of Stanford University, 16 March 2009 (powerpoint presentation).

Schumacher, E. (1973) *Small is Beautiful*, New York: Harper Torchbooks.

Sekine, T. (1992) *Broadening the Scope of Political Economy*, CDAS Discussion Paper No. 74, Montreal: McGill University.

Siemens (2010) 'Ultra HVDC transmission system', see: www.energy.siemens.com/co/en/power-transmission/hvdc/hvdc-ultra/#content=Benefits (accessed 3/2/12).

Simms, A., Johnson, V. and Chowla, P. (2010) 'Growth isn't possible: Why we need a new economic direction', London: New Economics Foundation, see: www.neweconomics.org/publications/growth-isnt-possible (accessed 8/3/12).

SIPRI (2010) 'Yearbook 2010', Stockholm International Peace Research Institute, see: www.sipri.org.

Smith, M. J. (1998) *Ecologism: Towards Ecological Citizenship*, Buckingham: Open University Press.

Sneddon C., Howarth, R. and Norgaard, R. (2006) 'Sustainable development in a post-Brundtland world', *Ecological Economics*, vol. 57, no. 2, pp. 253–268.

Snow, C. P. (1969) *The State of Siege*, New York: Charles Scribner's Sons.

Soskolne, C. (2008) 'Preface' to *Sustaining Life on Earth: Environmental and Human Health through Global Governance*, ed. C. Soskolne, New York: Lexington Books.

Soskolne C., Kotze, L., Mackey, B. and Rees, W. (2008) 'Conclusions: Challenging our individual and collective thinking about sustainability', in *Sustaining Life on Earth: Environmental and Human Health through Global Governance*, ed. C. Soskolne, New York: Lexington Books.

Soulé, M. (1995) 'The social siege of nature', in *Reinventing Nature: Responses to Postmodern Deconstruction*, eds M. Soulé and G. Lease, Washington, DC: Island Press.

Soulé, M. (2002) 'Debating the Myths of Wilderness', The Wilderness Society (Australia), calendar introduction for 2002 by Professor Michael Soulé, University of California.

Soulé, M. E. and Wilcox, B. A. (1980) 'Conservation biology: Its scope and its challenge', in *Conservation Biology: An Evolutionary-Ecological Perspective*, eds M. Soulé and B. Wilcox, Sunderland (MA): Sinauer.

Sovacool, B. (2011) *Contesting the Future of Nuclear Power: A Critical Global Assessment of Atomic Energy*, Singapore: World Scientific Publishing Co., see: www.worldscibooks.com/environsci/7895.html (accessed 3/2/12).

Spash, C. (2007) 'The economics of climate change impacts à la Stern: Novel and nuanced or rhetorically restricted', *Ecological Economics*, vol. 63, no. 4, pp. 706–713.

Specter, M. (2009) *Denialism: How Irrational Thinking Hinders Scientific Progress, Harms the Planet and Threatens our Lives*, New York: The Penguin Press.

Spratt, D. and Sutton, P. (2008) *Climate Code Red: The Case for Emergency Action*, Victoria, Australia: Scribe Publications.

Starke, L. and Mastny, L. (2010) *State of the World 2010: Transforming Cultures from Consumerism to Sustainability*, New York: Worldwatch Institute/Earthscan.

Stegner, W. (1969) *The Sound of Mountain Water*, New York: Garden City.

Stern, N. (2006) *The Economics of Climate Change* (Stern Review), London: Cambridge University Press.

Sukhdev, P. (2010) 'Preface' to *The Economics of Ecosystems and Biodiversity: Ecological and Economic Foundations*, ed. P. Kumar, London: Earthscan.

Sullivan, P. (1999) 'Sustainable soil management: Appropriate technology transfer for rural areas', see: www.soilandhealth.org/01aglibrary/010117attrasoilmanual/010117attra.html#nitrogen (accessed 5/11/11).

Swimme, B. and Berry, T. (1992) *The Universe Story: From the Primordial Flaming Forth to the Ecozoic Era*, San Francisco, CA: Harper Books.

Tacey, D. (2000) *Re-enchantment: The New Australian Spirituality*, Australia: Harper Collins.

Tainter, J. (1995) 'Sustainability of complex societies', *Futures*, vol. 27, pp. 397–404.

Tavris, C. and Aronson, E. (2007) *Mistakes Were Made (But Not By Me): Why we Justify Foolish Beliefs, Bad Decisions, and Hurtful Acts*, Orlando, FL: Harcourt Books.

Taylor, P. (1986) *Respect for Nature: A Theory of Environmental Ethics*, Princeton, NJ: Princeton University Press.

Taylor, P. (2010) *The Biochar Revolution: Transforming Agriculture and Environment*, Mt Evelyn, Victoria, Australia: Global Publishing Group.

Tempest Williams, T. (1999) 'A place of humility', *Wild Earth*, vol. 9, no. 3, 18–21.

Tempest Williams, T. (2003) In M. Tredinnick (2003) 'Writing the wild: Place, prose and the ecological imagination', Ph.D. Thesis, Richmond: University of Western Sydney.

Thomas, C., Cameron A., Green R., Bakkenes M., Beaumont L., Collingham Y., Erasmus B., Siqueira M., Grainger A., Hannah L., Hughes L., Huntley B., Jaarsveld A., Midgley G., Miles L., Ortega-Huerta M., Peterson A., Phillips, O. and Williams S. *(*2004) 'Extinction risk from climate change', *Nature*, vol. 427, pp. 145–148.

Thomashow, M. (1996) 'Voices of ecological identity', in *Ecological Identity: Becoming a Reflective Environmentalist*, ed. M. Thomashow, Cambridge, MA: MIT Press.

Thoreau, H. D. (1854) *Walden: Or, Life in the Woods*, New York: Dover Publications (current edition 1995).

Tredinnick, M. (2003) 'Writing the wild: Place, prose and the ecological imagination', Ph.D. Thesis, Richmond, NSW: University of Western Sydney.

Trenberth, K. (2011) 'Changes in precipitation with climate change', *Climate Research*, vol. 47, pp. 123–138.

Trenberth, K., Smith, L., Quian, T., Dai, A. and Fasullo, J. (2007) 'Estimates of the global water budget and its annual cycle using observational and model data', *J. Hydrometeor*, vol. 8, pp. 758–769.

Turner, G. (2008) 'A comparison of the *Limits to Growth* with 30 years of reality', *Global Environmental Change*, vol. 18, no. 3, pp. 397–411.

Turner, K. and Daily, G. (2008) 'The ecosystem service framework and natural capital conservation', *Environmental and Resource Economics*, vol. 39, pp. 25–35.

UCS (1992) 'World Scientists Warning to Humanity', Union of Concerned Scientists, see: www.ucsusa.org/about/1992-world-scientists.html (accessed 14/11/11).

UN (2007) *World Urbanization Prospects: The 2007 Revision*, New York: United Nations, see: www.unpopulation.org.

UN (2009) 'World population to exceed 9 billion by 2050', press release by United Nations Population Division, 11/3/2009, see: www.un.org/esa/population/publications/wpp2008/pressrelease.pdf (accessed 5/6/12).

UN DESA (2009) *Rethinking Poverty: Report on the World Social Situation, 2010*, New York: UN Department of Social Affairs, p. 89.

Ungunmerr, M. R. (1995) 'Dadirri', in *The Aboriginal Gift: Spirituality for a Nation*, ed. E. Stockton, Sydney, Millennium Books.

USGS (2011) 'Sulphur', see: http://minerals.usgs.gov/minerals/pubs/commodity/sulfur/mcs-2011-sulfu.pdf (accessed 6/3/12).

Van Emden, H. and Peakall, D. (1999) *Beyond Silent Spring: Integrated Pest Management and Chemical Safety*, London: UNEP/ICIPE, Chapman & Hall.

Vance, L. (1997) 'Ecofeminism and wilderness', *NWSA Journal*, vol. 9, no. 3, pp. 60–77.

Vitousek P., Aber, J., Howarth, R., Likens, G., Matson, P., Schindler, D, Schlesinger, W. and Tilman, D. (1997) 'Human alterations of the global nitrogen cycles: Sources and consequences', *Ecological Applications*, vol. 7, no. 3, p. 737–750.

Vitousek, P., Ehrlich, A. and Matson, P. (1986) 'Human appropriation of the products of photosynthesis', *BioScience*, vol. 36, no. 6, pp. 368–373.

Vitousek, P., Mooney, H., Lubchenco, J. and Melillo, J. (1997) 'Human domination of Earth's ecosystems', *Science*, vol. 277, pp. 494–499.

Vogt, W. (1948) *Road to Survival*, New York: William Sloan.

Wackernagel, M. and Rees, W. (1996) *Our Ecological Footprint: Reducing Human Impact on the Earth*, Gabriola Island, BC, Canada: New Society Publishers.

Wald, M. (2009) 'Dismantling nuclear reactors', *Scientific American*, March 2009, see: www.scientificamerican.com/article.cfm?id=dismantling-nuclear (accessed 5/6/12).

Walker, B. (1995) 'Conserving biological diversity through ecosystem resilience', *Conservation Biology*, vol. 9, no. 4, pp. 747–752.

Washington, H. (1991) *Ecosolutions: Solving Environmental Problems for the World and Australia*, Tea Gardens, NSW, Australia: Boobook Publications.

Washington, H. (2002) *A Sense of Wonder*, Sydney, Australia: Ecosolution Consulting.

Washington, H. (2006) 'The wilderness knot'. Ph.D. Thesis, Sydney: University of Western Sydney, see: http://arrow.uws.edu.au:8080/vital/access/manager/Repository/uws:4 (accessed 5/6/12).

Washington, H. (2010) *Gift of the Wild: The Nature Poetry of Haydn Washington*, Raleigh, NC: Lulu.com publishing, see: www.lulu.com/browse/search.php?fListing Class=0&fSearch=gift+of+the+wild (accessed 5/6/12).

Washington, H. and Cook, J. (2011) *Climate Change Denial: Heads in the Sand*, London: Earthscan.

WCC (2008) *Sustainability Charter*, Sydney Australia: Willoughby City Council, see: www.willoughby.nsw.gov.au/About-Council/Forms-Policies---Publications/Publications/?categoryid=303 (accessed 5/6/12).

WCED (1987) *Our Common Future*, World Commission on Environment and Development, London: Oxford University Press.

Weitzman, M. (2009) 'On modelling and interpreting the economics of catastrophic climate change', *The Review of Economics and Statistics*, vol. XCI, pp. 1–19.

Westman, W. (1977) 'How much are nature's services worth?', *Science*, vol. 197, pp. 960–964.

Weston, A. (1992) 'Between means and ends', *The Monist*, vol. 75, no. 2, pp. 236–249.

Westra, R. (2004) 'The "Impasse" debate and socialist development', in *New Socialisms: Futures beyond Globalisation*, eds R. Albritton, S. Bell, J. Bell and R. Westra, London: Routledge.

Westra, R. (2008) 'Market society and ecological integrity: Theory and practice', in *Sustaining Life on Earth: Environmental and Human Health through Global Governance*, ed. C. Soskolne, New York: Lexington Books.

Williams, J. and Dodd, C. (1980) 'Importance of wetlands to endangered and threatened species', in *Wetland Functions and Values: The State of Our Understanding*, eds P. Greeson *et al.*, Minneapolis, MN: American Water Resources Association.

Wilson, E. O. (1984) *Biophilia: The Human Bond with other Species*, Harvard, MA: Harvard University Press.

Wilson, E. O. (1992) *The Diversity of Life*, Cambridge, MA: Harvard University Press.

Wilson, E. O. (2002) *The Future of Life*, New York: Vintage Books.

Woodford, J. (2000) *The Wollemi Pine*, Melbourne: Text Publishing.

Woolf, D., Amonette, J., Street-Perrott, F., Lehmann, J. and Joseph, S. (2010) 'Sustainable biochar to mitigate global climate change', *Nature Communications*, vol. 1, no. 5, pp. 1–9.

Worster, D. (1994) *Nature's Economy: A History of Ecological Ideas*, Cambridge: Cambridge University Press.

Wright, J., Jones, C., and Flecker, A. (2002) 'An ecosystem engineer, the beaver, increases species richness at the landscape scale', *Oecologia*, vol. 132, no. 1, pp. 96–101.

Wright, M. and Hearps, P. (2010) *Australian Sustainable Energy Stationary Energy Plan*, Melbourne: University of Melbourne Energy Research Institute/Beyond Zero Emissions, see: http://beyondzeroemissions.org.

WWF (2010) 'Living Planet Report. World Wide Fund for Nature', see: www.wwf.org.uk/what_we_do/about_us/living_planet_report_2010/ (accessed 11/12/11).

WWF (2011) *The Energy Report: 100% Renewable Energy by 2050*, Switzerland: WWF, see: wwf.panda.org/what_we_do/footprint/climate_carbon_energy/energy_solutions/renewable_energy/sustainable_energy_report/ (accessed 3/2/12).

Zack, N. (2002) 'Human values as a source for sustaining the environment', in *Just Ecological Integrity*, eds P. Miller and L. Westra, Lantham, MD: Rowman & Littlefield.

Zerubavel, E. (2002) 'The elephant in the room: Notes on the social organization of denial', in *Culture in Mind: Toward a Sociology of Culture and Cognition*, ed. K. Cerulo, New York: Routledge.

Zerubavel, E. (2006) *The Elephant in the Room: Silence and Denial in Everyday Life*, London: Oxford University Press.

Zimmerman, M. (2001) *The Nature of Intrinsic Value*, Lanham, MD: Rowman & Littlefield.

Index

CPSIA information can be obtained at www.ICGtesting.com
Printed in the USA
LVOW10s1957040414

380406LV00003B/33/P